Theodor Storm's Novellen

UNC | COLLEGE OF ARTS AND SCIENCES
Germanic and Slavic Languages and Literatures

From 1949 to 2004, UNC Press and the UNC Department of Germanic & Slavic Languages and Literatures published the UNC Studies in the Germanic Languages and Literatures series. Monographs, anthologies, and critical editions in the series covered an array of topics including medieval and modern literature, theater, linguistics, philology, onomastics, and the history of ideas. Through the generous support of the National Endowment for the Humanities and the Andrew W. Mellon Foundation, books in the series have been reissued in new paperback and open access digital editions. For a complete list of books visit www.uncpress.org.

Theodor Storm's Novellen
Essays on Literary Technique

E. ALLEN MCCORMICK

UNC Studies in the Germanic Languages and Literatures
Number 47

Copyright © 1964

This work is licensed under a Creative Commons CC BY-NC-ND license. To view a copy of the license, visit http://creativecommons.org/licenses.

Suggested citation: McCormick, E. Allen. *Theodor Storm's Novellen: Essays on Literary Technique.* Chapel Hill: University of North Carolina Press, 1964. DOI: https://doi.org/10.5149/9781469657943_McCormick

Library of Congress Cataloging-in-Publication Data
Names: McCormick, E. Allen.
Title: Theodor Storm's novellen : Essays on literary technique / by E. Allen McCormick.
Other titles: University of North Carolina Studies in the Germanic Languages and Literatures ; no. 47.
Description: Chapel Hill : University of North Carolina Press, [1964] Series: University of North Carolina Studies in the Germanic Languages and Literatures. | Includes bibliographical references.
Identifiers: LCCN 64064253 | ISBN 978-0-8078-8047-0 (pbk: alk. paper) | ISBN 978-1-4696-5794-3 (ebook)
Subjects: Storm, Theodor, 1817-1888.
Classification: LCC PD25 .N6 NO. 47 | DCC 833/ .8

TABLE OF CONTENTS

		page
CHRONOLOGY OF STORM'S NOVELLEN.		iii
PREFACE		v
CHAPTER I.	The Two *Immensee's*	1
CHAPTER II.	*Am Kamin, Auf dem Staatshof,* and the Technique of "Ganz Wenig": Notes on Storm's Narrative Method	34
CHAPTER III.	Death and Survival in the Situation Tragedy: The Beginnings of Storm's Tragic Novellen.	70
CHAPTER IV.	Three Themes in *Aquis Submersus*	90
CHAPTER V.	*Hinzelmeier:* "Nachdenkliche Geschichte" as Problematic *Kunstmärchen.*	118
NOTES		153
BIBLIOGRAPHY		168
INDEX		180

CHRONOLOGY OF STORM'S NOVELLEN ACCORDING TO DATE OF COMPOSITION

1837	Hans Bär	1871	Draußen im Heidedorf
1847	Marthe und ihre Uhr	1871	Zwei Kuchenesser der alten Zeit
1848	Im Saal	1873	Beim Vetter Christian
1849	Immensee	1873	Viola Tricolor
1849	Posthuma	1873	Von heut und ehedem
1849	Der kleine Häwelmann	1874	Pole Poppenspäler
1850	Ein grünes Blatt	1874	Waldwinkel
1850	Hinzelmeier	1875	Ein stiller Musikant
1854	Im Sonnenschein	1875	Psyche
1855	Angelika	1875	Im Nachbarhause links
1856	Wenn die Äpfel reif sind	1876	Aquis Submersus
1858	Am Kamin	1876	Von Kindern und Katzen
1858	Auf dem Staatshof	1877	Carsten Curator
1859	Späte Rosen	1878	Renate
1860	Drüben am Markt	1878	Eekenhof
1861	Veronika	1878	Zur Wald- und Wasserfreude
1861	Im Schloß	1879	Im Brauerhause
1862	Auf der Universität	1879	Die Söhne des Senators
1862	Unter dem Tannenbaum	1881	Der Herr Etatsrat
1863	Abseits	1882	Hans und Heinz Kirch
1864	Von Jenseit des Meeres	1883	Schweigen
1864	Die Regentrude	1884	Zur Chronik von Grieshuus
1864	Bulemanns Haus	1884	Es waren zwei Königskinder
1864	Der Spiegel des Cyprianus	1885	John Riew'
1867	In St. Jürgen	1885	Ein Fest auf Haderslevhuus
1867	Eine Malerarbeit	1886	Bötjer Basch
1870	Lena Wies	1886	Ein Doppelgänger
1870	Der Amtschirurgus – Heimkehr	1887	Ein Bekenntnis
1871	Eine Halligfahrt	1888	Der Schimmelreiter

PREFACE

In his recent and substantial literary history of the nineteenth century Fritz Martini offers this summarizing comment on Theodor Storm's achievement as a writer of Novellen:

> Die Novelle mußte seine Erzählform werden. Er hat die Subjektivierung der Erzählweise, das Verweben von Geschehen und Erlebnisspiegelung, von Gegenständlichem und Gefühlsanschauung sehr verfeinert; ebenso die Kunst der Nuancen im Bildhaften, Atmosphärischen und Innerseelischen, in der stimmungsvollen Spiegelung und musikalischen Durchtönung. Er hat die Kunst des fragmentarischen Andeutens, der relativierenden und letzthin unausdeutbaren Verknüpfung verschiedenartiger Faktoren, die ein Geschick komplex zusammensetzen, erweitert. Sein Stil hat eine fast artistische Empfindlichkeit für das Leise, Mehrdeutige, Schwebende, Verdämmernde, Ungewisse erreicht. Er ist die Sprache seiner Spätzeit – so wie seine konstante Thematik von der vorgehenden Zeit, vom versäumten und zerfallenden Leben und seine Form der Erinnerungs- und Rückschauerzählung. Denn für ihn gewann das Leben aus der Geschichte seine Stimmungstöne.[1]

The student of Storm will find nothing startlingly new in this evaluation, which serves the present essays as corroboration rather than as *Ausgangspunkt*: our *Stormbild* is reasonably stable and our estimate of his novellistic achievement subject more to the vagaries of taste and the shifts and turns of critical (and historical) emphasis than to the promise of new discovery. Yet the challenge of the already familiar ought not to be slighted nor our appreciation of technique dulled by the awareness that Storm's forty-odd Novellen have been assigned their place – beyond the pale of fashion – with a certain finality.

With the possible exception of Paul Heyse, no other *Novellendichter* of the century showed a greater concern for form than this north German *Filigranarbeiter*. Not in the sense of daring innovation or exaggerated formalism but simply from a conviction that the "Dichtungsart, welche die spätere Hälfte meines Lebens begleitet hat," makes the greatest demands of any art form and permits the poet "auch in dieser Form das Höchste der Poesie zu leisten."[2] The five essays comprising this book are an attempt to investigate a few of the more significant aspects of Storm's literary technique, or more specifically, his *Novellenkunst* – whereby the second, more personal part of the compound is stressed. From the standpoint of *Novellentheorie* or even of the narrower question of Storm's novellistic art the essays are admittedly limited in perspective. For example, in the first chapter, there is a close comparison of the two versions of *Immensee* designed to illustrate Storm's scenic technique and the careful way in which he subjected his stories to revision. Other examples would have been equally valid and their inclusion would doubtless have strengthened the impact of the argument. Similarly, the treatment of *Hinzelmeier* might have been extended to other of Storm's *Märchen* and a fuller case made for the fairy tales as *Erzählungen* or as mixed rather than simple forms. And, finally, such frequently used terms as tragedy, guilt, *Andeute-Technik* (or, in my phrasing, the "ganz wenig" technique), etc. might have been explored in greater detail.

But if the discussions and analyses offered here do not in their sum present an exhaustive study of Storm's literary technique, we may still claim that, in following the dictates of a personal literary curiosity, we have cast additional light on some of the basic qualities and problems of one of German Realism's foremost representatives.

Dartmouth College   E. ALLEN MCCORMICK
June 1, 1963

CHAPTER ONE

THE TWO *IMMENSEE'S*

Two sketches, a vignette and a Novelle, written in the late 1840's and, with the exception of one of the sketches, first published in Karl Leonhard Biernatzki's *Volksbuch*, mark the emergence of Theodor Storm as a prose writer.[1] In 1851 these writings, together with a modest body of lyric poetry, were collected and published in book form by Alexander Duncker in Berlin. Storm's preface to the slender volume of *Sommergeschichten und Lieder* opens with this comment on his choice of a title: "Sommergeschichten habe ich auf den Titel geschrieben; um das Wesen dieser Geschichten zu bezeichnen, hätte ich 'Situationen' schreiben müssen."[2] While the remainder of the brief dedicatory preface offers no more than the charming sentiment that "Sommergeschichten" was chosen "lieber als eine Klassifikation" because of its appropriateness for his wife Konstanze, who loved this season of the year above all others, one is nevertheless struck by the author's awareness of the question of form, of what it was precisely that he was offering his public.

In a letter to Hartmuth Brinkmann which accompanied a gift copy of the book (intended for Brinkmann's wife Laura) Storm takes up in some detail the problem of classification alluded to so briefly in the preface, as though to stress the importance he gave to formal considerations: "Bei dem Ausdruck 'Situationen' in der Dedikation habe ich an eine Stelle in Gervinus' Literaturgeschichte

Bd. v, S. 697 gedacht, wo er sagt, die Novelle sei wesentlich Situation und als solche geeignet, der großen Gattung subordinierter Konversationspoesie, dem Roman, der sich im Gleise des modernen sozialen Lebens bewege, eine poetische Seite abzugewinnen durch Beschränkung und Isolierung auf einzelne Momente von poetischem Interesse, die sich auch im dürftigsten Alltagsleben finden.

In dem Sinne glaube ich, daß meine prosaischen Stücke recht eigentlich reine Novellen sind; denn eben dem Bedürfnis, nur das wirklich Poetische darzustellen, haben sie ihre knappe Form zu verdanken."[3]

The degree to which critics have ignored or taken issue with Storm's acceptance of Gervinus' description of the Novelle as situation or as isolated poetic moments is perfectly understandable in the light of what the history of the Novelle with its countless examples and its emphasis on the Goethean *Begebenheit* or the central *Geschehnis* has established as dictum. Yet one cannot but wonder if evaluation via definition does justice to Storm's intentions – or to his achievement within the confines of intent. Much of the adverse criticism of *Immensee*, for example, seems to stem from a critical overawareness of what that work *qua* Novelle ought to have done rather than from what Storm, the novice prose writer, actually succeeded in doing within the limits of his "Beschränkung und Isolierung auf einzelne Momente" and his full recognition of the fact that these earliest prose works are "reine Novellen" only in the sense of situation.[4] Storm's most recent biographer, Franz Stuckert, is to be commended for his refusal to accept conventional labels (*lyrische Novellen, Resignationspoesie, Stimmungsnovellen, Novellen der Liebesbeziehung,* etc.) and for returning instead to Storm's own description.[5] In his chapter on the beginnings of Storm's narrative art he speaks of *Situationsnovellen* and rightly stresses Storm's clearly discernible *Formwille*, placing it in the mainstream of Biedermeier literature.[6] And unless one gives the term Biedermeier itself pejorative overtones it is possible not only to evaluate fairly the plot-weak series of *Bilder* of which

Immensee consists, but even to admire the high compositional art of this early work.[7]

One of Storm's severest critics, the close friend and early collaborator Tycho Mommsen, dismissed *Immensee* with the well-known words "lebende Bilder, tote Kunst."[8] The version that so displeased Mommsen was the 1849 one, which appeared in Biernatzki's *Volksbuch* for 1850.[9] A comparison of the Biernatzki *Immensee*, which unfortunately has never been reprinted,[10] and the 1851 version printed in *Sommergeschichten und Lieder* shows to what extent Storm was groping toward, and to a remarkable degree succeeded in finding, adequate artistic expression for his Biedermeier attitude, his flight into a kind of idyllic nostalgia during the troubled years of early marriage, and for his early concept of the Novelle as consisting of individual moments of poetic interest. The following remarks will be concerned primarily with the last of these, Storm's concept of the Novelle, as it manifests itself in the revisions made in the first *Immensee*.

At five points in the story Storm undertook extensive revision: the strawberry hunt, the *Ratskeller* scene, the *Gartensaal* scene, the incident with the beggar girl, and the account of Reinhard's later life. We shall examine each of these major changes in some detail before attempting to offer an evaluation of Storm's "technical" progress from the Biernatzki *Volksbuch* version (B) to the standard one of the *Sommergeschichten und Lieder* (S).

The children's search for strawberries occurs in the chapter *Im Walde*, one of the two instances in the story where the standard version is appreciably longer than the Biernatzki one. This latter describes the children's walk into the woods in a scant nine lines, while S uses well over twice this number. Aside from mere length, S shows at least three significant innovations. The hare has been removed and with it the rather clumsy "Böse Zeichen!;" the landscape has been modified, and while it cannot be called less wild than that of B it is a different, more meaningful kind of wildness; finally, the almost laconic statement of B has become a full-blown

3

scene in the sense that an outline has been developed into a picture, a *Stimmungsbild*. In each instance one must speak of modification rather than substitution, for the symbolic value, while being increased, remains in essence the same. Reinhard's "Böse Zeichen!" is evidently a warning, a foreboding of the failure both of the children's little expedition and, in a much broader context, their entire future relationship. The same foreboding is expressed much more subtly in S: "Bald aber hörte er hinter sich Elisabeth seinen Namen rufen. Er wandte sich um. 'Reinhard!' rief sie, 'warte doch, Reinhard!' Er konnte sie nicht gewahr werden; endlich sah er sie in einiger Entfernung mit den Sträuchern kämpfen..." – lines much more in keeping with the role Reinhard and Elizabeth play (through their passivity, to be sure) in bringing about their own unhappiness than the purely external manifestation of superstition embodied in the hare. Altogether, the notion of *Entfernung*, of the distant and unattainable, is everywhere present in *Immensee*, whereas the picture of a hare springing across the children's path is totally isolated.

An earlier change in this chapter has led to a leveling of the landscape and a shift in emphasis from a real wilderness to one that is both real and symbolic. In B the region is first described as a "nahbelegenes Waldgebirge", and the party arrives at the beech grove after "Wandern und Steigen." In S it is "eine der nah gelegenen Holzungen," and their "Wandern und Steigen" has become simply "Wandern." The single sentence used in B to describe their arduous passage through the woods, "Die Wanderung wurde immer mühsamer; bald mußten sie über sonnige Halden, bald waren Felsstücke zu überklettern," is replaced by the lengthier description of a woods with "feuchte undurchdringliche Baumschatten," "dichtes Gestrüpp," "das Wirrnis der Kräuter und Stauden," etc. In the earlier passage in which the *Waldgebirge* is mentioned B offers an additional description of the fir grove through which the party passes: "die dunklen Kronen bildeten ein undurchdringliches Dach gegen die heiße Vormittagssonne." S deletes this line, or rather transforms it and puts it into Reinhard's and Elizabeth's private wilderness. The general effect of this change in landscape is to stress the feeling of isolation from the outside world shared by the two children. Storm has been at some pains to create the impression of a foreboding (and paradoxically, a protecting, isolating) enclosure. As a result, the vague, almost generic "Felsstücke," "schroffe Felskante," and "sonnige Halden" have given way to a detailed *Bild* whose wildness is the circle drawn about the haven Reinhard and Elizabeth find and share for a brief moment of their lives: the "freier Platz... wo blaue Falter zwischen den einsamen Waldblumen flatterten."[11] Storm's critics have noted the symbolic and "mood" value of the scene. Fritz Lockemann, for example, speaks of "symbolische Vorgänge" in *Immensee* and finds two such instances in this forest scene: "Das vergebliche Erdbeersuchen: die Liebe wird keine Frucht tragen; Elisabeth als Waldeskönigin wird dem Liebenden entrückt."[12] The first symbol is common to both versions and has approximately the same strength in both, the second has been made possible in S by the elaboration in landscape description and the children's struggle to stay together amidst the "dichtes Gestrüpp." The later version has thus been enriched symbolically and the scene welded more tightly to the story as a whole: Reinhard's and Elizabeth's struggle here for *Gemeinschaft*, lacking in B altogether, anticipates not only the entire later course of the story but specifically the later episode in which Reinhard contends (as does Elizabeth here) with nature, with the "glatte Stengel" of the water lilies.

The importance of this little scene for the atmosphere of the story is, then, obvious, although it is difficult to say exactly how the *Stimmung* is created. By adding the account of the children's struggle to stay together, by placing the scene in a solitary spot of forest and suggesting thereby that the conflict is and will remain a personal one (i.e., not really dependent for its outcome on others: Erich, Elizabeth's mother, etc.), and finally by repeating such symbolic actions in modified form throughout the remainder of the Novelle, Storm has here improved on the B version. In its new form the scene contributes substantially to the greater density of structure that characterizes the standard version.

The rewriting of the *Ratskeller* scene, which opens the chapter "Da stand das Kind am Wege," marks the second major step in tightening the structure of *Immensee*. In this instance Storm has shortened the entire scene by more than 50 lines, or approximately 50%. Here too the term "symbolische Vorgänge" seems appropriate in moving from B to S, for a considerable amount of direct statement and action has been deleted. The chapter's opening lines represent perhaps the most important single statement in the story in regard to motivation. Two sentences in particular arrest our attention: "Der phantastische Aufputz und die freien Verhältnisse des Studentenlebens entwickelten den ganzen Ungestüm seiner Natur," and "Irrthum und Leidenschaft begannen ihr Teil von seiner Jugend zu fordern." The summary narrative given in the opening paragraph of B – and especially in the two sentences just quoted – is unusual for *Immensee*; we expect rather the immediate scene, the stress on the event itself and its concrete details. A glance at the standard version confirms our suspicion that this transitional passage with its slight but nonetheless significant shift in point of view (from editorial back to neutral omniscience) was considered by its author to be a violation of the whole principle of situation, of "einzelne poetische Momente:" S omits the lines entirely, a change which has earned Storm the occasional reproach that *Immensee's* motivation is weak, the plot scanty, and Reinhard's transformation too sudden and unexpected, but which nevertheless reveals clearly the conscious attempt to throw the responsibility for transition, for connecting the series of *Bilder*, onto the reader.[13] One may say that in this sense Storm is asking the reader to be his own psychologist, and such a demand marks the beginning of his well-known *Andeute-Technik*.

If the summarizing statements of the first paragraph seem a travesty of Storm's technique of suggesting rather than stating, the subsequent episode in the *Ratskeller* must be placed at the opposite extreme. Nowhere else in the story, and indeed rarely in any of the later works, do we find a scene so drawn out and so filled with the bustle of life. In offering an explanation for the radical revision of this scene, we must consider first its role in regard to the entire Novelle. The glimpse into Reinhard's way of life at the university is evidently intended to serve a double purpose: to show the change in Reinhard's character and thus prepare us for certain later events (his *Befangenheit* with Elizabeth – certainly not attributable solely to his newly awakened love –, her mother's changed attitude to Reinhard, etc.), and to motivate Reinhard's self-imposed isolation, his refusal to continue the childhood idyl with Elizabeth. To this one might add a third, although in this case it is difficult to say if we are dealing with cause or effect: the scene (in both versions) stresses the fact that Elizabeth's and Reinhard's paths have parted and are now leading the couple in opposite directions.

Having thus granted a pivotal importance to the *Ratskeller* scene, it remains to show the major differences between B and S and to discuss their effects on the work as a whole. In addition to, and in keeping with, the removal of direct statement with its different point of view in the opening paragraph, we observe a toning down of the students' exuberance throughout the drinking scene: the deletion of the *Präsides*, the colored caps and other evidences of the *Burschenschaft;* the removal of one of the two *Zithermädchen;* the omission of Reinhard's song "Wein her! Es brennt mir im Gehirne" and the addition of the *Zithermädchen*'s "Heute, nur heute;" the deletion of the preparations for a card game; and the new motivation for Reinhard's sudden return to his room. The effects of these changes are threefold. First, a new note of moderation has been given to the entire scene. The *Gesellschaft* of students becomes in S simply "Reinhard mit andern Studenten;" "im Rathsweinkeller vor vollen Rheinweinflaschen" is abbreviated to "im Ratskeller;" "noch früh am Nachmittage" becomes "noch nachmittags," perhaps a hint that the bout is, for Reinhard at least, not quite so prolonged as before. The noise of tankards being struck together, Reinhard's lusty "vivat sequens!," the drinking songs, the presence of the *Korpsbrüder*, the lengthier exchange with the *Geigenpeter* (called *Geigenspieler* in S!) have been reduced, respectively, to the popping of a champagne cork, the remark that only a few people were present and that the waiters were leaning idly against the pillars, and the attempt to persuade the one remaining *Zithermädchen* to play for the group. Reinhard's openly erotic exchange with the zither girl, who is described as a gypsy type in S, also shares in the general toning down. In the standard version Reinhard can still drink to her "schöne sündhafte Augen," but he no longer says "sie haben mein Blut in Brand gesteckt;" and her "verzehrende Augen" are described in S merely as "schwarze Augen."

Secondly, the *Zithermädchen* has been given a more important role. While the two girls have been cut to one (who remains nameless in S) and their share of the entire scene reduced by several lines, the relative significance of the remaining girl has been greatly increased. In the Biernatzki version she is described as accompanying Reinhard's drinking song with both zither and "tiefer Altstimme;" the standard version introduces her own "Heute, nur heute," sung with "tiefer, leidenschaftlicher Stimme." In this new form she is both in harmony with the quieter atmosphere of the *Ratskeller* scene with its more subdued merry-making and at the same time so prominent a figure that the entire episode seems to center on the brief encounter between Reinhard and the girl. The pathos and melancholy of her song as well as the ominous message of the last two lines cast their shadow over the scene to such an extent that what was once an illustration of Storm's opening pronouncement concerning the *Ungestüm* of Reinhard's nature (and the rather unsubtle motivation for his neglect of Elizabeth) has become both an anticipatory motif and a highly effective means of pointing out an important aspect of Reinhard's own character. For it is surely inadequate to say, as critics generally do, that the *Zithermädchen* is a symbolic Elizabeth, a forlorn, cast-off creature in whom Elizabeth later sees her own fate. She is no less the thoughtless, fun- and lifeloving Reinhard who, even in the midst of revelry, recalls with pain the impermanence of *heute*. Her new role thus gives her the function of revealing to the reader at least a part of the reason for Reinhard's and Elizabeth's failure to transport the playhouse (*Die Kinder*) and the haven in the woods (*Im Walde*) into the adult world of later years.

Thirdly, Reinhard's departure from the *Ratskeller* conserves for him no small measure of the loyalty and devotion to his past which we expect of him in the light of earlier events in the story. In B his interruption of the revelry and the subsequent discovery of the Christmas package is explained by his need for gambling money: his pockets are empty, "er wußte, zu Haus in einer Schieblade seines Pultes lagen noch drei Gulden; er hatte sie zurückgelegt, um ein Weihnachtsgeschenk für Elisabeth dafür zu kaufen." After having told his companions that he would return immediately, he got up and "stieg eilig die Kellertreppe hinauf." The deletion of the scene with the card player, part of the process of toning down the whole episode, makes Reinhard's reason for leaving the Ratskeller without point. He must be removed in another way, and Storm does this by the convenient invention of a friend to tell him of the package in his room. The importance to Reinhard of this message from home is emphasized by the addition of a new theme: the *Zithermädchen* tells him to stay, Reinhard is tempted, hesitates briefly, then declares "Ich kann nicht." As the girl turns away, Reinhard "stieg langsam die Kellertreppe hinauf." In changing *eilig* to *langsam* Storm has introduced certain complications. The *eilig* of B is of course appropriate to Reinhard's haste in getting the money for the card game; there is no ambiguity either in his haste or his character as it is shown us during the entire *Ratskeller* scene (we recall that Storm is here illustrating his initial evaluation of Reinhard). Only when he discovers the Christmas package with the letters and, as a second reminder, sees on his way back to the *Ratskeller* the Christmas tree through a lighted window do these ghosts of his own past, his "verlorenes Paradies," force a change of plans. The standard version, however, leaves some doubt as to why Reinhard's return to his room was *langsam*. Are we to share Reinhard's reluctance to leave the pleasures of the *Ratskeller* and the inviting eyes of the zither girl, or are we to feel with him a sudden nostalgia and a sense of guilt at the news of the parcel from home? The evidence would seem to favor the latter explanation, especially in the light of both the milder tone of this chapter in S and the deletion of the second "reminder," the Christmas scene viewed from a cold seat on the *Treppengeländer*. In any case, the ambiguity is effective both as a necessary part of *Andeute-Technik* and as a reflection of Reinhard's ambivalent state at this point in the story.

Seen as a whole, the revisions in the *Ratskeller* scene offer valuable insights into Storm's search for a way to make his point unobtrusively, even silently. Not only is the brevity of this chapter in its new form more in keeping with the ideal of *Bilder* or situations; the eradication of virtually all evaluative statement pushes the reader, as we have observed, more and more into the role of participator and conspirator. This aspect of the early Storm's method serves as a kind of counter-agent to the frame technique, for if we must constantly fill out the silences ourselves, the sense of distance created by the frame tends to dissolve. Thus we can see in the elimination of such a comment as "Er fühlte etwas wie Reue oder Schmerz, es war ihm, als gehöre er zum ersten Male nicht mehr dazu" (Reinhard's reaction to the Christmas scene as observed from the dark stairs) a clear progression to the situation that serves as a speaking picture and the accompanying renunciation of author intrusion.

The third major change occurs in the chapter "Meine Mutter hat's gewollt." The first fifty lines or so, somewhat more than one-third of the chapter, have been rewritten with the result that Reinhard's account of his Venetian journey has vanished, his remarks on the nature of the folksong shortened, the reading of the poem "Meine Mutter hat's gewollt" given a purely accidental character, and the idyllic aspects of the scene elaborated on. Of these four changes the first and longest need concern us least. It is manifestly filler, i.e., its relation to the remainder of this chapter – and to all of *Immensee* – is slight. Therefore its omission from S must be regarded as yet another attempt to bring the situations of the story into more tightly knit form.

A more striking example of the move toward compactness and greater cohesiveness is offered by the new role accorded the folksong. In the Biernatzki version there are three instances where the *Lied* is used as an intrinsic part of the story: on his return from the picnic (strawberry hunt) Reinhard writes a poem in his notebook. "Reinhard hatte aber doch etwas gefunden; waren es keine Erdbeeren, so war es doch auch im Walde gewachsen." Love's awakening is here united with the lyric; it is the first instance of the insertion of poetry at a key moment in the story. One cannot of course speak of symbolic value here, for the *Waldeskönigin* and Elizabeth are a clear one-to-one equation. What is significant is the turn to the simple *Volksliedton* in order to express the characters' emotions in such critical situations, prose being inadequate for this. The same principle applies to the second occurrence of verse in B. After Reinhard discovers the Christmas package in his room and reads the letters from his mother and Elizabeth he speaks aloud the verses

> Er wäre fast verirret
> Und wußte nicht hinaus;
> Da stand das Kind am Wege
> Und winkte ihm nach Haus!

That Storm intends the reader to take this as genuine emotional crisis is borne out by Reinhard's subsequent action. He takes the money he had saved for Elizabeth's present (but later forgotten), then intended to use for the card game in the *Ratskeller*, and buys the present after all. To be sure, both the package with the letters and the Christmas tree scene supply sufficient motivation for Reinhard's change of heart, but the point is that at the critical moment (an emotional *Wendepunkt*) a simple lyric is inserted.

The third use of lyric poetry in B occurs in the episode under consideration, the *Gartensaal* scene. In addition to Reinhard's comments on the nature of the *Volkslied*, not necessarily appropriate to the scene as a whole, and the reading and singing of *Schnaderhüpfl*, etc., we are given the poem "Meine Mutter hat's gewollt." Reinhard had heard it, he says, "im vorigen Herbste in der Gegend unsrer Heimath... Die Mädchen sangen es beim Flachsbrechen; die Melodie habe ich nicht behalten können, sie war mir völlig unbekannt." This time it is not for Reinhard that the *Volkslied* speaks: Elizabeth recognizes her own unhappy life in the lines and quickly leaves the *Gartensaal*, thus ending the scene.

These uses of lyric poetry, either *Volkslieder* or *volksliedhafte Lieder*, are, as we have indicated, valuable parts of the Biernatzki *Immensee*. But there is still something occasional, even arbitrary, about them. They seem to represent and enhance single, isolated moments or scenes, and with no predictable frequency, throughout the story. The standard version has removed the occasional, non-related character and thereby strengthened their role considerably. The three occurrences of B have been increased to five and Reinhard's description of the folksong in the *Gartensaal* scene made more meaningful and "natural" by an earlier reference to his *Sammeltätigkeit*.[14] The standard version of the *Ratskeller* scene, we observed earlier, removed Reinhard's boisterous drinking song and added the important "Heute, nur heute" of the zither girl. The way of life led by Reinhard and embodied in the gypsy girl is summed up symbolically in the song's "message," which is the transiency of life and love and beauty. The recurrence of the song's final lines at a later point in the story emphasizes their importance, for at the moment when Reinhard realizes fully that Elizabeth is forever lost to him "ein altes Lied brauste ihm ins Ohr."

Another instance of the interweaving of motifs through folksong is the connecting of Reinhard's poem "Meine Mutter hat's gewollt" to a later incident. We have seen that in the Biernatzki version Reinhard read this song to his friends "on purpose," as it were. In S, on the other hand, Reinhard is made to say "Wir lesen auf gut

Glück... ich habe sie selber noch nicht durchgesehen" thus making his choice of this particular *Volkslied* purely accidental. The advantages of such a change are evident. Fate is given a far greater role in the events: it is not Reinhard who intentionally (or unthinkingly) chooses this song with its obvious connection to Elizabeth, but rather we are made to sense the inevitability of such an expression of "Unser eigenstes Tun und Leiden" at this particular gathering. It is thus inner necessity rather than intentional selection, a fact borne out by the song's last two lines,

> Ach, könnt ich betteln gehen
> Über die braune Heid!

The insertion of a short scene in the later chapter *Elisabeth* in which Elizabeth pours the contents of her purse into the hands of a beggar girl returns us to this *Gartensaal* scene in the same manner as the "Sterben, ach sterben/ soll ich allein" establishes a connection to the *Ratskeller* scene.[15]

A final change in the *Gartensaal* scene, the slight increase in emphasis on the idyllic aspects, is an attempt to give greater unity to *Immensee* in much the same way as the use of folksong discussed above. In this instance, however, the effects are less positive. For example, the deletion of Reinhard's totally irrelevant travel anecdote (Storm evidently realized that a sojourn in Italy could not help but have a retarding, disjunctive effect on the *Bilder* sequence) has caused the author to attempt a rounding off of the opening lines of the chapter. To the standard version he added the sentence "Die Türen standen offen; die Sonne war schon hinter den Wäldern jenseits des Sees," which has the purpose of supplying a smoother transition to Reinhard's *Volkslieder* and an appropiate nature setting for his and Elizabeth's spiritual reunion (continued of course on their walks in the following chapter). In adding this line it is quite possible that Storm momentarily forgot the passage which comes a page later and introduces the song "Meine Mutter hat's gewollt:" "ein roter Abendschein lag wie Schaum auf den

Wäldern jenseits des Sees." The point is admittedly a minor one, yet the dangers of excessive sentimentality in describing such a scene as this make the similarity in wording unfortunate because any hint of overworked phrasing, of the ready-made expression, immediately deprives the passage of its effectiveness.

Another minor modification raises the same problem of freshness versus stylization, of genuine spontaneity versus effect-creating. In B Reinhard has just read some Tyrolean *Schnaderhüpfl*, and Erich, in answer to Elizabeth's query as to their origins, replies

> "'das hört man den Dingern schon an, Schneidergesellen und Friseure! und derlei luftiges Gesindel!' Reinhard las hierauf das tiefsinnige 'Ich stand auf hohen Bergen.' Elisabeth kannte die Melodie, die so rätselhaft ist, daß man nicht glauben kann, sie sei von Menschen erdacht worden. Beide sangen nun das Lied gemeinschaftlich, Elisabeth mit ihrer etwas verdeckten Altstimme dem Tenor secondirend."

The standard version offers a much more elaborate scene:

> "Er nahm ein anderes Blatt: 'Ich stand auf hohen Bergen...' 'Das kenn ich!' rief Elisabeth. 'Stimme nur an, Reinhard, ich will dir helfen.' Und nun sangen sie jene Melodie, die so rätselhaft ist, daß man nicht glauben kann, sie sei von Menschen erdacht worden; Elisabeth mit ihrer etwas verdeckten Altstimme dem Tenor sekundierend.
>
> Die Mutter saß inzwischen emsig an ihrer Näherei, Erich hatte die Hände ineinandergelegt und hörte andächtig zu. Als das Lied zu Ende war, legte Reinhard schweigend das Blatt beiseite. – Vom Ufer des Sees herauf kam durch die Abendstille das Geläute der Herdenglocken; sie horchten unwillkürlich; da hörten sie eine klare Knabenstimme singen:
>
> > Ich stand auf hohen Bergen,
> > Und sah ins tiefe Tal...
>
> Reinhard lächelte: 'Hört ihr es wohl? So geht's von Mund zu Mund.'
> 'Es wird oft in dieser Gegend gesungen,' sagte Elisabeth.
> 'Ja', sagte Erich, 'es ist der Hirtenkaspar; er treibt die Starken heim.'
> Sie horchten noch eine Weile, bis das Geläute oben hinter den Wirtschaftsgebäuden verschwunden war."

In this little idyl Storm is trying to make nature, a thoroughly domesticated landscape, work for him. The introduction of a boy actually singing the folksong at such a propitious time would evidently serve to add *Stimmung* to a picture of simple people close to nature – and themselves singing the *Urtöne* which, Reinhard claims, arise spontaneously and are "an tausend Stellen zugleich gesungen." It is perhaps unnecessary to point out how dangerously close this *Bild* comes to the oversentimentalizing that lies at the heart of so much second-rate Biedermeier literature. In any case the little scene does not appear to effect much improvement in the earlier version. It is incidental but interesting to observe how the *Knabe* of the Biernatzki version, the "nackter, schwarzäugiger Bube," has been taken over into S and made into a *Hirtenknabe* who moves in a truly pastoral setting. In sum, one may accept and even mildly admire the elaboration which S offers, but one can scarcely call it an improvement over the scant seven lines of B.

The fourth major change in *Immensee*, the incident with the beggar girl, has already been discussed in connection with the use of folksong in the story. The entire scene of some 25 to 30 lines is an entirely new addition and has, as was indicated earlier, an intimate connection to the *Ratskeller* scene. The *Geigenspieler* has become a *Scherenschleifer*, but the identity is unmistakable: as he turns his grinding wheel he hums a *Zigeunermelodie*. And the girl "mit verstörten schönen Augen" causes Reinhard to call out a name and, getting no answer, to recall the eyes of the zither girl. Whether or not the identity is intended to be real or symbolic is of little consequence, for it is Reinhard's and Elizabeth's own fate, their childhood love, which has reappeared here wearing a death mask. At this moment both feel the beggar girl to be an answer to the question Reinhard had asked shortly before, "hinter jenen blauen Bergen liegt unsere Jugend. Wo ist sie geblieben?"

An additional justification for the addition of this scene to *Immensee* may be given. We have observed that a number of critical moments in the story are given with "double" motivation, that is, symbolic importance is stressed by offering a variation of the original action. The strawberry hunt, for example, is a symbolic action in that the fruits of the children's love are withheld. In the same episode their separation by nature and their struggle to come back together are a reinforcement of the same basic theme. Reinhard's decision not to return to the *Ratskeller* was made after his discovery of the package and letters from home; and in the same scene Storm has him catch a glimpse of the kind of Christmas he had known as a boy. The incident with the beggar girl represents in this sense a reinforcement of Reinhard's futile quest of the water lily. His failure to grasp the flower, "fern und einsam über der dunklen Tiefe" is of course his inability and guilt in not having seized the happiness that might have been his.[16] The beggar girl as a reminder of the past tells him a second time of his failure and the fate in store for him. Immediately after this scene Reinhard retraces the paths he had walked with Elizabeth during his visit, but it is a meaningless action. Symbolically and in reality he has taken the last step before fulfilling the gypsy girl's prophecy. Her words to Reinhard, "Ich will nichts mehr," are effectively ambiguous, for they apply both to herself and Reinhard and Elizabeth, both to the past with its warning and the future with its emptiness. The two versions of *Immensee* close this chapter with Reinhard's dramatic leave-taking, but the standard version has with admirable economy placed double emphasis on the necessity for this final step.

The last major change and the most important artistically and materially is the deletion of an entire chapter in the revision of *Immensee*. In an essay written in 1880 Erich Schmidt, literary historian and personal friend of Storm, gives his reaction to the omission: "Da erzählt die erste Fassung zu unserm Befremden, daß Reinhard später eine brave Hausfrau heimführte, den mit Jubel begrüßten Knaben früh, die Gattin nach dreißig Jahren verlor und dann – nach dreißig Jahren – sein Auge vereinsamt auf die im Abenddämmerschein auftauchende Wasserlilie heftete. Hier war ein dicker Strich geboten."[17] With his customary terseness Schmidt has touched the chapter's most vulnerable spot

– "nach dreißig Jahren" – for psychologically Storm's explanation for the old man's *Träumerei* after the death of wife and son and the passage of three decades is as unlikely as it is impossible to accept aesthetically. Additional reasons for deleting this chapter were perhaps so self-evident to Schmidt as to require no explanation. Certainly the reader's *Befremden* is just as warranted here as in those other instances where B has failed to maintain economy of story line, notably in the *Ratskeller* and *Gartensaal* scenes. But other equally severe objections to the chapter may be raised. There is firstly the way in which these later events violate the story's symbolism. The water lily (an even more important symbol in B than in S, which adds the "Sterben, ach sterben" motif), being just out of reach, condemns Reinhard to solitude. Hence his marriage and the birth of his son are so irrelevant or even contrary to what *Immensee* is about as to represent an outright violation of the remainder of the story. Secondly, one may object in particular to the birth of Reinhard's son: "Er gerieth dadurch in die aufgeregteste Freude, er lief in die Nacht hinaus und schrie es in die Winde: 'Mir ist ein Sohn geboren!'" Disregarding for a moment the artistic irrelevancy of this event, we may call it one of the three central happenings of the story, the other two being Reinhard's secret, his unwillingness to declare himself to Elizabeth before returning to the university, and his leave-taking from the *Immenhof*. Both of the latter are shrouded in silence, this one ought to be also.

Finally, the architecture of the whole is weakened, for the *Bilder* of which *Immensee* consists do not attempt to cover longer stretches of time or a number of situations at once. At the risk of affecting hindsight and working backwards from the standard to the Biernatzki version, we may insist on the non-essentiality of this chapter by noting briefly its place in the structure of *Immensee*. Two short chapters (entitled *Der Alte* in S) act as a frame and give the story its circular form; following the first chapter and preceding the last are two pairs of chapters, dealing with Reinhard and Elizabeth in analogous situations: *Die Kinder* and *Im Walde* offer the childhood idyl with its undertone of future unhappiness; *Meine Mutter hat's gewollt* and *Elisabeth* are the futile attempt to recapture the idyl and the final separation. Or one might describe them as the adult tragedy (anti-idyllic) with its undertone of idyllic past. In the center are the four remaining chapters, of which the first, *Da stand das Kind am Wege*, represents the preparation for reunion after the revealing student chapter, and the last, *Immensee*, Reinhard's and Elizabeth's final reunion. The core of the Novelle is found in the two chapters *Daheim* and *Ein Brief*. Interestingly enough, if we omit the episode dealing with Reinhard's marriage, the exact center of *Immensee* falls between these two chapters, both of which deal with the story's main "fact:" the failure of the two children to stay together. Thus the novellistic *Mittelpunkt* toward which all else is directed occurs in the two year span of silence between Reinhard's Easter visit and the letter from his mother. And not only is this central act outside the story, its *post facto* transmission requires a scant 19 lines, making *Ein Brief* the shortest chapter in *Immensee* with the sole exception of the concluding one (which is in effect but a reiteration of the story's opening.)

It is thus apparent that the account of Reinhard's later years destroys the careful symmetry of the other episodes. Moreover, it does not offer a *Bild* or an everyday situation raised to the level of poetry but rather the same kind of summary we observed at the beginning of the *Ratskeller* scene. A brief review of Storm's treatment of time in *Immensee* shows clearly this second asymmetrical aspect of the episode:

Der Alte: flashback to youth, offering the rudiments of frame.
  Duration: a few minutes.
Die Kinder: Reinhard is 10, Elizabeth 5.
  Duration: a few hours or less.
Im Walde: Seven years later.
  Duration: half a day.
Da stand das Kind am Wege: a few months later.
  Duration: early afternoon to following morning, with the passing of night indicated in one line.

Daheim: approximately three months later.
Duration: Easter vacation of some six weeks. (Two summarizing paragraphs, one scene with *Goldfinken* and *Maiblume,* one scene describing children's farewell).
Ein Brief: two years later. The letter of some 10 lines deals only with Elizabeth's *Jawort.*
Immensee: "Wiederum waren Jahre vorüber"
Duration: several days. (All but one paragraph is devoted to two scenes: Reinhard's arrival at Immensee and Erich's surprise for Elizabeth; Reinhard sees the figure of a woman beside the *Abendbank*).
Meine Mutter hat's gewollt: "Einige Tage nachher."
Duration: from early evening to night. (Two scenes: the *Gartensaal* scene and Reinhard's quest for the water lily.)
Elisabeth: "Am folgenden Nachmittag."
Duration: afternoon and night, comprising three scenes: the walk with Elizabeth (ending with the beggar girl incident), Reinhard's solitary walk, and his last night at Immenhof (ending with his farewell to Elizabeth.)
[Reinhard]: "Nach einigen Jahren."
Duration: perhaps 40 to 50 years (death of Reinhard's mother soon after the *Immenhof* scene; "so gingen mehrere Jahre hin"; marriage and death of wife after thirty years; unspecified lapse of time that carries the reader up to the closing scene).
Der Alte: return to opening scene of the Novelle.
Duration: a few minutes.

The foregoing remarks proceeded from Storm's own concept of the Novelle as he found it embodied in *Immensee* and a few other early prose attempts. Our comparison of the two *Immensee*'s has shown the consistency with which he pursued his goal of creating a series of single situations or scenes linked together by inner action. We may summarize the effects of Storm's revisions under five headings:

1. An economy of narration has been achieved, primarily through elimination of irrelevant passages and scenes. The standard version, we recall, represents a shortening of B by some 10%.
2. A greater degree of unity has been given to the story, chiefly through reiteration of motifs and symbols and the deletion of summarizing, "transitional" lines.
3. A few author intrusions have been omitted, the editorial "we" of B giving way to straight objective narration.
4. The already scant plot of B has been further "verinnerlicht;" mood has been heightened and connecting narration(points 1 & 3) reduced to a minimum.
5. The technique of suggestion and the general artistic principle of silence have been evolved to such a point that (a) any choice between stating and rendering (to use the Jamesian terms) is made in favor of the latter, (b) psychological analysis is virtually eliminated, and (c) major acts are placed offstage: the Novelle's critical moments are wrapped in silence, understatement and dramatic gesture generally serving in place of such action.

It should be noted that these effects are fundamentally one and the same inasmuch as economy, unity through motif and symbol, *Verinnerlichung*, the tendency to compress and suggest, etc., all point to one basic fact in Storm's early novellistic art as it is revealed in his revision of the 1849 *Immensee*: the movement of the short prose work toward the poem, both in general structure and in details of composition. The point has of course been made many times before – one need only recall the frequency with which Storm's remark, "Meine Novellistik hat sich aus der Lyrik entwickelt," has been quoted – but its importance for an appreciation of Storm's theory of composition cannot be overestimated. Not that one can accept without reservation the notion of the shorter prose pieces developing effortlessly from a body of lyric poetry modest in size but substantial in quality. The continuity, if there actually is one, exists primarily between Storm's youthful ghost stories, fairy tales, and anecdotes – in oral rather than written form – and his earliest published stories.[18] It is rather the attitude lying behind both poem and prose work that makes the latter seem *gedichthaft*. In his *Grundbegriffe der Poetik* (p. 60 & 66) Emil Staiger equates lyric style with recollection (*lyrischer Stil: Erinnerung*) and explains that "Vergangenes als Gegenstand einer Erzählung gehört dem Gedächtnis an. Vergangenes als Thema des Lyrischen ist ein Schatz der Erinnerung... So dürfen wir sagen, daß der Erzähler Vergangenes vergegenwärtigt. Der lyrische Dichter vergegenwärtigt das Vergangene so wenig wie das, was jetzt geschieht. Beides ist ihm vielmehr gleich nah und näher als alle Gegenwart. Er geht darin auf, das heißt, er 'erinnert.' 'Erinnerung' soll der Name sein für das Fehlen des Abstandes zwischen Subjekt und Objekt, für das lyrische Ineinander." Storm's use of frame, even in a rudimentary stage, suggests a qualification to this explanation of *Erinnerung*, but no reader will question the general appropiateness of the lines to Storm's early prose.

In *Immensee* particularly one is able to see Staiger's distinction between *Gedächtnis* and *Erinnerung*, for the dissolution of plot as a narrative flow into a series of genre-like scenes represents a commitment to the lyrical *Ineinander* that requires no audible or visible linking, i.e., no connecting narration and a minimum of epithets. The result of such dissolution is not, however, a turn to impressionistic art, as has been suggested on occasion,[19] but a pronounced approach to the formal structure of the poem. Johannes Klein, one of the supporters of the term *lyrische Novellen* for the early stories, makes this telling comparison:

> Auch die Technik ist die eines Gedichtes. Das Ganze ist in Kapitel eingeteilt, die die Funktion von Strophen haben. Die Kapitel sind mit Versen und Gedichten nach Eichendorffscher Art durchsetzt und enthalten Seitenstücke zu Storms Lyrik, wie jenes Motive der leidgezeichneten Hände. – Die Handlung tritt zurück hinter der Stimmung, und nur die markanten Stimmungs-Augenblicke sind festgehalten.[20]

The division into chapters is a part of the work of revision. But since B also clearly indicates the points of chapter separation (by means of a heavy black line and wider spacing) the addition of chapter titles in S can hardly be called a major change. Nonetheless, the greater emphasis given by these titles – themselves appropriate for poems – to the *Bilder* as separate, *markante* situations serves to suggest stanzas of a poem, in which the spaces between hint at another kind of continuity than mere narrative. And the silence of these spaces is neither an avowal of ignorance nor an intentional withholding of unimportant parts of the narrative but rather a special kind of communication.

THE *IMMENSEE* REVISIONS

Biernatzki	Standard (Böhme, vol. I, pp. 243-82)
1. no chapt. title	243 *Der Alte*

Except for minor punctuation changes, this first chapter is the same in both versions.

2. no title	244 *Die Kinder*
Hier war er nicht allein; denn bald trat die anmuthige Gestalt eines kleinen Mädchens zu ihm.	244 Bald trat die anmutige Gestalt eines kleinen Mädchens zu ihm.
Der winkte ihm mit der Hand und ging gerade in die Felsen hinein; da stand der Mann auf und folgte ihm, und sie gingen ungehindert weiter mitten durchs Gestein, und bei jedem Schritt, den sie vorwärts thaten, wurden vor ihnen die Felsen donnernd aufgerissen. So erzählte Reinhardt; Elisabeth hatte aufmerksam zugehört.	245-46 Der winkte ihm mit der Hand und ging dann gerade in die Felsen hinein. Elisabeth hatte aufmerksam zugehört.
"Das weiß ich nicht", antwortete er; "aber es giebt doch keine."	246 "Das weiß ich nicht", antwortete er.
3. no title	247 *Im Walde*

der junge Adler gelobte, an der armen Krähe Rache zu nehmen	247 der Adler gelobte an der grauen Krähe Rache zu nehmen
aber immer überkam ihn das Gefühl, als dürfe er diese uralten Geschichten nicht antasten.	248 aber er wußte nicht weshalb, er konnte immer nicht dazu gelangen.
Nun wollte man noch einmal sich und die Natur zusammen in Heiterkeit empfinden. Dazu wurde eine Landpartie nach dem nahbelegenen Waldgebirge in größerer Gesellschaft veranstaltet.	248 Nun wollte man noch einmal einen festlichen Tag zusammen begehen. Dazu wurde eine Landpartie nach einer der nahe gelegenen Holzungen in größerer Gesellschaft veranstaltet.
Ein Tannengehölz mußte zuerst durchwandert werden; die dunkeln Kronen bildeten ein undurchdringliches Dach gegen die heiße Vormittagssonne; es war kühl und dämmerig und der Boden überall mit feinen Nadeln bestreut. Nach halbstündigem Wandern und Steigen kam man...	248–49 Ein Tannengehölz mußte zuerst durchwandert werden; es war kühl und dämmerig und der Boden überall mit feinen Nadeln bestreut. Nach halbstündigem Wandern kam man...
Auf einem Platze, über welchem uralte Buchen mit ihren Kronen zu einem durchsichtigen Laubgewölbe emporstrebten, machte die Gesellschaft Halt.	249 Auf einem Platze, über welchem uralte Buchen mit ihren Kronen zu einem durchsichtigen Laubgewölbe zusammenwuchsen, machte die Gesellschaft Halt.
Zum Frühstück erhält jetzt ein Jeder von Euch zwei trockene Wecken; die Butter ist zu Hause geblieben, die Zukost muß sich ein Jeder selber suchen.	249 Zum Frühstück erhält jetzt ein jeder von euch zwei trockene Wecken; die Butter ist zu Hause geblieben, die Zukost müßt ihr euch selber suchen.
So gingen sie in den Wald hinein: als sie eine Strecke gegangen waren, sprang ein Hase über den Weg. "Böse Zeichen!" sagte Reinhardt. Die Wanderung wurde immer mühsamer; bald mußten sie über weite sonnige Halden, bald waren Felsstücke zu überklettern. "Wo bleiben Deine Erdbeeren?" fragte Elisabeth, in-	250–51 Elisabeth knüpfte die grünen Bänder ihres Strohhutes zusammen und hing ihn über den Arm. "So komm", sagte sie, "der Korb ist fertig." Dann gingen sie in den Wald hinein, tiefer und tiefer; durch feuchte undurchdringliche Baumschatten,

dem sie stehen blieb und einen tiefen Athemzug that.
    Sie waren bei diesen Worten um eine schroffe Felsenkante herumgegangen. Reinhardt machte ein erstauntes Gesicht. Hier haben sie gestanden, sagte er...

wo alles still war, nur unsichtbar über ihnen in den Lüften das Geschrei der Falken, dann wieder durch dichtes Gestrüpp, so dicht, daß Reinhard vorangehen mußte, um einen Pfad zu machen, hier einen Zweig zu knicken, dort eine Ranke beiseite zu biegen. Bald aber hörte er hinter sich Elisabeth seinen Namen rufen. Er wandte sich um. "Reinhard!" rief sie, "warte doch, Reinhard!" Er konnte sie nicht gewahr werden; endlich sah er sie in einiger Entfernung mit den Sträuchern kämpfen; ihr feines Köpfchen schwamm nur kaum über den Spitzen der Farrenkräuter. Nun ging er noch einmal zurück und führte sie durch das Wirrnis der Kräuter und Stauden auf einen freien Platz hinaus, wo blaue Falter zwischen den einsamen Waldblumen flatterten. Reinhard strich ihr die feuchten Haare aus dem erhitzten Gesichtchen; dann wollte er ihr den Strohhut aufsetzen und sie wollte es nicht leiden; dann aber bat er sie, und dann ließ sie es doch geschehen.
    "Wo bleiben denn aber deine Erdbeeren?" fragte sie endlich, indem sie stehenblieb und einen tiefen Atemzug tat.
    "Hier haben sie gestanden", sagte er.

"Als wir uns im Walde verirret hatten"   253 (title of the poem not given)

Die blauen Fliegen blitzen
Und summen durch die Luft.

253 Die blauen Fliegen summen
Und blitzen durch die Luft.

4. no title

254 *Da stand das Kind am Wege*

24

Reinhardt hatte in einer entfernten Stadt die Universität bezogen. Der phantastische Aufputz und die freien Verhältnisse des Studentenlebens entwickelten den ganzen Ungestüm seiner Natur. Das Stilleben seiner Vergangenheit und die Personen, welche dahinein gehörten, traten immer mehr zurück; die Briefe an seine Mutter wurden immer sparsamer, auch enthielten sie keine Märchen für Elisabeth. So schrieb denn auch sie nicht an ihn, und er bemerkte es kaum. Irrthum und Leidenschaft begannen ihr Theil von seiner Jugend zu fordern. So verging ein Monat nach dem andern.

Endlich war der Weihnachtabend herangekommen. – Es war noch früh am Nachmittage, als eine Gesellschaft von Studenten an dem alten Eichtische im Rathsweinkeller vor vollen Rheinweinflaschen zusammensaß. Die Lampen an den Wänden waren angezündet, denn hier unten dämmerte es schon. Die Studenten sangen ein lateinisches Trinklied, Rheinwein-und die Präsides, welche zu beiden Enden des Tisches saßen, schlugen bei jedem Endrefrain mit den blanken Schlägern aneinander, die sie beständig in den Händen hielten. Die Meisten aus der Gesellschaft trugen rothe oder blaue silbergestickte Käppchen, und außer Reinhardt, welcher mit in der Zahl war, rauchten alle aus langen mit schweren Quasten behangenen Pfeifen, welche sie auch während des Singens und Trinkens unaufhältlich in Brand zu halten wußten. – Nicht weit davon in einem Winkel des Gewölbes saßen ein Geigenspieler und zwei Zittermädchen; sie hatten ihre Instrumente auf dem Schooß liegen und sahen gleichgültig dem Gelage zu.

(this passage deleted from the standard version)

254 Weihnachtabend kam heran. Es war noch nachmittags, als Reinhard mit andern Studenten im Ratskeller am alten Eichentisch zusammensaß. Die Lampen an den Wänden waren angezündet, denn hier unten dämmerte es schon; aber die Gäste waren sparsam versammelt, die Kellner lehnten müßig an den Mauerpfeilern. In einem Winkel des Gewölbes saßen ein Geigenspieler und ein Zithermädchen mit feinen zigeunerhaften Zügen; sie hatten ihre Instrumente auf dem Schooße liegen und schienen teilnahmlos vor sich hinzusehen.

Am Studententische knallte ein Champagnerpropfen. "Trinke, mein böhmisch Liebchen!" rief ein junger Mann von junkerhaftem Äußern, indem er ein volles Glas zu dem Mädchen hinüberreichte.

"Ich mag nicht", sagte sie, ohne ihre Stellung zu verändern.

"So singe!" rief der Junker und warf ihr eine Silbermünze in den Schoß. Das Mädchen strich sich langsam

25

Am Studententische wurde ein Rundgesang beliebt; Reinhardts Nachbar hatte eben gesungen. "Vivat sequens!" rief er und stürzte sein Glas herunter. Reinhardt sang sogleich:
Wein her! Es brennt mir im Gehirne;
Wein her! Nur einen ganzen Schlauch!
Wohl ist sie schön, die braune Dirne,
Doch eine Hexe ist sie auch!
Dann hob er sein Glas auf und that, wie sein Vorgänger.
"Brandfuchs!" rief der eine Präses und füllte Reinhardt's leeres Glas, "Deine Lieder sind noch durstiger, als Deine Kehle."
"Vivat sequens!" rief Reinhardt.
"Holla! Musik!" schrie der dritte; "Musik, wenn wir singen, verfluchter Geigenpeter!"
"Gnädiger Herr," sagte der Geigenspieler, "die Herren Barone belieben gar zu lustig durcheinander zu singen. Wir können's nicht gar so geschwind."
"Flausen, vermaledeite braune Lügen! Die schwarze Lore ist eigensinnig; und Du bist ihr gehorsamer Diener!"
Der Geigenpeter flüsterte dem Mädchen etwas ins Ohr; aber sie warf den Kopf zurück und stützte das Kinn auf ihre Zitter. "Für den spiel' ich nicht." sagte sie.
"Gnädiger Herr," rief der Geigenpeter, "die Zitter ist in Unordnung, Mamsell Lore hat eine Schraube verloren; die Käthe und ich werden uns bemühen, Euer Gnaden zu begleiten."
"Herr Bruder," sagte der Angeredete und schlug Reinhardt auf die Schulter, "Du hast uns das Mädel totalement verdorben! Geh, und bring' ihr die Schrauben wieder in Ordnung, so werde ich Dir zum Recompens Dein neuestes Liedel singen."

mit den Fingern durch ihr schwarzes Haar, während der Geigenspieler ihr ins Ohr flüsterte.
"Für den spiel' ich nicht", sagte sie. Reinhard sprang mit dem Glase in der Hand auf und stellte sich vor sie.

(deleted)

"Bravo!" riefen die Übrigen, "die Käthe ist zu alt, die Lore muß spielen."
Reinhardt sprang mit dem Glase in der Hand auf, und stellte sich vor sie.
"Was willst Du?" fragte sie trotzig.
"Deine Augen sehn."
"Was gehn Dich meine Augen an?"
Reinhardt sah funkelnd auf sie nieder.
"Ich weiß wohl, sie sind falsch; aber sie haben mein Blut in Brand gesteckt." Er hob sein Glas an den Mund. "Auf Deine schönen, sündhaften Augen!" sagte er und trank.
Sie lachte, und warf den Kopf herum. "Gieb!" sagte sie; und indem sie ihre verzehrenden Augen in die seinen heftete, trank sie langsam den Rest. Dann griff sie einen Dreiklang, und indem der Geigenpeter und das andere Mädchen einfielen, secondirte sie Reinhardt's Lied mit ihrer tiefen Altstimme.
"Ad loca!" riefen die Präsides und klirrten mit den Schlägerklingen. Nun ging der Rundgesang die Reihe durch, dazu klangen die Gläser und die Schläger klirrten beim Endrefrain, und die Geige und die Zittern rauschten dazwischen. Als das zu Ende war, warfen die Präsides die Schläger auf den Tisch und riefen: "colloquium!" Nun schlug ein dickwanstiger Bursche mit der Faust auf den Tisch: "Jetzt werde ich den Füchsen einigen Unterricht angedeihen lassen!" rief er, "das wird ihnen über die Maaßen wohlthun. Aufgemerkt also! Wer nicht antworten kann, trinkt drei pro poena."
Die Füchse und die Brandfüchse standen sämmtlich auf und faßten jeder ihr Glas. Nun fragte das bemooste Haupt: "Was für ein Abend ist heute Abend?"
"Weihnachtabend!" riefen die Füchse wie aus einer Kehle.

255 "Was willst du?" fragte sie trotzig.
"Deine Augen sehen."
"Was gehen dich meine Augen an?"
Reinhard sah funkelnd auf sie nieder.
"Ich weiß wohl, sie sind falsch!" – Sie legte ihre Wange in die flache Hand und sah ihn lauernd an. Reinhard hob sein Glas an den Mund. "Auf deine schönen, sündhaften Augen!" sagte er und trank.
Sie lachte und warf den Kopf herum. "Gib!" sagte sie, und indem sie ihre schwarzen Augen in die seinen heftete, trank sie langsam den Rest. Dann griff sie einen Dreiklang und sang mit tiefer, leidenschaftlicher Stimme:

> Heute, nur heute
> Bin ich so schön;
> Morgen, ach morgen
> Muß alles vergehn!
> Nur diese Stunde
> Bist du noch mein;
> Sterben, ach sterben
> Soll ich allein.

Während der Geigenspieler in raschem Tempo das Nachspiel einsetzte, gesellte sich ein neuer Ankömmling zu der Gruppe.
"Ich wollte dich abholen, Reinhard", sagte er. "Du warst schon fort; aber das Christkind war bei dir eingekehrt." "Das Christkind?" sagte Reinhard, "das kommt nicht mehr zu mir."
"Ei was! Dein ganzes Zimmer roch

27

Der Alte nickte langsam mit dem Kopfe. "Ei, ei!" sagte er, "die Füchse werden immer klüger. Aber nun kommt's: "Wie viel der heiligen Könige erschienen an der Krippe zu Bethelehem?"
"Drei!" antworteten die Füchse.
"Ja," sagte der Alte, "ich dachte nicht daran; Ihr seid ja eben erst hinter'm Katechismus weggelaufen. Aber nun geht's an die Hauptfrage! Woher, wenn 's zu Bethelehem der heiligen Könige nur drei waren, woher kommt es, daß heute Abend ihrer dennoch vier erscheinen werden?"
"Aus Deiner Tasche kommt es!" sagte Reinhardt. "Heraus mit dem Buch der vier Könige, Du eingefleischter Spielteufel!"
"Du knackst alle Nüsse, mein Junge!" sagte der Alte und reichte Reinhardten über den Tisch weg die Hand. "Komm, ich geb' Dir Revange für Deine silbernen Tressen, die Du gestern vom Sonntagscamisol herunterschneiden mußtest. Aber heute geht's um baar Geld!" Dabei schlug er an seine Westentaschen und breitete ein vergriffenes Spiel Karten auf dem Tisch aus. – Reinhardt griff in seine Taschen; es war kein Heller darin. Eine hastige Röthe stieg ihm in's Gesicht; er wußte, zu Haus in einer Schieblade seines Pultes lagen noch drei Gulden; er hatte sie zurückgelegt, um ein Weihnachtsgeschenk für Elisabeth dafür zu kaufen, und dann wieder darum vergessen. "Baar Geld?" sagte er, "ich habe nichts bei mir; aber wart' nur, ich bin gleich wieder da." Dann stand er auf und stieg eilig die Kellertreppe hinauf.

Er stolperte die Treppe hinauf und trat in seine Stube. Er wollte sofort im

nach Tannenbaum und braunen Kuchen."
Reinhard setzte das Glas aus der Hand und griff nach seiner Mütze.
"Was willst du?" fragte das Mädchen.
"Ich komme schon wieder."
Sie runzelte die Stirn. "Bleib!" rief sie leise und sah ihn vertraulich an.
Reinhard zögerte. "Ich kann nicht", sagte er.
Sie stieß ihn lachend mit der Fußspitze. "Geh!" sagte sie. "Du taugst nichts." Und während sie sich abwandte, stieg Reinhard langsam die Kellertreppe hinauf.

256 er stolperte die Treppe hinauf und trat in seine Stube. Ein

Dunkeln das Pult aufschließen und das
Geld herausnehmen; aber ein süßer Duft
schlug ihm entgegen

Dann trat er plötzlich an sein Pult, nahm
das Geld heraus und ging wieder auf die
Straße hinab. Hier war es mittlerweile
stiller geworden, die Umzüge der Kinder
hatten aufgehört, der Wind fegte durch
die einsamen Straßen, Alte und Junge
saßen in ihren Häusern familienweise
zusammen. Auch die Weihnachtsbäume
hatten ausgebrannt; nur aus einem Fenster brach noch ein heller Kerzenschein
in das Dunkel hinaus. Reinhardt stand
still und suchte auf den Fußspitzen einen
Blick in das Zimmer zu gewinnen; aber
es waren hohe Läden vor den Fenstern,
er sah nur die Spitze des Tannenbaums
mit der Knittergoldfahne und die obersten Kerzen. Er fühlte etwas wie Reue
oder Schmerz, es war ihm, als gehöre
er zum ersten Male nicht mehr dazu.
Die Kinder da drinnen aber wußten
nichts von ihm, sie ahnten es nicht, daß
draußen Jemand, wie er es zuvor von
hungrigen Bettelkindern gesehen hatte,
auf das Treppengeländer geklettert war
und sehnsüchtig in ihre Freude wie in ein
verlorenes Paradies hineinsah. Zwar
hatte ihm in den letzten Jahren seine
Mutter keinen Baum mehr aufgeputzt;
aber sie waren dann immer zu Elisabeths
Mutter hinübergegangen. Elisabeth hatte
noch jedes Jahr einen Weihnachtsbaum
erhalten und Reinhardt hatte immer das
Beste dabei gethan. Am Vorabende hatte
man immer den großen Menschen auf's
eifrigste damit beschäftigt finden können, Papiernetze und Flittergold auszuschneiden, Kerzen anzubrennen, Eier und
Mandeln zu vergolden und was sonst

süßer Duft schlug ihm entgegen

258 Dann trat er an sein Pult, nahm
einiges Geld heraus und ging wieder
auf die Straße hinab. – Hier war es
mittlerweile stiller geworden; die
Weihnachtsbäume waren ausgebrannt, die Umzüge der Kinder
hatten aufgehört. Der Wind fegte
durch die einsamen Straßen; Alte
und Junge saßen in ihren Häusern
familienweise zusammen; der zweite
Abschnitt des Weihnachtabends
hatte begonnen. –

(deleted)

noch zu den goldnen Geheimnissen des Weihnachtsbaums gehörte. Wenn dann am folgenden Abend der Baum angezündet war, so lag auch immer ein kleines Geschenk von Reinhardt darunter, gewöhnlich ein farbig gebundenes Buch, das letzte Mal das sauber geschriebene Heft seiner eigenen Märchen. Dann pflegten die beiden Familien zusammen zu bleiben, und Reinhardt las ihnen aus Elisabeths neuen Weihnachtsbüchern vor. So trat allmählig ein Bild des eignen Lebens an die Stelle des fremden, das vor seinen Augen stand; erst als in der Stube die Kerzen ausgeputzt wurden, verschwanden beide. Drinnen wurden Zimmerthüren auf- und zugeschlagen, Tische und Stühle zusammengerückt; der zweite Abschnitt des Weihnachtsabends begann. – Reinhardt verließ seinen kalten Sitz und setzte seinen Weg fort. Als er in die Nähe des Rathskellers kam, hörte er aus der Tiefe die rostige Stimme des Dicken die Karten beim Landsknecht aufrufen, dazu Geigenstrich und den Gesang der Zittermädchen; nun klingelte unten die Kellerthür, und eine dunkle, taumelnde Gestalt schwankte die breite, matt erleuchtete Treppe herauf. Reinhardt ging rasch vorüber; dann trat er in den erleuchteten Laden eines Juweliers; und nachdem er ein kleines Kreuz von rothen Korallen eingehandelt hatte, ging er auf demselben Wege, den er gekommen war, wieder zurück. –	(deleted) 258 Als Reinhard in die Nähe des Ratskellers kam, hörte er aus der Tiefe herauf Geigenstrich und den Gesang des Zithermädchens; nun klingelte unten die Kellertüre, und eine dunkle Gestalt schwankte die breite, matt erleuchtete Treppe herauf. Reinhard trat in den Häuserschatten und ging dann rasch vorüber. Nach einer Weile erreichte er den erleuchteten Laden eines Juweliers; und, nachdem er hier ein kleines Kreuz von roten Korallen eingehandelt hatte, ging er auf demselben Wege, den er gekommen war, wieder zurück.
5. no title	259 *Daheim*
Um eine bestimmte Unterhaltung zu haben, brachte er in Vorschlag, Elisabeth	260 Um während der Ferienzeit eine bestimmte Unterhaltung zu haben,

während der Ferienzeit in der Botanik zu unterrichten, womit er sich...	fing er an, Elisabeth in der Botanik zu unterrichten, womit er sich...
6. no title	264 *Ein Brief*
7. no title	264 *Immensee*
Nur die Stunden vor dem Abendessen, wie die ersten des Vormittags, blieb Reinhardt arbeitend auf seinem Zimmer. –	269 Nur die Stunden vor dem Abendessen, wie die ersten des Vormittags, blieb Reinhard arbeitend auf seinem Zimmer. Er hatte seit Jahren, wo er deren habhaft werden konnte, die im Volke lebenden Reime und Lieder gesammelt und ging nun daran, seinen Schatz zu ordnen und womöglich mit neuen Aufzeichnungen aus der Umgegend zu vermehren. –
Sie stand unbeweglich und, wie er beim Näherkommen zu erkennen meinte, zu ihm hingewandt, als wenn sie ihn erwarte.	270 Sie stand unbeweglich und, wie er beim Näherkommen zu erkennen meinte, zu ihm hingewandt, als wenn sie jemanden erwarte.
8. no title	270 *Meine Mutter hat's gewollt*
Einige Tage nachher, es ging schon gegen Abend, saß die Familie, wie gewöhnlich um diese Zeit, im Gartensaal zusammen. Reinhardt erzählte von seinen Reisen: "Sie leben noch immer träumerisch in dem Glanz der alten Zeiten," sagte er. "Der Tag ging zu Ende, da wir uns durch einen nackten, schwarzäugigen Buben nach Venedig übersetzen ließen. Als nun im letzten Sonnenglanz die leuchtende Stadt aus dem Wasser aufstieg, da mußte ich, von ihrer Schönheit bewältigt, sie laut in ihrer eignen Sprache begrüßen: "'O bella Venezia!'" rief ich, die Arme ausstreckend. Der Knabe sah mich trotzig an und hielt im Rudern inne. "'E domi-	270 Einige Tage nachher, es ging schon gegen Abend, saß die Familie, wie gewöhnlich um diese Zeit, im Gartensaal zusammen. Die Türen standen offen; die Sonne war schon hinter den Wäldern jenseit des Sees.

(deleted) |

nante!'" sagte er stolz und tauchte die Ruder wieder ein. Dann stimmte er eins von jenen Liedern an, die dort ewig neu entstehen und, bis wieder neuere sie ablösen, von allen Kehlen gesungen werden. Das Ritornell am Ende jeder Strophe ließ er langsam, wie rufend, über den Wasserspiegel hinausschallen. Der Inhalt dieser Lieder ist meist ein sehr anmuthiger."
"Dann," sagte die Mutter, "müssen sie anders sein, als die deutschen. Was hier die Leute bei der Arbeit singen, ist eben nicht für verwöhnte Ohren."
"Sie haben zufällig eins der schlechtern gehört." sagte Reinhardt. "Das darf uns nicht irre machen. Das Volkslied ist wie das Volk, es theilt seine Schönheit, wie seine Gebrechen, bald grob, bald zierlich, lustig und traurig, närrisch und von seltsamer Tiefe. Ich habe manche davon aufgezeichnet, noch auf dieser letzten Wanderung. Nun wurde Reinhardt um Mittheilung des Manuscripts gebeten; er ging auf sein Zimmer und kam gleich darauf mit einer Papierrolle zurück, welche aus einzelnen flüchtig zusammengeschriebenen Blättern bestand. Man setzte sich an den Tisch, Elisabeth an Reinhardts Seite, und dieser las nun zuerst einige Tyroler Schnaderhüpferl, indem er beim Lesen je zuweilen die lustigen Melodien mit halber Stimme anklingen ließ. Eine allgemeine Heiterkeit bemächtigte sich der kleinen Gesellschaft. "Wer hat denn aber die schönen Lieder gemacht?" fragte Elisabeth. "Ei," sagte Erich, der bisher in behaglichem Zuhören seinen Meerschaumkopf geraucht hatte, "das hört man den Dingern schon an, Schneidergesellen und Friseure! und derlei luftiges Gesindel."

(deleted)

271 Reinhard wurde um die Mitteilung einiger Volkslieder gebeten, welche er am Nachmittage von einem auf dem Lande wohnenden Freunde geschickt bekommen hatte. Er ging auf sein Zimmer und kam gleich darauf mit einer Papierrolle zurück, welche aus einzelnen sauber geschriebenen Blättern zu bestehen schien.
Man setzte sich an den Tisch, Elisabeth an Reinhards Seite. "Wir lesen auf gut Glück", sagte er, "ich habe sie selber noch nicht durchgesehen." Elisabeth rollte das Manuskript auf. "Hier sind Noten", sagte sie, "das mußt du singen, Reinhard."
Und dieser las nun zuerst einige Tyroler Schnaderhüpferl, indem er beim Lesen je zuweilen die lustige

Reinhardt las hierauf das tiefsinnige "Ich stand auf hohen Bergen". Elisabeth kannte die Melodie, die so rätselhaft ist, daß man nicht glauben kann, sie sei von Menschen erdacht worden. Beide sangen nun das Lied gemeinschaftlich, Elisabeth mit ihrer etwas verdeckten Altstimme dem Tenor secondirend. "Das sind Urtöne," sagte Reinhardt, "sie schlafen in Waldesgründen. Gott weiß, wer sie gefunden hat." Dann las er das Lied des Heimwehs "Zu Straßburg auf der Schanz".

"Nein," sagte Erich, "das kann doch wohl kein Schneidergesell gemacht haben."
Reinhardt sagte: "Sie werden gar nicht gemacht; sie wachsen, sie fallen aus der Luft, sie fliegen über Land wie Mariengarn, hierhin und dorthin, und werden an tausend Stellen zugleich gesungen. Unser eigenstes Thun und Leiden finden wir in diesen Liedern, es ist, als ob wir alle an ihnen mitgeholfen hätten." Er nahm ein anderes Blatt. "Dies Lied," sagte er, "habe ich im vorigen Herbste in der Gegend unsrer Heimath gehört. Die Mädchen sangen es beim Flachsbrechen; die Melodie habe ich nicht behalten können, sie war mir völlig unbekannt."

Melodie mit halber Stimme anklingen ließ. Eine allgemeine Heiterkeit bemächtigte sich der kleinen Gesellschaft. "Wer hat doch aber die schönen Lieder gemacht?" fragte Elisabeth.
"Ei", sagte Erich, "das hört man den Dingern schon an; Schneidergesellen und Friseure und derlei luftiges Gesindel."
Reinhard sagte: "Sie werden gar nicht gemacht; sie wachsen, sie fallen aus der Luft, sie fliegen über Land wie Mariengarn, hierhin und dorthin, und werden an tausend Stellen zugleich gesungen.

271 Unser eigenstes Tun und Leiden finden wir in diesen Liedern; es ist, als ob wir alle an ihnen mitgeholfen hätten."
Er nahm ein anderes Blatt: "Ich stand auf hohen Bergen..."
"Das kenne ich!" rief Elisabeth. "Stimme nur an, Reinhard, ich will dir helfen." Und nun sangen sie jene Melodie, die so rätselhaft ist, daß man nicht glauben kann, sie sei von Menschen erdacht worden; Elisabeth mit ihrer etwas verdeckten Altstimme dem Tenor sekundierend.

Die Mutter saß inzwischen emsig an ihrer Näherei, Erich hatte die Hände ineinandergelegt und hörte andächtig zu. Als das Lied zu Ende war, legte Reinhard das Blatt schweigend beiseite. – Vom Ufer des Sees herauf kam durch die Abendstille das Geläute der Herdenglocken; sie horchten unwillkürlich; da hörten sie eine klare Knabenstimme singen:

                                   Ich stand auf hohen Bergen
                                   Und sah ins tiefe Tal...

                                Reinhard lächelte: "Hört ihr es wohl? So geht's von Mund zu Mund."
                                "Es wird oft in dieser Gegend gesungen", sagte Elisabeth.
                                "Ja", sagte Erich, "es ist der Hirtenkaspar; er treibt die Starken heim."
                                Sie horchten noch eine Weile, bis das Geläute oben hinter den Wirtschaftsgebäuden verschwunden war.
                                "Das sind Urtöne", sagte Reinhard. "sie schlafen in Waldesgründen; Gott weiß, wer sie gefunden hat."
                                Er zog ein neues Blatt heraus.

als er zu Ende war, schob Elisabeth leise ihren Stuhl zurück und ging schweigend in den Garten hinab. Ein strenger Blick der Mutter folgte ihr.	273	als er zu Ende war, schob Elisabeth leise ihren Stuhl zurück und ging schweigend in den Garten hinab. Ein Blick der Mutter folgte ihr.
Reinhardt blickte noch eine Weile auf die Stelle, wo Elisabeths feine Gestalt zwischen den Laubgängen verschwunden war; dann rollte er sein Manuscript zusammen und ging mit der Bemerkung, daß er seinen Abendspaziergang machen wolle, durchs Haus an das Wasser hinab.	273	Reinhard blickte noch eine Weile auf die Stelle, wo Elisabeths feine Gestalt zwischen den Laubgängen verschwunden war; dann rollte er sein Manuskript zusammen, grüßte die Anwesenden und ging durchs Haus an das Wasser hinab.
Endlich war er der Blume so nahe gekommen, daß er die silbernen Blätter deutlich im Mondlicht unterscheiden konnte; zugleich aber fühlte er sich in einem Gewirr von Wasserpflanzen wie in einem Netze verstrickt...	274	Endlich war er der Blume so nahe gekommen, daß er die silbernen Blätter deutlich im Mondlicht unterscheiden konnte; zugleich aber fühlte er sich wie in einem Netze verstrickt...
Bei seinem Eintritt in den Gartensaal fand er...	275	Als er aus dem Garten in den Saal trat, fand er.....
"Wen haben Sie denn so spät in der	275	"Wo sind Sie denn so spät in der

Nacht besucht"? rief ihm die Mutter entgegen.	Nacht gewesen?" rief ihm die Mutter entgegen.
9. no title	275 *Elisabeth*
Er sah auf ihr jenen feinen Zug geheimen Schmerzes, der sich so gerne schöner Frauenhände bemächtigt, die Nachts auf kranken Herzen liegen.	279 Er sah auf ihr jenen feinen Zug geheimen Schmerzes, der sich so gern schöner Frauenhände bemächtigt, die nachts auf krankem Herzen liegen. –

	279 Er wollte sie aufhalten, aber er besann sich und blieb an der Treppe zurück. Das Mädchen stand noch immer auf dem Flur, unbeweglich, das empfangene Almosen in der Hand. "Was willst du noch?" fragte Reinhard. Sie fuhr zusammen. "Ich will nichts mehr", sagte sie; denn den Kopf nach ihm zurückwendend, ihn anstarrend mit den verirrten Augen, ging sie langsam gegen die Tür. Er rief einen Namen aus, aber sie hörte es nicht mehr; mit gesenktem Haupte, mit über der Brust gekreuzten Armen schritt sie über den Hof hinab.
	
	    Sterben, ach sterben
	    Soll ich allein!
	
	Ein altes Lied brauste ihm ins Ohr, der Atem stand ihm still; eine kurze Weile, dann wandte er sich ab und ging auf sein Zimmer.

Reinhardt ging auf sein Zimmer; er setzte sich hin, um zu arbeiten...	Er setzte sich hin, um zu arbeiten...
10. no title	(episode deleted completely)
Nach einigen Jahren finden wir Reinhardt an der nördlichsten Grenze des	

Landes in weiter Entfernung von den eben beschriebenen Scenen wieder. Nach dem bald erfolgten Tode seiner Mutter hatte er hier ein Amt gesucht und gefunden, und sich so in den Gang des täglichen Lebens eingereiht. Seine amtliche Stellung noch mehr als das natürliche Bedürfniß des Umganges hatte ihn mit den verschiedensten Menschen beiderlei Geschlechts zusammengeführt, und was er erfahren und geliebt hatte, trat vor den Anregungen der Gegenwart, obwohl sie mit den früheren an Stärke nicht verglichen werden konnten, mehr und mehr in den Hintergrund. So gingen mehrere Jahre hin. Allmählig kam die Gewöhnlichkeit und nutzte die frische Herbigkeit seines Gefühls ab oder schläferte sie wenigstens ein, und es wurde in den Dingen des äußerlichen Lebens mit ihm, wie mit den meisten Menschen. Endlich nahm er auch eine Frau. Sie war wirthschaftlich und freundlich, und so ging Alles seinen wohlgeordneten Gang. Dennoch mitunter, wenn auch selten, machte sich der Zwiespalt zwischen Gegenwart und Erinnerung bei ihm geltend. Dann konnte er stundenlang am Fenster stehen und, scheinbar in die Schönheit der unten ausgedehnten Gegend verloren, unverwandten Blickes hinaussehen; aber sein äußeres Auge war dann geblendet, während das innere in die Perspektive der Vergangenheit blickte, wo eine Aussicht tiefer als die andere sich abwechselnd eröffnete. Dies war meistens der Fall, wenn Briefe von Erich eingelaufen waren; mit den Jahren aber kamen sie immer seltner, bis sie endlich ganz aufhörten, und Reinhardt erfuhr nur noch zuweilen von durchreisenden Freunden, daß Erich und

Elisabeth nach wie vor in ruhiger Thätigkeit, aber kinderlos, auf ihrem stillen Gehöfte lebten. Reinhardten selber wurde im zweiten Jahre seiner Ehe ein Sohn geboren. Er gerieth dadurch in die aufgeregteste Freude, er lief in die Nacht hinaus und schrie es in die Winde: "Mir ist ein Sohn geboren!" Er hob ihn an seine Brust und flüsterte mit weinenden Augen die zärtlichsten Worte in das kleine Ohr des Kindes, wie er sie nie im Leben einer Geliebten gesagt hatte. Aber das Kind starb, ehe es jährig geworden, und von nun an blieb die Ehe kinderlos. Nach dreißig Jahren starb auch die Frau, sanft und still, wie sie gelebt hatte, und Reinhardt gab sein Amt auf und zog nördlich über die Grenze in das nördlichste deutsche Land. Hier kaufte er sich das älteste Haus in einer kleinen Stadt, und lebte in sparsamem Umgange. Von Elisabeth hörte er seitdem nichts wieder; aber je weniger ihn jetzt das gegenwärtige Leben in Anspruch nahm, desto heller trat wieder die entfernteste Vergangenheit aus ihrem Dunkel hervor, und die Geliebte seiner Jugend war seinem Herzen vielleicht niemals näher gewesen, als jetzt in seinem hohen Alter. Sein braunes Haar war weiß geworden, sein Schritt langsam und seine schlanke Gestalt gebeugt, aber in seinen Augen war noch ein Strahl von unvergänglicher Jugend.

11. no title	281 *Der Alte*
So haben wir ihn zu Anfang dieser Erzählung gesehen; wir haben ihn selbst auf sein abgelegenes Zimmer und dann seine Gedanken auf ihrer Wanderung in die alte Zeit begleitet. – Der Mond schien nicht mehr...	(deleted) 281 Der Mond schien nicht mehr...

CHAPTER TWO

AM KAMIN, AUF DEM STAATSHOF,
AND THE TECHNIQUE OF "GANZ WENIG:"
NOTES ON STORM'S NARRATIVE METHOD

I

Auf dem Staatshof, written in 1857, is Storm's first full-fledged *Ich-Novelle*. It is also one of the more successful combinations of *Geschichtenvertellen* and memory technique in his entire novellistic production. Much has been made of these two aspects of Storm's style, primarily because they are present in varying degree in virtually all the Novellen, but also because they seem to reflect a fundamental attitude of the author toward his art, if not toward life altogether.[1] In his Berlin reminiscences, *Der Tunnel über der Spree*, Fontane records a conversation on the occasion of one of the Tunnel's *Storm-Abende*:

> Denselben Abend erzählte er [Storm] auch Spukgeschichten, was er ganz vorzüglich verstand, weil es immer klang, als würde das, was er vortrug, aus der Ferne von einer leisen Violine begleitet. Die Geschichten an und für sich waren meist unbedeutend und unfertig, und wenn wir ihm das sagten, so wurde sein Gesicht nur noch spitzer, und mit schlauem Lächeln erwiderte er: "Ja, das ist das Wahre; daran können Sie die Echtheit erkennen; solche Geschichte muß immer ganz wenig sein und unbefriedigt lassen; aus dem Unbefriedigten ergibt sich zuletzt die höchste künstlerische Befriedigung.[2]

Even if we take into account Storm's desire to counter his friends' reproach with a show of slyness – as if to imply that he alone possessed the secret of "true" fictional art – the tradition of oral narration nevertheless remained his real criterion for determining whether or not his stories had achieved the desired effect. The *ganz wenig* and the *Unbefriedigte* offered here as rebuttal are raised to an artistic principle in such a work as *Auf dem Staatshof*, and it is surely not an exaggeration to speak, as Storm does, of highest artistic satisfaction arising from what is only hinted at or not said at all.

A more striking though not necessarily a better example of this stress on oral story telling is the collection of ghost stories called *Am Kamin*, in which the narrator-listener relationship is kept in the foreground by a constant interweaving of *gesellige Unterhaltung* throughout. One such story concerns a dream which the narrator's friend once told him. It is introduced this way:

> Von ihren mancherlei Geschichten ist mir indessen – verzeih, Klärchen! – nur ein Traum im Gedächtnis geblieben!
> "Es existierte" – so erzählte sie mir – "vorzeiten in unsrer Gegend eine reiche holländische Familie, welche allmählich fast alle großen Höfe in der Nähe meiner Vaterstadt in Besitz genommen hatte – vorzeiten, sage ich, denn das Glück der van der A... hatte nicht standgehalten. In meiner Kindheit lebte von der ganzen Familie nur noch eine alte Dame, die Witwe des längst verstorbenen Pfenningmeisters van A..., die übrigen Glieder der Familie waren gestorben, zum Teil auf seltsame und gewalttätige Weise ums Leben gekommen; und von den ungeheuren Besitzungen war nur noch ein altes Giebelhaus in der Stadt zurückgeblieben, in welchem die letzte dieses Namens den Rest ihrer Tage in Einsamkeit verlebte."

While the relation this story bears to *Auf dem Staatshof* is quite evident so far as subject matter is concerned, its position in the chronology of the Novellen is uncertain. Böhme, who rediscovered the *Am Kamin* stories in 1911 and subsequently published them in his Storm edition, dates the collection from 1857, thus making it contemporary with, or slightly earlier than, *Auf dem Staatshof*.[3] Until recently this date remained unchallenged; however, in his 1955 Storm biography Franz Stuckert points out that the author himself was uncertain as to the exact time of composition. In a letter to his children Storm decides, though not at all firmly, on the year 1859.[4] The later date, if correct, is of some significance, for the common assumption that one of the *Am Kamin* stories is a proto-form of *Auf dem Staatshof* becomes untenable,[5] and we are then confronted with a series of little *Spukgeschichten* which, despite their apparent *Unfertigkeit* and otherwise incidental character, are not (and were certainly not intended to be) mere preliminary stages for later, more artistic endeavors. To some this might appear unnatural, as was the case with Stuckert, who, while admitting that *Am Kamin*'s date of composition was relatively late, nevertheless insists that it goes back to "weit ältere Anregungen."[6]

But there seems to be no compelling reason to insist on early origins, "Anregungen," or the like for *Am Kamin* – unless of course the generally known fact that experiences, scenes, characters, etc., from Storm's past recur throughout almost all of his work is to be cited as proof! Aside from Storm's own conjecture, one might adduce a second bit of evidence favoring a later date of composition. In a letter to his father dated December 19, 1858 Storm writes:

> Auch du, lieber Vater, wirst, denke ich, meine Geschichte aus der Marsch, die mir jetzt aus der Ferne als die reizendste Gegend erscheint, mit einiger Teilnahme lesen. Außer einer dunklen Anschauung des alten eiderstedtschen Staatshofes aus der Zeit, wo er noch verödet stand, und wo wir einmal von Friedrichsstadt mit jungen Leuten beiderlei Geschlechts eine Tour dahin machten, ist alles darin reine Dichtung. Doch muß ich hinzufügen, daß die Stamp mir einmal erzählt hat, wie in ihrer Kinderzeit eine alte Frau von Ovens in Friedrichsstadt gelebt habe, die letzte einer großen Familie, welche noch an 100 Höfe besessen habe. Die Idee zu dieser Geschichte kam mir in der Nacht, als wir beide auf der Rückkehr von Heiligenstadt in Göttingen bei Herrn Bettmann schliefen.[7]

The letter accompanied a copy of the *Argo Jahrbuch* for 1859, which included *Auf dem Staatshof*. While the Stamp's story of the family with 100 *Höfen* could already have furnished another story (namely, the old friend's dream in *Am Kamin*) with this fragment of plot, it is highly unlikely, for otherwise Storm would surely have mentioned it. Moreover, it seems equally improbable that such additional details as the one remaining *Hof*, the rumors of improper business transactions, the visit of a party of young people to the *Hof* – things common to both the dream story and the Novelle – would have been used before in much the same combination. When Storm says that the idea for his story came to him on a certain night in Göttingen, we can hardly be expected to accept the existence of another, earlier story in which the very same idea was used!

As already indicated, the issue is of more importance than simply one of accurate dating, for in our opinion the peculiarities of style inherent in Storm's *Geschichtenvertellen* cannot be relegated to early, short, and *unfertige* works that served as models for later, longer, and more developed ones. True, *Auf dem Staatshof* is a more fully developed story form, but its central fact is the same careful combination of oral and memory technique we find in *Am Kamin*. And the same is true of most of Storm's Novellen, from *Immensee* and before to the *Altersnovellen* of the 1880's. There seems, in a word, little evidence to support the notion that Storm moved away to any appreciable degree from the *ganz wenig* principle of composition apparent in the ghost stories narrated in the *Tunnel über der Spree*.[8]

Both of the works to be considered in this chapter make use of Storm's favorite device, the frame. In *Am Kamin* it is the traditional one as we know it from the *Arabian Nights* to Boccaccio, through Goethe and into the 19th century: a collection of separate stories bound together by a common situation or setting and having the primary purpose of entertainment. Two additional binding factors, theme and the effect of improvisation given by the thread of conversation running through the work, replace the frame plot common to many traditional examples. Both factors are clearly indicated in the opening lines of the story:

> "Ich werde Gespenstergeschichten erzählen! – Ja, da klatschen die jungen Damen schon alle in die Hände." "Wie kommen Sie denn zu Gespenstergeschichten, alter Herr?" "Ich? – das liegt in der Luft. Hören Sie nur, wie draußen der Oktoberwind in den Tannen fegt! Und dann hier drinnen dies helle Kienäpfelfeuerchen!"

The studied informality of these lines tends to conceal the fact that they are crammed with the information necessary to establish a full and effective frame: the narrator, one of Storm's favorite devices, as an old man who tells most of the stories (first person narration); the group of carefree young people gathered round a fire; and the contrasts that create the mood (by suggestion and reader association, not by direct descriptive means): youth – old age, fireside – dismal, windy landscape outside, lighthearted *Geselligkeit* – ghost stories. The eight stories in this frame (six are told by the *alter Herr*, two by other members of the group) are divided into two sections of four each. The first section closes with the lines: "– Warum erzählst du auch so dumme Geschichten!" "Nun! So mag es denn die letzte sein; ich wüßte für heute nichts Besseres zu erzählen."

The second section, clearly labeled as such by Storm, begins with the remark "Aber es ist noch einmal wieder Sommer geworden, alter Herr! Wo bleiben da unsre Geschichten? Ein Kaminfeuer läßt sich doch bei sechzehn Grad Wärme nicht anzünden!" But the narrator is not to be deterred; it is, he says, "immerhin schon dicht an den November," and the tea table with hissing tea kettle as accompaniment serve as well as the winter fire. While this change in setting would at first appear to be without point, the symmetry of the work and the emphasis on contrast suggest an underlying motive. The work's final lines close the frame and offer a clue to the reason for the type of frame used, the symmetrical division of *Am Kamin*, and the apparent disparity between setting and theme.

> Wenn wir uns recht besinnen, so lebt doch die Menschenkreatur, jede für sich, in fürchterlicher Einsamkeit; ein verlorener Punkt in dem unermessenen und unverstandenen Raum. Wir vergessen es; aber mitunter dem Unbegreiflichen und Ungeheuren gegenüber befällt uns plötzlich das Gefühl davon; und das, dächte ich, wäre etwas von dem, was wir Grauen zu nennen pflegen.
> Unsinn! Grauen ist, wenn einem nachts ein Eimer mit Gründlingen ins Bett geschüttet wird; das hab ich schon gewußt, als meine Schuhe noch drei Heller kosteten.
> Hast recht, Klärchen! Oder wenn man abends vor Schlafengehen unter alle Betten und Kommoden leuchtet, und ich weiß eine, die das sehr eifrig ins Werk setzen wird. Es könnte sogar sehr bald geschehen, denn es ist spät, meine Herrschaften; Bürger-Bettzeit, wie ich fast in dieser ausgewählten Gesellschaft gesagt hätte.

Winter or summer, the *heitere Gesellschaft* is virtually all that is needed as setting for the supernatural. The constant interruptions in story telling, on the part of both narrator and listeners, the underlying idea of isolation and horror within the gay and carefree group, and the ultimate victory of the latter over the former point out a message Storm is here conveying.

It is worthwhile to note the precise nature of these ghost tales. Three are concerned with dreams, one with a visible ghost, the others with coincidence that goes beyond the natural, with premonitions, visions, and those things related to the North German "zweites Gesicht." Inherent in all such *Spukgeschichten* is of course the mysterious, unexplainable quality, and it is typical of Storm that no answers are even attempted. The manner of narration emphasizes this enigmatic aspect in at least two ways. The first is through contrast, such as we have observed it already in the frame-ghost story relationship. *Am Kamin*'s second tale shows the contrast clearly:

> Es war das schönste Sommerwetter; das Gras auf den Fennen funkelte nur so in der Sonne, und die Stare mit ihrem lustigen Geschrei flogen in ganzen Scharen zwischen dem weidenden Vieh umher. Die Gesellschaft im Wagen, der sanft über den ebenen Marschweg dahinrollte, befand sich in der heitersten Laune; niemand mehr als unser junger kaufmännischer Freund. Plötzlich aber, als wir eben an einem blühenden Rapsfeld vorüberfuhren, verstummte er mitten im lebhaftesten Gespräch, und seine Augen nahmen einen so seltsamen glasigen Ausdruck an, wie ich ihn nie zuvor an einem lebenden Menschen gesehen hatte. Ich, der ich ihm gegenüber saß, ergriff seinen Arm und schüttelte ihn. Fritz, Fritz, was fehlt dir? fragte ich. Er atmete tief auf; dann sagte er, ohne mich anzusehen: Das war 'mal eine schlimme Stelle!

This is an interlarding of everyday life at its pastoral best with grotesque and alien elements. The tale from which the passage is taken has the young man pass over the *schlimme Stelle* a second time. When his horse returns with empty saddle, a party is sent out to search for the missing friend. "Als sie mit ihren Handlaternen an jenes blühende Rapsfeld kamen, fanden sie ihn tot am Wege liegen. Was die Ursache seines Todes gewesen, vermag ich nicht mehr anzugeben."

The closing sentence illustrates, as a second way of emphasizing enigma, a device in Storm's prose previously encountered in our analysis of *Immensee* and in the passage quoted from the supposed proto-form of *Auf dem Staatshof*. In the standard view it is the well known *Erinnerungstechnik*; however, in *Am Kamin* – and, indeed, in perhaps a majority of Storm's Novellen – it is a special kind of memory, the intentionally faulty one that amounts to an avowal of ignorance on the narrator's part. Point of view, to give it its technical name, is thrice removed from the objective "truth" of *Am Kamin*'s subject matter (itself enigmatic!) – or one may say that it is intentionally subjected to triple limitation. Considerable critical attention has been paid to this kind of disassociation in Storm's Novellen, and it would not be to our purpose to attempt an overall evaluation or explanation of it here.[9] More relevant to our discussion would be the question of what happens in this particular Novelle when first person narration is used, when the events of the *Innenerzählungen* are in the past (relative to the time of narration), when the recounting is intentionally spotty, and when the narrator acts solely as reporter rather than interpreter.

The story of the widow van A..., we recall, is introduced by the explanation that only one of the many stories the narrator has heard remains in his memory. The reference to the narrator as *alter Herr* and his frequent suggestion that the stories he is relating happened long ago convince the reader that the narrator does in effect have the right to forget more than he remembers. Selection is thus not a responsibility of either author or narrator but of something as difficult to describe precisely as fate or coincidence. The frequent interruptions, another touch of realism we may call *stimmunggebend*, also convince us that the narrator is not interpreting but simply reporting those things offered up by a reluctant memory. The story ends thus:

> Dann erzählte sie mir, wie sie in denselben Nächten im Traum genau dasselbe erlebt hatte wie ich. – Später hat sich indessen der Traum bei uns nicht wiederholt.

And the frame conversation continues:

Woher ist die tote Frau gekommen?
Ich kann Ihnen hierauf leider keine Antwort geben.

The narrator in *Am Kamin* reports this tale as he heard it; indeed, so careful is he to keep his distance that he has the *alte Freundin*, source of his tale, speak in the first person. We note the quotes within quotes at the end of the story and the resumption of the old narrator's authority in the frame conversation: "Ich kann... keine Antwort geben."

The consistency with which this principle of a highly limited point of view is applied in *Am Kamin* may be shown by the following schematic view of the other stories in the collection:

1st story   After two interruptions by his audience, the narrator tells in the third person of the son of his home-town doctor, a four-year-old who dreams that a wolf is about to devour him. The following day the boy's affectionate aunt says that she dreamed she had turned into a wolf and was about to eat the little boy.
"Hu! Weißt du nicht, wieviel Uhr es gewesen?" – "Es muß nach Mitternacht gewesen sein; genauer kann ich es nicht bestimmen."
"Nun, und weiter, alter Herr?"
"Nichts weiter; damit ist die Geschichte aus."

3rd story   This tale is told in the third person. The narrator has heard it from his barber, who told it of his father. The latter, apprenticed as a youth to a cloth weaver, finds that the room in which he is quartered is visited at full moon by something that makes a sweeping sound. Returning to his room one evening in bright moonlight, he looks up at his window. "Da saß oben ein Ding, ungestaltig und molkig, und guckte durch die Scheiben in den Garten hinab." The apprentice spends the night elsewhere and on the following day quits his master and leaves town, "ohne jemals erfahren zu haben, womit er so lange in einer Kammer gehaust habe."
"Kann ich mir auch nicht 'bei denken."
"Geht mir ebenso, alter Herr."

45

"Ich dächte doch, das wäre eine echte rechte Spukgeschichte; oder was fehlt denn noch daran?"
"Sie hat keine Pointe."

4th story The narrator, after promising something more obvious to his listeners, tells of an experience from his own school days. The mother of a school friend is old and infirm. Shortly before the narrator's departure for the university, she becomes ill and the narrator pays what he realizes will be his last visit to her. "Was nun folgte, habe ich später aus dem Munde meines Freundes gehört; denn ich selbst verließ schon am Tage darauf die Stadt." The remainder of the tale is therefore third person narration: overcome with fatigue from his bedside vigil, the son is persuaded to go to his room and seek rest. At daybreak he is gently forced out of his sleep; looking up, he sees his door opened, and a hand appears holding a white handkerchief. He rushes to his mother's room and finds her corpse. In her hand is a white handkerchief.

6th story During a visit to his brother's home, the narrator meets the owner of the neighboring estate, who tells a story illustrating the proverb "Gott gibt's den Trägen im Schlaf." Herr B once discovered evidence of repeated theft from his granary but was unable to solve the mystery. In a dream he sees one of his old workers enter the granary, but at that moment the man catches sight of him standing at the window and disappears. The next day the hired man comes and confesses, saying that he had been frightened by the owner's face in the window. "Hier schwieg der Erzähler. Von meinem Bruder erfuhr ich später, daß er dem alten Martin damals gründlich geholfen... – Da hätten wir also eine Geschichte, wo der Wachende durch den Träumenden zum Visionär wird. – Aber der Tee dürfte indessen fertig sein..."

7th story "Aber Herr T wird Ihnen die Geschichte erzählen, die ich ihm schon seit lange am Gesichte angesehen habe." The new narrator's story is told by the story's central figure: "Als ich vor einigen Jahren, es war um Ostern, in B. in Garnison stand – so erzählte mir der Hauptman von K. –" The *Hauptmann*-narrator participates in the arrangements for a ball that is to take place in a large dilapidated house, whose upper story is used for storing grain. During the preparations the captain is transferred, and his best friend takes his place. In his new post, the narrator has occasion to write a letter to his friend. As he is writing he looks up and sees the friend in the room making a strange motion as if to pull something out of his mouth. They seemed to be kernels of grain, the narrator explains. Some days later he learns that the upper story of the house had collapsed with its load of grain and killed his friend.

8th story A third narrator, Alexius, is introduced. He has heard the other stories and wants now to complete the ring: "Es bleibt nur noch eins übrig; und wenn ihr hören wollt, so werde ich mich nicht scheuen, diesen letzten Schritt zu tun... Ich habe diese seltsame Geschichte von einem nahen Verwandten, der sie zum Teil selbst erlebt, teils später aus nächster Quelle erfahren hat." The mode of narration is the most elaborate in *Am Kamin*. Alexius tells the story in the third person. A relative is present at a gathering one evening when the conversation turns to "die Fortexistenz der Seele nach dem Vergehen des Körpers." One of the group, an old medical officer, tells (first person) of a common friend Z who dies of heart trouble. Z's greatest fear, the medical officer explains, was that his body would be dissected after death. And so the medical officer solemnly promises not to dissect. However, he is called away from the city and finds on his return that the friend has died and that his body has been dissected by Professor X, a colleague who had helped treat the patient. As the medical officer concludes his story, the group is silent; but suddenly his expression changes and he is heard to say "das ist entsetzlich." He excuses himself, explaining that he has just learned something. Alexius continues the story. The old *Medizinalrat* visits the home of Professor X, removes some books from his bookcase and pulls out a jar containing a large human heart. "Es ist das Herz meines

Freundes... ich weiß es, aber der Tote muß es wiederhaben; noch heute, diese Nacht noch!" The heart is placed in the coffin that same night.

That Storm is himself aware of the range of supernatural possibilities given in these stories is suggested by the narrator of the final tale: "Es bleibt nur noch eins übrig." The spectrum is a total one and progresses from the intrusion of man into the *dunkle Region* and from there back into everyday life. The examples move from the bad dream of a four-year-old to the waking experience of a man of science who, in the very midst of a social gathering, is visited by the spirit of his friend. The point could hardly be made more forcefully. Man, we remember, is called a "verlorener Punkt in dem unermessenen und unverstandenen Raum;" the feeling of horror that comes over one is the momentary awareness of man's position in a chaotic cosmos. At least this is the explanation Storm puts in the mouth of the *alter Herr*. But the means of combating or resisting remain unstated. We are reminded of Klärchen's retort to the old narrator's theory of *Grauen:* "Unsinn! Grauen ist, wenn einem nachts ein Eimer mit Gründlingen ins Bett geschüttet wird." The line may be interpreted in a number of ways, but coming as it does at the end of *Am Kamin* (the very last lines belong to the *alter Herr*, but he merely agrees with Klärchen and reminds the group that it is *Bürger-Bettzeit*), we are forced to accept it as more than a humorous, childish dismissal of that quality underlying all eight stories. The *Grauen* is there, all right, but according to Storm it can be banned by the very social order that exposes it.

The ending of *Am Kamin* is admittedly a simplification of the substance of life, but to Storm it seems more typical than not that he should express his light-hearted simplification in a way that makes it appear to be the very form of life. We note in this connection that the listeners' reactions parallel the gaiety-to-horror-to-gaiety movement: "Ach – Träumen!" / "Nun, und weiter, alter Herr?" / "Pfui! Die Tante ist ein Werwolf gewesen!" / "Aha, unser poetischer Freund improvisiert." / "Kann ich mir auch nichts 'bei denken... Sie hat keine Pointe." / "Und Ihr Freund? – Wie ist es dem ergangen?" / "Oh – mir graut nicht." "Aber du weinst ja!" "Ich? – Warum erzählst du auch so dumme Geschichten!" / "Woher ist die tote Frau gekommen?" / "Pfui! Wer befreit mich von diesem Schauder?" These reactions, given in abbreviated form, move with reasonable consistency from skepticism and criticism to acceptance without, however, losing the sense of *Geselligkeit* so important to the story.

Our review of *Am Kamin*'s ghost stories reveals the elaborateness of the means used to attain disassociation. Rarely is anyone willing or able to assume full authority, and the establishing of such authority as there is becomes increasingly more difficult until, in the final tale, we are faced with this stiuation: the central narrator gives way to a listener. The listener has heard the tale from a relative; the relative experienced it only in part, the remainder coming to him from a close source; the actual tale is told in the first person by one of the characters; at approximately the half-way point, the story moves into the present (the actual narrator's present) and changes narrators; the relative resumes the narration in the third person. If we compare this with the relatively simple structure of the first tale, and if we recall the other lines of movement discussed above, an explanation of sorts for the unusual structure of *Am Kamin* seems to emerge.

Ghost stories, perhaps more than anything else, are based on a sense of incompleteness and therefore tend to excite the imagination, to incite the reader to *Weiterdichten und Ergänzen*. Theme is also one of the two external unifying forces in *Am Kamin*, the other being the frame. Since we have in effect not one but eight stories plus the framing situation, there can be no gaps in plot or meaning other than those obviously created by the enigmatic subject matter. But a second possibility for silence exists: the narrator may plead ignorance and thus throw the responsibility for interpretation onto the listener or reader. In *Am Kamin* this technique becomes quite elaborate; several narrators are used (thus linking the frame more intimately to the stories), the stories are generally introduced by a statement as to their origin, a series of contrasts emphasizes the extremes of *gesellige Unterhaltung* and *Spukgeschichten* but, paradoxically, also tends to bring them together; the respective narrator is at times almost tedious in his efforts to cite his sources and let the fullest authority tell the story; and the stories are offered without interpretation from either narrator or listener. The former complains constantly of a faulty memory or of the same ignorance as to the meaning or point of his story that his listeners profess.

Through subject matter, we may conclude, Storm lets in the incredible; through technique he shows man's reaction to it, that is, his questioning, uncertain stand. The setting, the social gathering at fireside or tea table that ties the stories together, has the double effect of stressing, through contrast, the groups or units that comprise the separate ghost stories (technically not related to frame), a design which produces the effect of gaps or troughs of silence. But we have discovered a measure of deceit here: the repartee inserted between the various tales is in many ways the heart of the matter. Without them we should miss more than just a frame to hold the eight tales, for nothing less than a view of life is suggested in the way in which the *Grauen* of these supernatural stories is captured and put to the task of entertainment by Storm's reality, his *Geselligkeit*.

At the technical level we have observed a most elaborate bit of machinery operating in the gaps. Multiple shifts in point of view within the tales are caused by uneasy narrators searching for authority. Memory fails at times and the relation of narrator to narration is a chance thing. The audience is generally not up to interpretation (a fault shared by the narrators) and must ask "what does it mean?" Because the reader knows the answer, and because he is also aware of the fact that machinery has been used, he is likely to feel that Storm has overstated his case, or that *Am Kamin* is not good artistically. This is perhaps true – we stated at the beginning of this chapter that *Auf dem Staatshof* is a more developed story form – but he should be reminded that the writer needs a more elaborate apparatus to achieve his effects than the reader to understand them.

We should be grateful for the fact that *Am Kamin*'s devices, if not the entire process of composition, are all too visible, for it enables us to probe with more profit into another work, one whose joints seem more organic than mechanical.

II

Were it not for the fact that nearly all literary works possess multiple meaning or different levels, we might be justified in introducing an analysis of *Auf dem Staatshof* with such a formula. For Storm's mind ran naturally to the kind of concretized projections we have elsewhere called *Bilder* or situations, and a retelling of this Novelle's fable would reveal this fact of different levels expressed primarily through symbolic forms. At what level and from what angle should this work be read? Of contemporary critics, Johannes Klein offers what may doubtless be considered a conventional view: *Auf dem Staatshof* is a Novelle of "soziales Schicksal" and shows "den Untergang des Adels und den Sieg des Bürgertums." Two leitmotifs, we are told, illustrate this polarity, the *Staatshof* and the *Pavillon*. The former is also the symbol of a declining social class that had once misused its power. Additionally, "die Verlobung wird Sinnbild für die Erstarrung in der Überlieferung," Klaus Peters' appearance towards the end of the Novelle represents the new, stronger class, Anne Lene's death in the pavilion points out that a union of the rising and falling ways of life is impossible, and finally the sea at the horizon is both the inevitable course of history and the melancholy *Todes-Schicksal* of Storm's world.[10]

Fritz Lockemann, to cite another example, gives us a similar reading of the story's symbols but places them in a somewhat different context: "Den wahrhaft Geliebten, den Erzähler, mag sie [Anne Lene] nicht in den Strom des Vergehens hineinziehen, von dem sie sich schon ergriffen fühlt. Sie entzieht sich ihm halb mit Willen, halb unwillkürlich, indem sie durch den morschen Fußboden des Pavillons ins Wasser stürzt. Nur wahre Liebe kann im Strom des Vergehens Halt geben. Und ihr zu folgen, fehlt der Heldin Mut und innere Kraft. Die Verlobung mit dem Ungeliebten bedeutet wieder endgültige Wende; Verrat an der Liebe ist nicht gut zu machen."[11]

To accept both readings is not merely to indicate richness, although both may be justified and still others found. It is rather an admission that something else in the work, or about it, permits and even encourages the search for levels at which it is to be read. A working hypothesis for our analysis of *Auf dem Staatshof* might be that its "story," which yields meanings according to the kind of reading given it, illustrates its subject rather than presents it. Story is thus secondary, and interpretations derived from it are necessarily secondary as well.

A demonstrable fact about *Am Kamin*, we have seen, is the disconnectedness of plot in the sense that nine stories (the frame and eight tales) are told. Beyond or beneath these we locate the center of the work. The superficially discrete units tie themselves together through what we have called the *ganz wenig* technique; and if the reader is to go beyond an interest in spooks it is in the gaps that he finds what meaning *Am Kamin* has to offer. By hypothetical analogy, then, *Auf dem Staatshof*'s subject is not to be found where Klein and Lockemann looked for it, but at some less obvious point onto which a good deal of weight is heaped. Here too we may begin with avowed ignorance:

> Ich kann nur einzelnes sagen; nur was geschehen, nicht wie es geschehen ist; ich weiß nicht, wie es zu Ende ging und ob es eine Tat war oder nur ein Ereignis, wodurch das Ende herbeigeführt wurde. Aber wie es die Erinnerung mir tropfenweise hergibt, so will ich es erzählen.

We may list the more obvious things about this introduction to *Auf dem Staatshof* first. The frame (rudimentary) states the situation: a narrator recalls to an assumed group of listeners – *sagen*, not *schreiben*! – something from his youth. "Nur einzelnes" suggests the *Bild-Technik* much as we see it in *Immensee*, and the frequent qualifications (*nur* – three times – *ich weiß nicht, tropfenweise*) point to the faulty memory and the avowal of ignorance evident in *Am Kamin*. The emphasis on *was* rather than *wie* informs us that this is to be a report rather than an interpretation. Finally, the statement that the narrator intends to tell the story as his memory doles it out, drop by drop, places him in precisely the same situation as his listeners: the meaning will have to be arrived at *during* the narration.

Two less apparent hints are also given. Storm is at pains to distinguish between *Tat* and *Ereignis*, or rather he is careful to point out that *he* is unable to make the distinction. This we take to be a kind of anticipation that the story will have a central event, act, deed, happening, incident – we must pin precise meanings onto these two terms before listening further. *Ereignis*, to begin with the second term, is the most general word for incident or event. Its connection to the notion of the real or visible restricts its application to specific happenings. Its proximity to *Tat* in the passage above suggests that its meaning is event as incident, for Storm states that he does not know if the center of his narrative was a *Tat* or *merely* an *Ereignis*. The former term also contains the suggestion of something visible, something seen plastically. While it too may refer to a definite event, its stress is more on the dramatic quality and the larger proportions of that event. In this passage its closest equivalent is event as deed. Thus a comparison of the terms – which Storm demands simply by using them both – reveals that something of great moment, something vivid or dramatic, may have happened. And he suggests that, if this was the case, there is more than a hint of the active about it, that is, its doer (as an individual) must be considered also. Or, Storm continues, perhaps it was only an accident, something definite, to be sure, but primarily an incident without an active, "doing" will behind it.

A second hint lies in the words "wie es zu Ende ging" and "wodurch das Ende herbeigeführt wurde." Of these two phrases the first is the most puzzling, for any standard reading of the Novelle would seem to belie the assertion. *Auf dem Staatshof* is manifestly the story of Anne Lene and her tragic (or near tragic) inability to respond to Marx' plea that she join him who knows "den Weg zur Welt zurück." And there is surely no doubt in the reader's mind concerning the outcome! However, we may suspend final judgement on the line for the time being and examine instead the second phrase. The end, we are told, was brought about by the *Tat* or *Ereignis*. Any attempt to get at the precise meaning of this statement must therefore return us to our distinction between the two possible kinds of event and to the first use of *Ende* in the passage. In claiming that he does not know how it ended, Storm is either guilty of misleading us or else he intends to say that the assertion "ich weiß nicht, wie es zu Ende ging" exposes the narrator's ignorance not specifically of *what* happened but rather of his own role in the happening. Both the failure to make a choice between *Tat* and *Ereignis* and the use of the passive, impersonal construction in his second reference to the ending ("wie das Ende herbeigeführt wurde") suggest that an ultimate mystery will remain in this story despite the apparent clarity of its ending.

These extensive linguistic labors over a scant five lines of text are, we believe, justified both by the pains Storm takes to remove himself, i.e., as the narrator Marx, from the center of action and by the actual events of Anne Lene's death. We may recall the scene in brief:

> "O Anne Lene", rief ich und trat auf die Stufen, die zu dem Pavillon hinanführten, "ich – ich hole sie! Gib mir die Hand, ich weiß den Weg zur Welt zurück!"
> Aber Anne Lene beugte den Leib vor und machte mit den Armen eine hastige abwehrende Bewegung nach mir hin. "Nein", rief sie, und es war eine Todesangst in ihrer Stimme, "du nicht, Marx; bleib! Es trägt uns beide nicht." Noch auf einen Augenblick sah ich die zarten Umrisse ihres lieben Antlitzes von einem Strahl des milden Lichts beleuchtet; dann aber geschah etwas und ging so schnell vorüber, daß mein Gedächtnis es nicht zu bewahren vermocht hat. Ein Brett des Fußbodens schlug in die Höhe; ich sah den Schein des weißen Gewandes, dann hörte ich es unter mir im Wasser rauschen.

All accounts of *Auf dem Staatshof* with which I am familiar treat this scene as clear and unambiguous. Lockemann explains that

Anne Lene plunges through the rotten floor of the pavilion and makes the action her own. It is, in a word, a *Tat*, and we admire the scene for its dramatic and plastic qualities. Klein on the other hand is equally explicit in drawing Marx into the action. His resumé of the Novelle concludes with these words: "Sie erschrickt: 'Du nicht! Es trägt uns beide nicht!' Zu spät. Die Bohlen tragen nicht; sie stürzt ins Wasser und ertrinkt." This too suggests *Tat*, but Storm's words make it clear that Klein has not read carefully. We are not told that Marx actually steps onto the pavilion floor; on the contrary, it is probable that not even Anne Lene's "abwehrende Bewegung" of a moment before caused the floor to give way. There was a moment of stillness, and during that brief span Marx tells us that he sees her form bathed in a beam of light. To say, as Klein does, that "Marx tötet, wo er retten will,"[12] is to have the narrator step into the pavilion. But this is not in the text.

If we are to insist on nuances it must be said that what happens here, on the surface at least, is witnessed, not caused, by the narrator. If this climactic scene is to be called a *Tat*, then the doer might well be Anne Lene herself (as Lockemann believes) or, at a symbolic level, the acquisition of "unrecht Gut" or the passage of time that destroys family name and wealth as well as the floor (or foundation in a broader sense) of the last physical remnant of luxury and grandeur. If it is but an accident, an *Ereignis*, then we must consider fate the offender and accept this dramatic scene as the circumstance rather than the cause of Anne Lene's death.

This mystery can be resolved only at the level of interpretion, for it is apparent that Storm has withheld full information. We shall offer a possible interpretation at the end of this chapter. For the time being, however, it is enough to observe that the opening lines of *Auf dem Staatshof* are more than a mere convention intended to supply a frame or move the events of the story into the area of memory. They offer the expected avowal of ignorance, the inability to evaluate, and the warning that the story will be *ganz wenig* and thus leave us in many ways as *unbefriedigt* as the ghost stories related on the *Storm-Abend* in Berlin.

We may return to the death scene. One moment the girl is illuminated by a ray of soft light, the next something happens – so quickly that the narrator's memory is unable to hold it. Then the plank gives way and Anne Lene falls to her death. The insertion is undeniably odd. What happened, we must ask, that deserves mention at this dramatic moment, that merits insertion between the two inevitably successive steps of a tragedy? One finds a series of possible answers to the question: The narrator's lapse of memory at a critical moment is the unconscious concealment of his own role in the tragedy. We are not told that Marx actually caused Anne Lene to fall, but the deeper meaning of the story supports the argument for guilt. Marx is a member of the class which has replaced the aristocracy of the *Staatshof*. The story's final paragraph is concerned with the *Staatshof*'s new owner, the *Bürger* Klaus Peters, and his prosperity. Marx' attempt to save Anne Lene by stretching out his hand and offering her a way back to the world is therefore a *symbolischer Vorgang*. Anne Lene cannot be saved, and so Marx' actual participation in the *Tat* (as Klein would have it) is unnecessary; his very presence is the symbolic action necessary for destruction. The lapse of memory, then, may be called Marx' *Tat* in this scene; he does nothing else.

A second possibility may be considered. Lockemann, we recall, suggests that Anne Lene withdraws from Marx "halb mit Willen, halb unwillkürlich." The basic flaw is in the heroine herself because she lacks inner strength and courage, but something resembling fate intrudes to the degree that her drowning is only partly self-willed. Thus the final distinction between *Tat* and *Ereignis* is not made: it is both a deed and an incident, both personal and impersonal.

It will be evident from the foregoing discussion – which we hope saves itself from the reproach of quibbling by the fact that one encounters *ganz wenig* in the two most crucial places in the Novelle – that at least one vital point is outside the story. Moreover, there is evidence that Storm purposely placed it there and then led us to this fact by pleading ignorance (but also by offering possible avenues of approach) at the beginning and in the major scene of the Novelle. The reader, we may say in summary, is not misled but he is forced to look at certain gaps in the narration more intently than at the narration itself.

The choice of two scenes from *Auf dem Staatshof* to illustrate Storm's special technique should not be taken to mean that the principle of silence is necessarily more evident here than elsewhere. The apologia with which the Novelle opens is reiterated, although in less intense form, throughout. In the analysis to follow we shall list the more important devices of silence and discuss their contribution to the underlying principle of saying *ganz wenig*.

As in so many Novellen (*Renate, Aquis Submersus, Grieshuus,* etc.) Storm begins the actual narration of *Auf dem Staatshof* by placing the reader in a landscape, describing it for him in some detail, and telling of his frequent walks through the region as a youth.[13] The form is almost as predictable as the *Natureingang* of the medieval German allegory: on such a walk, usually in summertime, the narrator meets someone (*Renate*) or comes upon a particular spot or object about which there is a story to tell (*Grieshuus, St. Jürgen, Halligfahrt*). In this instance the narrator's recollection of the scene combines three devices often employed by Storm.

> Hier bin ich in meiner Jugend oft gegangen; ich mit einer anderen. Ich sehe noch das Gras im Sonnenschein funkeln...

Besides relating the narrator to the story's setting, reference is made in briefest fashion to a second figure (who, it is safe to assume, will figure prominently in the story), and the entire scene is recalled visually. However, nothing in these early paragraphs demands close recollection; the setting is intentionally given expected familiarity by making it a part of the narrator's own *Lebenswelt*. We might note a few of the specific features of *Auf dem Staatshof*'s setting. The narrator's home is a small town on the edge of the north German fen country. Several miles to the north is the sea, and in the area lying between, the *Staatshof*. The house is at the end of a path leading across the fens "seitwärts von der Straße;" it is set in the center of a (*düsteren*) group of elms and poplars, "wie sie kein anderes Besitztum dieser Gegend aufzuweisen hat," and its *Graft* (water-filled ditch or moat) is especially wide and deep. One part of an empire of 90 estates belonging to the van der Roden family (cf. the *Am Kamin* story), the *Staatshof* is now the sole possession of the family, which itself has been reduced to an old woman and her four-year-old granddaughter.

At this point in the description the narrator's story, i.e., the specific, non-habitual or non-introductory part of his recollection can begin ("zur Zeit, wo meine Erinnerung beginnt"). Significantly, the narrator sees only the end of a family chronicle, only the final episode of a decline that is carefully explained in this introduction to the story proper. "Unrecht Gut" had somehow come into the family's hands and from that point on its fortunes had sunk; also, we are told that the last male heir had died a violent death by drowning. We have seen that Storm makes this point, and, more generally, offers us this brief history of the ill-fated family to suggest that the narrator is destined to remain a spectator no matter how future events unfold. He will be powerless to intervene positively in the long and inevitable decline.

The first specific scene in the Novelle begins with the explanation that the narrator's father was business adviser to the old Frau van der Roden. He continues,

> Gehe ich rückwärts mit meinen Gedanken und suche nach den Plätzen, die von der Erinnerung noch ein spärliches Licht empfangen, so sehe ich mich als etwa vierjährigen Knaben.

The image of the scanty light of memory falling upon isolated spots is an appropriate one, for again the recollection is primarily visual. However, other senses come to Storm's aid here, and the entire scene is filled with references to *how* the scene is experienced (non-rationally, as is fitting for a four-year-old boy) by the narrator Marx:

> So sehe ich mich als etwa vierjährigen Knaben...
> Ich fühle plötzlich den Sonnenschein...
> Ich sehe eine alte Frau im grauen Kleide...
> Noch rieche ich...den strengen Duft der Atlantwurzel...
> Ich sehe auch noch meinen Vater...

We have listed all such occurrences in the scene up to now in the order in which they are given. Their frequency, five in only nineteen lines, the interruption "dann aber verläßt mich die Erinnerung," and the resumption of examples ("Ich sehe an den... Wänden") show that Storm is consciously concerned to give double authenticity to this part of his narrative. He makes both plausible and vivid the early experience that brings Marx and Anne Lene together; and he makes his loss of memory the more convincing, for the trough created here is decidedly *un*important to this part of the story. But there will be occasion later to insert other, important gaps, and the sudden silences must not come unexpectedly.

This first scene at the *Staatshof* contains other references to the narrator's memory, instances that is to say, when he no longer remembers or when he pointedly remarks that this much at least remains in his mind. The function of this scene with its constant mention of *Erinnerung* is perhaps revealed in the closing lines. The child's excursion to the *Staatshof* has ended. It was a day, explains Marx, "von dem ich bei ruhigem Nachsinnen nicht außer Zweifel bin, ob er ganz in der erzählten Weise jemals dagewesen, oder ob nur meine Phantasie die zerstreuten Vorfälle verschiedener Tage in diesen einen Rahmen zusammengedrängt hat." For convenience and compactness Storm has of course condensed; at least it is unlikely that the details of one day so long ago would stand out so sharply, especially when one considers the narrator's age. But the condensation was necessary – Storm frequently begins his stories with early childhood (one thinks of how many childhood scenes his Novellen contain!) and lets his characters grow to maturity, often even to old age, in the course of a short Novelle. More than this brief childhood experience is not needed, for its major narrative device, the memory technique used by a storyteller, has been firmly installed in the Novelle, the major characters introduced, and certain symbolic actions and objects (ravens, the elegance of the house, the pavilion standing on thin wooden piles over the water, the boy's fear of entering the pavilion, etc.) presented for later use in the story.

A final point may be made about the *Staatshof* scene. It is not set off from the introductory paragraphs by means of wide spacing, in the way that other scenes or episodes are separated.[14] Consequently, these paragraphs serve both to introduce the setting of the entire story and the first scene itself, the visit to the *Staatshof*.

The second scene, which we may call the dance scene, repeats the structure discussed above. Introduced by the vague *späterhin*, it tells briefly of the old woman's town life, young Marx' regular visits to Frau Ratmann and Anne Lene, the particular Sunday afternoon on which Marx and Anne Lene dance the minuet, and the unwelcome interruption by Simon. Or more generally formulated, the scene begins with a larger setting, then depicts an habitual scene – Marx' Sunday visits –, and finally focuses on the main event, the dance. References to the narrator's faulty memory are less frequent, but this may be explained by the fact that a step of some years has been taken toward the present. Moreover, the habitual nature of much of the scene (we are told that several years passed "in dieser Weise") and Marx' strong feeling of shame during the main incident make the clarity of detail with which the entire scene is related quite plausible.

Viewing the scene as a whole, we may say that its purpose is amplification. Nothing new has been introduced, but shifts of emphasis have occurred, sides of character brought out more clearly, and the symbols enriched in number and weight. If the primary fact of the first scene was the imperfect point of view due to faulty memory, this one may be said to concentrate on contrast. This was of course a significant feature of the opening scene as well – we think immediately of the pavilion, the pastoral scene depicted on its walls, Marx' reluctance to enter, etc. – but here the contrasts are both a substitute for the painfully elaborate reconstruction of the past and the primary way of delineating Anne Lene and stressing her social isolation. We may examine a few of the more important contrasts and show their use as devices of suggestion that bear the principal burden of communication.

In an early admission of uncertainty, Marx says "ich weiß nicht mehr, war es das kleine zierliche Mädchen, das mich anzog, oder war es die alte Schatulle, deren Raritäten ich in besonders begünstigter Stunde mit ihr beschauen durfte; die goldenen Schaumünzen, die seidenen bunt bemalten Fächer oder oben auf dem Absatz der Schatulle die beiden Pagoden von chinesischem Porzellan." During the course of the dance scene we come to realize that the narrator is not making a true distinction at all. His fascination for old and elegant objects, things normally outside the prosaic burghal sphere of which he is a part, shares a common source with his growing admiration and fondness for Anne Lene. When she appears before him his eyes move from her white summer dress (worn by most of Storm's female characters) to her blue sash, and rest finally on the old fan she holds in her hand. They dance the minuet together, one of the "altfränkische Künste," Anne Lene holds an open fan in her hand, Marx' mother is unable to take her eyes off the "kleine schwebende Gestalt" executing the figures of the old dance, and the entire episode takes place on a Sunday afternoon. This remnant of rococo is suddenly and grossly intruded upon by *dickköpfiger* Simon, son of a cobbler. On weekdays, Marx tells us, he plays cops and robbers with Simon, but now the invasion by this boy with the large hobnailed shoes causes a painful scene:

> die kleine Patrizierin schien durch die Gegenwart dieser Werkeltags-Erscheinung in ihrer idealen Stimmung auf eine empfindliche Weise gestört zu sein. Sie legte den Fächer auf den Tisch und sagte: "Laß Marx nur mit dem Jungen spielen."

It is perhaps regrettable that these symbols and the contrasts they offer are not better concealed. Certainly, this quote cannot be mustered into the ranks of the under- or unstated things with which we are above all concerned. Yet the contrasts do represent, whether too obviously or not, a kind of mirror for an interior never fully exposed in the course of the Novelle. Fächer: Nagelschuhe, Sonntag: Werktag, Minuett: Räuber- und Soldatenspiel – these opposites are, more than mere symbols, analogies of two classes or worlds in collision. What saves this scene is surely the fact that Simon slinks off, Marx is totally captivated, and Anne Lene of course victorious.

In the third scene two things in particular hold our attention. The first is an event: the old grandmother dies and Marx' father assumes legal guardianship of Anne Lene, who comes to live with them. The second is an extended habitual scene, the Sunday afternoons spent by the two children at the *Staatshof*, where they wander through the deserted and dilapidated rooms and the once tended garden that is now a *Blütenwald*, a wilderness as solitary as the house itself. The pavilion is locked, its floor has become unsafe and one can look through the cracks at the water below. Storm's treatment of time is noteworthy for its similarity to that in the preceding scene. Besides the references to their frequent visits to the *Staatshof* ("und wie oft sind wir diesen Weg gegangen!"; "denn mir ist, als habe an jenen Sonntagnachmittagen immer die Sonne geschienen"), the passage of time is alluded to twice, at the beginning, when we are told that the scene begins "etwa ein Jahr später," and in the closing paragraph, which offers the summary "so verging die Zeit." To emphasize the longer lapse of time Marx says that Anne Lene has grown up "ehe ich mich dessen versehen."

The action of this third scene begins when Marx returns from a vacation trip, sees the door to Anne Lene's house open, and enters. The lapse of a year (as well as wide spacing in the text) marks the start of a new episode. But there is a subtle connection between this and the preceding scene. At the end of the dance scene Marx has realized that Anne Lene's dancing feet have confused his youthful heart, and he spends all his money to buy her some sweets. When he visits Anne Lene at the beginning of this scene his avowed purpose is to give her the *Kleinigkeit* he has bought for her on the way home. Direct statement is avoided here, and it is of course unnecessary, for silence has taken the form of gesture.

The cementing of the children's relationship, which is the main point of this second *Staatshof* scene, is likewise revealed through certain gestures and actions rather than statement. But more important, we are shown their respective worlds and the position they are destined to take in them. Anne Lene's character undergoes virtually no change. She remains aloof from Marx' childhood games, and even though her clothing becomes simpler the inevitable touch of luxury and elegance remains, as in the dance scene. "Sie trug immer die feinsten englischen Handschuhe, und da sie dessen ungeachtet sich nicht scheute überall damit hinzufassen, so mußte das getragene Paar bald durch ein neues ersetzt werden." The narrator, an older Marx looking back over many years, offers an implied evaluation of this habit – his adjectives betray as much: "Meine bürgerlich sparsame Mutter schüttelte vergebens darüber den Kopf" – but we have no indication that the young boy in the story possessed this degree of insight.

Beyond his feelings for Anne Lene, clearly recognized and stated as such, Marx sees that his friend is somehow special and not of his world. When he is told of the grandmother's death and the decision to bring Anne Lene into his home, he hears only the part concerning Anne Lene. And when she embraces and kisses him he scarcely notices, for his imagination is too busy with the prospect of being with her. The grandmother's funeral is covered in a few lines; Marx' recollection, a precise one despite its brevity, consists of the unpleasant *Feiertagsgefühl* aroused by the sights and sounds of the *Sterbehaus* hovering in perfect balance with the sense of *Grauen* at this awesome splendor. Only after the funeral does Marx realize that their life together will consist of something more than the Sunday hours he so closely associates with Anne Lene. And it has been observed already that Anne Lene wants no part of the *Knabenspiele* – they bear no connection whatever to the *Staatshof*.

This scene, then, makes one major point and in doing so clearly prepares for the tragedy to come. Without realizing it, Anne Lene is totally committed to the past, to the fading, decaying *Staatshof*. Marx, who sees things too late or never at all, shares that world with her, but only as an outsider. The point is made symbolically in the passage describing their Sunday afternoon at the *Staatshof* (the composite or habitual scene standing for many). Wandering aimlessly in their *Blütenwald*, the children work their way toward an arbor in one corner of the garden only to find themselves standing before the pavilion – a scene that will be repeated in the story's final scene. The wording betrays their relationship to this decaying haven, "nicht selten glückte es," and their reaction to its locked doors suggests both a yearning for this pastoral past and the futility of trying to escape into it:

> Dann sahen wir durch die erblindeten Fensterscheiben nach dem zärtlichen Schäferpaar hinüber, das noch immer, wie vor Jahren, auf der Mitte der Wand im Grase kniete, und rüttelten vergebens an den Türen.

Storm does not insist on equating the *Schäferpaar* with Anne Lene and Marx (as these two might have been had fate dealt otherwise with them), yet the similarity is apparent enough to make us realize that reality and the inexorable course of time will overcome that which the idyllic picture in the pavilion represents.

The fourth scene, Marx' farewell visit to the *Staatshof* before leaving for the university, is central to the Novelle in a number of ways. It is the actual midway point of the story, there being three scenes preceding and three succeeding this one. It is also the shortest of the seven, filling only slightly more than two pages. On the side of content, the symmetry is even more striking: of the two episodes comprising the scene, one points backward in a summarizing way, the other to the future in a warning way. Further, both parts are concerned with specific rather than habitual scenes and both offer action rather than description; and both, finally, are told with a greater measure of authority than most of the other scenes and situations in the Novelle.

In regard to the technique of silence, this pivotal scene assumes a greater importance than perhaps any other in the story, except for the death scene already discussed. Certainly, it cannot be said that either of its two episodes contributes in any substantial way to plot or action. Thus we have a kind of paradox in that the stress is on action while the action itself is important not *per se* but solely as symbol. In this respect too the scene occupies a central position, representing as it does the crest of a curve moving from non-symbolic or marginally symbolic scenes to the total symbol and back again.

If we examine the scene as an instance of action as symbol (i.e., rather than to advance the story) and seek to determine the degree to which the symbols are explained through certain kinds of silence rather than explicitly, we find a consistent duality throughout. The two brief incidents comprising the scene both involve *Zank*. The first takes place on the way to the *Staatshof*, the second at the *Staatshof* itself; the first places the populace on one side and Marx and Anne Lene on the other, the second is concerned with Anne Lene and the beggar woman, with both Marx and Wieb seeking to intervene in different ways; in both incidents *Zank* takes the form of an act of violence: in the first Marx and Anne Lene are subjected to a shower of *Schimpf-* and *Neckworten*, in the second the beggar woman showers ill-concealed accusations at Anne Lene's ancestors and, through them, at Anne Lene herself. Furthermore, Marx intervenes and drags the beggar woman away by force.

The symbolic meaning such actions hold underlines the broader issue of duality in the Novelle. We have stated that one episode points backward and the other foreward. More precisely, there are two kinds of intrusion into Marx' and Anne Lene's idyllic world. In the first incident bourgeois reality (*Umwelt*) and the present remind the reader that the basic issue is what Klein has called *Adel* versus *Bürgertum*, in the second the beggar woman offers a grim reminder of the past for the sake of her dire prophecy. One admires the interweaving of past, present, and future: the villagers' mockery stresses the children's isolation from the present (Marx must be included here as an unwitting if not unwilling participant) and in this sense points to Anne Lene's past *and* future. The beggar woman's broad hints and her claim to *Muttergut* expose the precariousness of the present, the ugly mysteries of the past, and the fearful consequences in the future.

This farewell scene is, then, symbolic in the dramatic rather than the pictorial sense. The substantial measure of authority in the narration at this point is due principally to the fact that Marx witnesses *and* participates directly in the two incidents. For this reason, and despite the fact that Marx as narrator offers a severely limited field of vision, we might expect the scene to furnish little evidence of *ganz wenig* other than its importance as total symbol. But in actual fact the reverse is true, for there is an unmistakable note of restraint lying at the base of the entire scene. For example, the secret of the *Staatshof* was hinted at broadly by the narrator early in the story. The sketchy history of the family (only the conclusion of which, we recall, is experienced by Marx) is further qualified by "so hieß es" and "sagten die Leute." In this central scene the secret is touched on again. We have Marx' explanation of the *Bettlerin*, her dark and prophetic words to Anne Lene, her "geheimnisvolle Gebärde" to Wieb, and her unsubtle accusation, "mein Muttergut such ich, womit ihr die Löcher in eurem alten Dach zugestopft habt." All that remains to be stated is surely the explanation which Anne Lene demands of Wieb and the reader already knows. It is of course given – but at this critical moment Marx leaves the scene. We are not impressed by his excuse for creating a void: "da ich glaubte, die Alte werde das Gemüt des Mädchens leichter zur Ruhe sprechen, wenn sie allein sich gegenüber wären," but the symbolic substitute for overt explanation should impress us. A few days later, Marx says, he observed that Anne Lene had removed the diamond cross, this "Zeichen alten Glanzes," from her throat. The moment of evaluation is again no more than an objective observation based on the visual. The meaning of Anne Lene's act is abundantly clear: she is making a concession to the very thing she has sought to separate herself from and is thereby sacrificing part of her past.

But the real force of removing the cross is brought out by a second symbol, placed in direct contrast to this one. As the beggar woman is taunting Anne Lene, she suddenly removes her shoes (*Schlumpen!*) and offers them to the motionless girl. "Greif zu, Goldkind", rief sie, "greif zu! Es sind Bettelmannsschuhe, du kannst sie bald gebrauchen." Although Anne Lene remains silent, the extremes of diamond cross and beggar's shoes are meaningful to her; actual impoverishment comes two scenes later, but her renunciation of the jewelry indicates a not entirely unconscious admission of guilt and impending defeat.

Two gestures, then, condense the meaning of this two-part scene, which presents Anne Lene's two basic quarrels, one with the present, the other with the future. Both present and future have been condemned, as it were, by the past, and the two symbols discussed here illustrate both the condemnation and Anne Lene's partial acceptance of it. Typically, very little happens in this "action" scene, for the events serve as symbols which, along with gesture (at once a form of action and of silence), tell us all we need to know.

The fifth scene tells of Anne Lene's engagement to the *Kammerjunker*. It employs action as symbol, centers on two *Vorfälle* (which Marx soon afterward forgets for a time), portrays violence, and unites past and present. The engagement scene represents a violation of the story's time sequence in that Marx, on receiving the news of the engagement, remembers two "trivial" incidents from the past that once aroused his implacable hostility to the young aristocrat. They are recalled here as attempts to find reasons for his uneasiness on learning of the betrothal. Once, while sitting at afternoon coffee, Marx had observed how his adversary cast occasional looks at Anne Lene. There was, he says, something in them that infuriated him. Anne Lene too was conscious of the junker's eyes and went to sit with Marx' mother, as if to seek protection. At this point the junker seized a fly and began to torture it. Suddenly tiring of his game, he stabbed the insect with his pen and dropped it before him on the table. "Ich hatte wie gebannt diesem Vorgange zugesehen, und Anne Lene schien es ebenso ergangen." A few days later Marx found Anne Lene in the garden leaning against a young tree. The junker had just left the scene, and so again Marx sees only the end of something. "Zufällig aber hatte ich bemerkt, daß die Krone des kleinen Baumes wie von einem Pulsschlage in gleichmäßigen Pausen erschüttert wurde, und es überkam mich eine Ahnung dessen, was hier geschehen sein könne."

Marx' rage at the way in which the junker looked at Anne Lene, his horror at seeing the insect tortured, and his *Ahnung* of what happened in the garden are, to be sure, clear evidence that he is evaluating the scene as he later recalls it; for the facts so obvious to the reader – the junker's indifference to Anne Lene herself, his cold calculation and display of cruelty to both fly and betrothed – remain for Marx at the level of *Zorn* and *Ahnung* as they occurred as well as later, when he recalls them in this engagement scene. While the incidents are clear examples of action as symbol, and while the narrator's field of vision is almost as restricted as it was in the first *Staatshof* scene, the stress cannot be said to fall on either of these. Their real importance seems to be rather to offer a counterpart to the violence of the preceding scene. There Anne Lene was the victim, was helplessly exposed first to the taunts of the people, then to the accusations of the beggar woman. Here the violence is inside the characters. Without resorting to overt statement, Storm makes it evident that Anne Lene will fail in her attempt to save herself and her world by remaining within it. The junker's cruelty and hence his inability to save Anne Lene is demonstrated in his act of violence committed with the same casualness and impersonalness that Marx saw (but failed to evaluate) in the aristocrat's "läßigem Anschauen."

As for Anne Lene, her reaction to her fiancé's ruthlessness is likewise a transfer of violence to a point outside herself. As the junker's cruelty can be seen only in a silent act that concerns no one directly, so does Anne Lene's violent reaction manifest itself silently and in an object totally outside the story's sphere of action. The use of a trembling sapling to express her grief and agitation – nature's response to man's agony of isolation and silence – is scarcely a coincidence; one finds a number of parallels in other Novellen by Storm. There is, for example, the murmuring of the sea in *Aquis Submersus* as nature's reply to Johannes, who has lost Katherina and his son and at the end is left in appalling isolation. The effectiveness of this use of nature lies in what silence or the unspoken things mean to the story. In most cases – and certainly here in this scene beneath the tree – resignation, frustration, failure, and an inner violence are given expression through nature imagery and what may be called silent response.

The sixth scene tells of Anne Lene's impoverishment, the dissolving of the engagement, the burning of her fiancé's letters and the promise not to wait for him any longer, her decision to learn house-keeping, and her reluctant, awkward attempt to work. In regard to Storm's use of silence this series of incidents and facts presents nothing new. On the contrary, the frequent use of symbols, symbolic actions and gestures as substitutes for statement gives way to straight-forward narration. Admittedly suggestive in larger context, the events stand primarily for themselves in this scene. They serve as bearers of plot and as a means of disposing of the *Kammerjunker* (whose role began late and – if the focus on Anne Lene is not to be weakened – must end early) and preparing for the final scene, in which the burghal Marx will try unsuccessfully to save Anne Lene from an inevitable yet self-willed fate.

Two suggestive references to the broader lines of the story fail to attain the symbolic value we might expect. Marx discovers Anne Lene burning the letters. "Nein, Marx", sagte sie endlich und mühte sich, ihrer Stimme einen festeren Klang zu geben, "ich verspreche es dir, ich will nicht länger auf ihn warten." The action itself was plain enough, the statement that follows pushes explicitness to an extreme – and obviously well beyond symbol. And a few lines later, as Marx attempts to persuade her to leave the *Staatshof* and return to the town, she exclaims "nein, nicht unter Menschen!" We know this already. Intentional social isolation was effectively expressed in the dance scene by the mention of the fan, and again in the second *Staatshof* scene by the gloves. Here the urge for isolation is overtly stated, and the sense of restraint established earlier in the story threatens to vanish. Moreover, the habitual scene that closes this section appears to drop all pretense of both faulty memory and the limited field of vision. Anne Lene is of course unsuccessful in her attempt to learn her trade. "Allein man fühlte leicht, daß die Teilnahme an diesen Dingen nur eine äußerliche war; eine Anstrengung, von der sie bald in der Einsamkeit ausruhen mußte." But the assertion of authority is fitting, for when the story becomes as explicit as this the devices that aid silence lose their reason for being.

The final scene in its entirety offers a recapitulation and evaluation, implied rather than stated, of past events and of the scenes and incidents in Anne Lene's life as Marx experienced them. Some of the devices of silence discussed above are employed, others abandoned almost completely. For the bulk of this scene narrator memory, for example, is fully restored: "Mir ist aus jenen Stunden noch jeder kleine Umstand gegenwärtig." Also overt statement is resorted to, "nun fällt alles zusammen. Ich kann es nicht halten, Marx." Gesture, nature as symbolic response, and more generally, symbolic action are present to a degree, but since *symbolische Vorgänge* lie at the heart of most of Storm's early Novellen, there is little point in isolating them and offering them here as those devices necessary for understanding the scene as a whole.

Yet here too the principle of *ganz wenig* emerges as central to the scene's meaning, for if taken as evaluative summary the final scene arrives at little that is explicit. But if taken as a kind of replica in small of the whole Novelle its general shape makes up for the lack of explicitness or overt statement. We may therefore discuss the scene as an example of structure as symbol, or of structure as a way to express meaning.

A party at the *Staatshof* encloses the course of action. Its similarity to another *Staatshof* visit made years before is apparent, but the similarity is primarily for the sake of contrast. On the first occasion the old generation sits amidst decaying but still obvious elegance; on this second occasion it is the young who dominate the scene. Time bears symbolic meaning: Sunday afternoon in summer is a necessary part of Marx' and Anne Lene's past; indeed, the narrator's entire recollection of Anne Lene's world and his own life in it is a picture of many Sunday afternoons. This will of course be the last and it too will represent a composite. The central figure in the first *Staatshof* visit is the old lady, whose words "Du mußt dich immer hübsch gerade halten, Kind!" instil once and for all a sense of respect in Marx; in the last visit the young, robust brewer's son Claus Peters dominates the gathering. Marx of course dislikes him and reserves his respect for Anne Lene.

Other scenes and incidents from the past are repeated here in new form. The tranquil, overgrown garden is turned into a playground, and the pair of old linden trees at the *Hoftor* must submit to the indignity of a rope swing. The meaning of this gay party of young people is that the entire *Staatshof*, beginning with the garden, is to be revitalized. But the embodiment of rejuvenation, the party's leader, is also the embodiment of coarseness, insensitivity, gross vitality. The introduction of Claus Peters at this point in the story, long after our sympathies have been enlisted in the cause of the old, betrays the artificiality of revitalization. A further example is suggested by the *Blumenleuchte*. The crystal chandelier is gone from the ballroom and a new one has to be made – by nailing together two strips of wood! Flowers are picked from the garden and woven into garlands which are then wrapped around the wooden improvisation to conceal its plainness. Anne Lene accompanies the girls as they look for flowers, "aber sie selber stand dabei; sie pflückte nichts." We sense her reluctance to see the *Verwilderung* of once cultivated, ordered nature subjected to change, to cleaning up; and both reader and Anne Lene realize that any such restoration will be temporary and hence artificial.

The dance, intended as the high point of the youthful gathering, repeats an earlier scene and adds a revealing point: Anne Lene and Marx want to dance the minuet together as they had once done long ago. But the old musician, who earned his bread "bald mit der Nadel, bald mit dem Fiedelbogen," no longer carries this kind of music with him, and they have to make do with a waltz instead. Anne Lene herself establishes the connection to their earlier dance, "nicht wahr, Freund Simon darf dabei sein?" Their second dance also holds Marx completely under its spell, but here there is more pathos and a greater sense of something forever lost: "ich war allein mit ihr; diese festen klingenden Geigenstreiche hatten uns von der Welt geschieden; sie lag verschollen, unerreichbar weit dahinter." In both scenes the dance is a form of escape; here, however, the world on which the dance is based has either vanished or its remnants attacked from within.

A number of other symbols support the picture of final collapse. The *Schäferpaar* on the pavilion walls is "halb erloschen" and the wallpaper on which the scene is depicted hangs loosely. Anne Lene remarks on this herself and shows her awareness of the *Schäferpaar* as a representation of a happy pastoral past. But this does not lessen its worth as symbol, it is rather a sign that the reality of a new time has taken over before Anne Lene's eyes. The *Graft* likewise takes on a new aspect. Early in the Novelle this moat-like canal is referred to very briefly; it is "weit und tief" and surrounds the *Heuberg*. A later, oblique reference may be seen in the statement that Marx learns how to cross the *Gräben* by means of a *Springstock*, while Anne Lene must use the footplank. The *Graft*'s importance as symbol lies in the fact that Marx is able to cross the object of separation and isolation at will, whereas Anne Lene cannot. For her it represents both a danger and an impassable abyss. Toward the end of the third scene we learn for the first time that the pavilion floor has become unsafe; "hier und dort konnte man durch die Ritzen in den Dielen auf das darunterstehende Wasser sehen."

And in this last scene we encounter a series of references to it.
After dancing their waltz, the couple leave the group and wander
toward the orchard until they come to the *Graft*. They follow its
course and find themselves at length in their childhood *Spielplatz*
and, shortly afterward, before the old pavilion. In this passage the
Graft is called "breit und schwarz." Beyond it, on the other side
where the fens lie, Marx can hear the cows grazing. The peaceful-
ness of the scene, effectively contrasting the ominous *Graft*, is
suddenly shattered by the strident cry of a gull, which awakens
Marx to the surge of the sea not far off. "Ein Gefühl der Öde und
Verlorenheit überfiel mich; fast ohne es zu wissen, stieß ich Anne
Lenes Namen hervor und streckte beide Arme nach ihr aus."
As in the engagement scene, nature is a kind of communication –
but neither Marx nor Anne Lene understands its warning. Immediately afterward, Anne Lene steps into the pavilion, whose
floor gives way and drops her into the *Graft*. The word *Graft* is
used three times (and *Graben* once) in the remainder of the paragraph, but with one exception – "die Graft war tief, aber ich war
kein ungeübter Schwimmer" – its attributives have been dropped.
After the catastrophe it loses its sinister properties because its
symbolic function as barrier is lost with Anne Lene's death.

This partial listing of symbols, juxtapositions, correspondences,
and themes shows how meaning and action are ordered into a whole,
that is to say, how events, objects and effects are gathered up and
placed in final combination. To show how and for what purpose
this combination tends to reproduce the whole we may review in
bare outline the structure of *Auf dem Staatshof*, its final scene, and
the main points of similarity and dissimilarity between the two.
Seen schematically, the Novelle offers this sevenfold division:

A Introductory statement: mode of narration, avowal of ignorance.

B General setting; narrator is placed in the landscape; introduction
to the *Staatshof*.

1 First visit to the *Staatshof* by the four-year-old narrator.
2 Dance scene. Anne Lene leaves the *Staatshof* and lives in town.
3 Grandmother's death. Anne Lene in the narrator's home. The children's visits to the *Staatshof*. Anne Lene grows up.
4 Farewell visit to the *Staatshof;* incidents with the villagers and the *Bettlerin*.
5 Anne Lene's engagement; the fly and tree incidents.
6 Anne Lene's impoverishment, her life at the *Staatshof*, her renunciation of the junker.
7 Party at the *Staatshof;* Anne Lene's death.

B Closing paragraph as general setting: Claus Peters at the new *Staatshof*.

A Avowal of ignorance: "Ich bin aber niemals wieder dort gewesen."

The seven scenes comprising the Novelle fall rather naturally into three main groups, each of which corresponds to a section of the final scene. The first group (scenes 1-3) corresponds to the events of scene seven up to the moment when the young people enter the ballroom, the second group (scene 4) to the ballroom scene, and the third (scenes 5-7) to the death scene, which begins with the nocturnal walk and ends when Anne Lene's body is found in the *Graft*.

By using scene four and its counterpart in the final scene, the events centering on the ballroom, we may show how Anne Lene's fate is repeated in symbolic form. Marx' farewell visit to the *Staatshof* combined past and future, i.e., pointed backward and foreward by means of two incidents. The waltz beneath the artificial *Blumenleuchte* in the delapidated ballroom is an intentional recovery of the past in surroundings and circumstances that represent a fulfillment of the beggar woman's prophecy. Moreover, Anne Lene's failing health is the actual cause for leaving the ballroom and thus concluding the central scene: "Als aber Anne Lene mit der Hand nach dem Herzen griff und zitternd mit dem Atem rang, da bat ich sie, mit mir in den Garten hinabzugehen."

She goes to her death, and we cannot ignore the fact that Marx has invited her to do so.

Similarly, the first part of scene seven is a symbolic reiteration of the Novelle's first three scenes: the Sunday afternoon party with its carefree spirit, the gradual intrusion of decay and poverty, of the jarring notes of social differences, and of the attempts to escape reality and the passing of time. Anne Lene's total identification with the old and the taking over of the *Staatshof* by the young (seen in her refusal to use the rope swing or to pick flowers with the others) correspond to her marks of distinction in earlier scenes – the gloves, fan, and diamond cross – and to her financial ruin. Together they lead to the central scene discussed above, in which clear warnings of ultimate destruction are given.

The final three scenes, two of which are concerned with Anne Lene's attempt (and failure) to escape her fate through marriage, describe the destruction which the central scene has already shown to be inevitable. A number of similarities and contrasts between these three scenes and the last part of scene seven are evident: the young nobleman as rescuer, who in his brutality and *Versagen* as human being makes a telling statement on Anne Lene's aristocratic world, fails just as the young bourgeois doctor does; nature is used as communication in the incident beneath the tree in scene five and again in the last scene, when Marx hears the surging sea just before he loses Anne Lene in the "ungeheueren Raum;"[15] finally, Anne Lene's burning of her fiancé's letters is the same admission of defeat and acceptance of fate that we see (but with greater finality) in her judgement of the *Schäferpaare*, who "wollen sich auch empfehlen."

The final section to be considered, the death scene, is the point at which both structures – the total one of the Novelle and the symbolic, reiterative one of scene seven – coincide and unite. What is said in this scene is said through symbols and they apply both to scene and Novelle. The principal one is concentrated in Anne Lene's ambiguous words to Marx as he is on the point of entering the pavilion: "du nicht, Marx; bleib! es trägt uns beide nicht."

In our earlier discussion of this scene two possible explanations for Anne Lene's death were offered. She committed suicide by moving about on a surface unable to support her at length; or Marx contributed to her death, not by actually entering the pavilion, but by preparing to do so. In his role as bourgeois companion he bears symbolic guilt. The final evaluation of Anne Lene's death was deferred, for the significant thing about the scene was found in Storm's refusal to dissolve the residuum of mystery.

It is still not possible to do so fully at this point. However, the combination of symbols observed in our analysis of scene seven offers at least a better grounded explanation for the death than it has been possible to find heretofore. The pavilion, it is obvious, is a sign of aristocracy and elegance; its position above the water and its thin legs suggest insubstantiality and potential collapse; the floor was referred to earlier as equivalent to the foundation of aristocratic wealth, and its rotten state coincides with the loss of all property. Anne Lene, who is shortly to leave the *Staatshof* forever, realizes that the pavilion floor cannot support them both; indeed, it can hold her only because she is scarcely more substantial than the remnant of grandeur to which she clings! Marx' presence, not in the pavilion but at its threshold, is no cause for alarm to Anne Lene. At this point she feels totally isolated ("sie haben mich ganz allein gelassen") and does not consider Marx as a possible rescuer. But when he makes a move to join her in her precarious position, she realizes the danger to – him!

Yet the events of the Novelle make it apparent that her withdrawal to the pavilion as a haven against an unacceptable social reality is not to offer her more than a brief respite; they make it clear that her death is a logical and necessary end to the ill-fated family, whose last male descendent, we recall, died violently also. Marx' role is thus reduced to witness, or at most to Anne Lene's constant reminder that she is not a part of the world that grows in strength as her own falters and vanishes. The "abwehrende Bewegung," our sole bit of evidence that Marx inadvertantly brought about her fall, possibly makes the catastrophe appear avoidable.

But this cannot be the case. The *Unding* that races through Marx' mind immediately afterwards is perhaps the recognition of death or the fear that he may have contributed to it. Storm leaves this unexplained and hence leaves a critical question unanswered in the narrator's mind. Yet Anne Lene's alienation from life has been so carefully documented in the course of the Novelle that, regardless of Marx' actions or his interpretation of the action, we must conclude that Anne Lene's act was a suicide of the kind that involves both *Tat* and *Ereignis*. The former lies in her answering fidelity to a family and a class doomed to vanish, the latter in the fact that time has run out, that Claus Peters and all he represents have taken over.

It is the function of the seventh scene to show this by gathering together those things which reformulate the meaning of *Auf dem Staatshof* and to offer thereby an expressive frame in which author and narrator silence (or perplexity) is maintained while the heart of the matter, the communication of experience, is conveyed.

CHAPTER THREE

DEATH AND SURVIVAL IN THE SITUATION TRAGEDY:
THE BEGINNINGS OF STORM'S TRAGIC NOVELLEN

Traditionally the word "tragic" is reserved for Storm's later Novellen, specifically the series that begins with *Aquis Submersus* (1875/76) and closes with the *Schimmelreiter* (1888). While there has been little argument as to whether these "Novellen tragischer Spannung" (Fritz Lockemann) are in fact tragic or merely sad, the broader and more difficult question of Storm's basic view of life has been raised again and again in the attempt to show a development running from *Immensee* to the Novellen of the 1880's or to show the tragic-idyllic duality (Franz Stuckert) that gave rise to such works as *Beim Vetter Christian* and *Die Söhne des Senators* in closest proximity to tragic ones like *Draußen im Heidedorf* and *Eekenhof*. Yet regardless of where the emphasis is placed – on Storm's steady growth from the early, non-tragic *Stimmungskunst* to the portrayal of man's conflict with his cosmos in the later works, or on the existence of a tragic *Kern* in all his Novellen, even the most idyllic ones – there is general agreement that for approximately half of his forty years of novellistic activity Storm was essentially a *Tragiker*.

The point of division between the two periods of novellistic production is also a matter of critical agreement: the years from 1867 to 1870 or 1871 mark Storm's departure (by no means abrupt) from the lyric, nostalgic "windstille Zeit des literarischen Vormärz"[1] to the more dramatic, tragic, and starkly realistic world of Hauke

Haien. Such neat categories, even if we allow a few years for the *Übergangszeit*, are of course misleadingly simple, but a comparison of the *Halligfahrt* with *Draußen im Heidedorf* (both published in 1871) does take us with one seemingly sudden stride into another world, one which is frequently and consistently portrayed from *Aquis Submersus* on.

If we disregard the facts of Storm's private life and concern ourselves rather with those aspects of his works that reveal a turn to tragedy, we are forced to renounce the convenience of periodization and search out the elements comprising or contributing to the tragic where they first manifest themselves in reasonable strength and clarity. Not surprisingly, the evidence takes us back to a work as early as 1849, to *Posthuma*, published the same year as *Immensee*. It will be the intent of this chapter to discuss incipient tragedy in a few of Storm's works up to the *Heidedorf* Novelle, with which his "major" period begins. For convenience in isolating the elements contributing to tragedy we shall reverse the chronological order and examine the later examples first.

Of the 29 stories written in the years from 1837 to 1871, only three deal with the death of one of the principal characters, *Posthuma*, *Auf dem Staatshof*, and *Auf der Universität*.[2] To these should be added Storm's plan for a Novelle to be called *Im Korn*, which in his own words was to be "tiefer, tragischer, schlüssiger" than its literary "source", Auerbach's *Joseph im Schnee*.[3] In a letter to Constanze he describes his new work and asks for her reaction:

> Meine neue Dichtung heißt "Im Korn"; ich weiß nur noch nicht, ob ich sie in "rime" oder in "prosa" schreibe. Ein junger Gutsherr hat die Tochter des Schullehrers verführt unter Eheversprechen. Er hält dies Versprechen nicht, und ein Abstandsgeld, das er ihr geben will, schlägt sie aus. Der Vater stirbt und hinterläßt sie in Armut; sie ist gezwungen, auf Tagelohn auszugehen und das Kind einer alten stumpfen Frau, bei der sie wohnt, zu überlassen. So geht es ein paar Jahre. Hinter dem Dorf hat der Gutsbesitzer sein reichstes Kornfeld, eine einzige unübersehbare Fläche. Die Ähren sind reif, es ist in diesem Jahre eine Überfülle des goldenen Segens. Das Kind, das die Mutter, die dem Erwerb nachgehen muß, nicht überwachen kann, entläuft der Alten und verirrt sich in dieses Kornmeer. Die Welt zwischen dem Kornwalde, die Seelenstimmung des Kindes werden

79

> Gegenstand der Darstellung; die Angst, die Raserei der Mutter, das vergebliche Suchen. Du erinnerst, daß vor Jahren auf solche Weise ein Kind bei Berlin zugrunde ging. Der junge Gutsherr, dem das Häuschen, wo Mutter und Kind wohnen, ein steter Vorwurf war, der oft einen großen Umweg machte, um dort nicht vorbeizumüssen, ist währenddes abwesend als Geschworener in der nächsten Stadt. Er reitet heim. Eine Flinte, die er in der Stadt beim Büchsenmacher gehabt, hängt er über seiner Schulter. Die letzte Sache ist ein Kindesmord gewesen; es hat tiefen Eindruck auf ihn gemacht. Er sieht noch, wie beim Abgehen der Richter die junge Verbrecherin von der Bank heruntergleitet mit ausgestreckten Armen. "Ach, meine Herren, haben Sie Barmherzigkeit mit mir!" Es ist ihm gewesen, als sei *sie* es, auch sie hätte nun durch ihn dort auf der Anklagebank sitzen können. Er kommt an sein prachtvolles Kornfeld; er überschlägt den Wert der Ernte, er beschließt, daß es geschnitten werden soll. Da sieht er hundert Schritt vom Wege zwei Raben über einer bestimmten Stelle auf eine auffallende Weise flattern, hinabtauchen, wieder auffliegen. Er nimmt seine Flinte und erschießt den einen. Er bindet sein Pferd an einen Baum, er geht in's Korn nach der Stelle. Er findet sein Kind; es liegt mit dem Kopf auf den beiden aufeinandergelegten Händchen, aber das Gesicht ist wächsern. Er erkennt es, er sieht alles. "Verhungert – mitten im Korn – in seines Vaters Reichtum". Er fühlt seine Schuld an seines Kindes Tod, die Gedanken kommen, die sich anklagen und entschuldigen."Aber warum hat sie das Geld nicht genommen, sie hätte dann nicht zu tagelöhnern, ihr Kind nicht ohne Aufsicht zu lassen brauchen!" – "Pfui, Rudolf, du bist ein Schuft!" – usw. Er bringt der Mutter ihr Kind. Große Erschütterungen, Versöhnung, eine stille Hochzeit.
>
> Das ist der Plan; ich habe noch nie einen so guten gehabt...[4]

One may or may not share Storm's enthusiasm for his story, but it can hardly be denied that *Im Korn*, as given here, is decidedly transitional in that it offers distinct possibilities both for *Stimmungskunst* and for tragedy. For the former we might imagine a treatment, especially of the discovery scene, or possibly the "Verirrung im Kornwalde," similar to some of the *Bilder* in *Immensee* or *Auf dem Staatshof*; for the latter we should of course have to disregard Storm's laconic description of the ending. Such speculations, admittedly pointless in many respects, nevertheless afford an opportunity to consider plausible reasons why Storm dropped the plan. The scanty criticism of this fragment is concerned primarily with "Gründe schaffenspsychologischer Art" (Stuckert) or with even more conventional arguments based on biographical data.

Böhme, for example, argues that (1) Storm's legal duties and the voluminous correspondence with publishers and magazine editors made such great demands on his time and energies that he was unable to let the plan ripen slowly ("Ich werde es langsam reifen lassen und für jetzt noch nicht schreiben"[5]); (2) Storm's general feeling of literary sterility in the ensuing months made its completion impossible. As evidence for this Böhme cites two remarks made by Storm in the summer of 1862, one to the effect that he was "unfähig zu produktiver Arbeit," the other that his "innere Unruhe" prevented him from writing any Novellen; (3) Storm himself saw the "stoffliche Schwierigkeiten" and lamented his inability "über das belebende Beiwerk zu kommandieren" – in contrast to Auerbach, "der vom Dorfe ist."[6]

Stuckert argues, somewhat more cogently in our opinion, that (1) his "rein konstruktive Planung" did not correspond to Storm's manner of creating. As a "schauender Künstler" he created scenes and *Bilder* which grew together into Novellen "ihm selber fast unbewußt;" (2) the plan for *Im Korn* offered in itself too little "Bild- und Erlebnisgehalt;" (3) the rigid determinism of guilt and atonement was alien to Storm's way of thinking. The happy end, while compatible with burghal "Harmoniebedürfnis," was not acceptable to Storm's own nature or to the basic social theme of the story.[7]

The danger of accepting fully any of these "reasons" should be apparent to all but the most confirmed biographical critic, for the problem of author intent and of how far information about the author helps us to understand his creation, in itself a difficult one, becomes virtually insolvable in the face of the unfinished work. Still, the *Im Korn* plan has a definite value beyond the pleasures of speculation it affords: it was conceived in June 1862, only shortly after the completion of *Auf der Universität*. Storm considered this latter work to be one of his best; he wrote to Fontane that "nichts von allen meinen Sachen eine originellere Stormsche Dichtung ist als eben diese,"[8] and as late as 1884 he was insisting (to Erich Schmidt) that his most recent works were not better than this one.[9]

The ending of *Auf der Universität* is, in the context of Storm's Novellen, a tragic one which derives its meaning from a combination of factors that include guilt, coincidence, and fate.

Any or all of these might be cited for *Im Korn* as well. Guilt in particular appears to have been foremost in Storm's mind if we may judge from a remark made in the letter in which he describes his plan: "Das Verirren des Kindes wurzelt hier in der Schuld der Eltern, und sie wird gebüßt durch ein Leid, das ihr künftiges Leben dem tiefsten Ernste weiht."[10] To any reader of Storm's enthusiastic letter the question of guilt must seem a critical, and perhaps obvious, one. From the meager evidence at hand, however, one is tempted to raise objections to the wording. Why "Schuld der Eltern" rather than "Schuld des Vaters"? And on what grounds – artistic as well as human – is one to justify an ending (of a story, we recall, to which Storm himself applies the phrase "tiefer, tragischer, schlüssiger") that joins, through "Versöhnung" and "stille Hochzeit," the guilty pair in communal mourning? Still another question arises in the light of Storm's statements: whose tragedy is this? Storm's answer would seem to say that it belongs to the parents, and by implication the child's death is reduced to the role of catalyst. To go on living and suffering is hence the real tragedy, the parents' joint dedication to "tiefster Ernst" its manifestation.

Novellen pre- and postdating this fragment offer ample support for Storm's hypothetical answer. To take but one example – and the most obvious parallel to *Im Korn* – *Aquis Submersus* contains at least two important motifs anticipated in the plan: the marriage between members of different social classes and the death of a child through neglect by its parents. Storm proves the youthful narrator's *culpa patris* as an explanation of the first two letters of the enigmatic C.P.A.S. to be correct, yet the old manuscript in which Johannes tells his story leaves strong doubt as to whether the father alone bears the principal burden of guilt. Storm himself added to the difficulty – and started the still unsettled controversy concerning tragic guilt in the Novelle – with his well-known statement:

> Man würde durchaus fehlgehen, wenn man in 'Aquis Submersus' in der, freilich die bestehende Sitte außer Acht lassenden, Hingebung des Paares die Schuld der Dichtung suchen wollte. Das hat dem Dichter ebenso ferngelegen wie etwa Shakespeare bei Romeo und Julia. Die Schuld, wenn man diese Bezeichnung beibehalten will, liegt auf der anderen Seite, hier auf dem unerbittlichen Geschlechterhasse, dort auf dem Übermute eines Bruchteils der Gesellschaft, der ohne Verdienst auf die irgendwie von den Vorfahren eroberte Ausnahmestellung pochend, sich besseren Blutes dünkt und so das menschlich Schöne und Berechtigte mit der ererbten Gewalt zu Boden tritt. Nicht zu übersehen ist, daß es eben diese feindliche Gewalt ist, die das Paar einander fast blindlings in die Arme treibt.[11]

This criticism is in our opinion demonstrably weak, but it has at least the merit of consistency. Storm has created a "situation," a social sphere in direct opposition to any possible heroic action on the part of the central characters. And such action as there is will therefore arise from the collision of the individual against external forces. In Storm's Novellen the struggle is almost invariably weighted in favor of the latter, generally in the form of *Schicksal* or some similar deterministic factor. More important to our present discussion, however, is the fact that Storm explicitly rejects guilt on the part of Johannes and Katherina; indeed, there is more than a suggestion that he did not consider the issue of guilt ("wenn man diese Bezeichnung beibehalten will"), on whichever side, a vital one at all. It is rather a matter of something external, in this instance a "feindliche Gewalt."

To be sure, there is danger in judging a work strictly from the modern point of view, especially where tragedy is concerned. But in this case we are reassured that our objections are not without validity; Gertrud Storm quotes the author's reaction to a contemporary reader's complaint that the characters in his Novellen "ohne eigene Schuld zugrunde gingen." Storm's rebuttal contains perhaps his best known formulation of tragedy:

> Wenn das ein Einwand gegen mich sein soll, so beruht er auf einer zu engen Auffassung des Tragischen. Der vergebliche Kampf gegen das, was durch die Schuld oder auch nur die Begrenzung, die Unzulänglichkeit des Ganzen, der Menschheit, von der der (wie man sich ausdrückt) Held ein Teil ist, der sich nicht abzulösen vermag, und sein oder seines eigentlichen Lebens herbeigeführter

> Untergang scheint mir das Allertragischste. (Karsten Kurator, Renate, Aquis Submersus, bei welchem ich an keine Schuld des Paares gedacht habe.)[12]

As late as 1880, when these words were written, Storm is still concerned less with what his characters do than with what happens to them. One is struck by the adjective *vergeblich* and by the words "der sich nicht abzulösen vermag." They appear to say that, beyond any question of individual guilt (a term Storm uses somewhat reluctantly, we have seen), the forces of fate – expressed through nature, society, or some other limiting agent – are the determinants of tragedy, the possibility for which is given to man with his very existence.

It is but a short step from "vergeblicher Kampf" and the "Unzulänglichkeit des Ganzen" to man's perilously heavy burden of freedom and his ability (and necessity) to make a choice. But Storm is reluctant to let his characters take that step; or to put it another way, he seems to insist on making an Hebbelian assumption in overemphasizing external hindrances to human, and hence tragic, activity.

To return to the ending of *Im Korn*, we recall that the child's death brings about a realization of guilt, and the parents are joined in a "stille Hochzeit." We may assume – more than this, we are told – that silent suffering and bitter memory comprise their lifelong atonement. Similarly, Johannes and Katherina atone, and the only thing different about their situation is that the suffering is without benefit of *Beisammensein*. If one is to accept Storm's suffering and *Vereinsamung* as valid constituents of tragedy, as substitutes for the protagonists' death, it is possible to call *Im Korn* a tragedy. It is also possible to understand the sharing of guilt by both parents (*culpa patris* is applicable to the *Gutsherr* in precisely the same sense that it applies to Johannes) in the light of Storm's emphasis on passive rather than active protagonists, on situations, that is to say, which characters stumble into rather than create.

Situation tragedy, as Storm's peculiar version of the mode may be called, arises when an individual must contend with forces outside himself. The active causes of conflict are attributable more to fate, to demonic and often supernatural powers, than to any element of hamartia in the individual or to any major act of will. Stuckert describes Storm's concept of tragedy this way:

> So wurzelt auch Storms Gefühl des Tragischen in dem Bewußtsein des unabänderlichen Verfallenseins alles menschlichen Lebens an die überlegenen Mächte der Natur und des Schicksals.[13]

And to these two forces he suggests the addition of a third, that of society; these are, according to Stuckert, the main tragic motifs in Storm's Novellen.[14] Singly or in combination they emerge as the dominant factors in a majority of the Novellen after 1871. The earlier period, however, offers no such picture. We have observed that in only three stories is the approach to tragedy apparent, while our fourth example, *Im Korn*, holds a problematic position by virtue of a tragic situation with a "deeply serious" but, except in Storm's peculiar view, basically non-tragic outcome. One of the reasons Stuckert gives for Storm's failure to write *Im Korn* is, we recall, the incompatibility of its happy end with Storm's *Wesen* and the story's social theme. Our thesis has been that *Im Korn*'s ending is anything but happy, that it represents in Storm's special view of tragedy a form of atonement weakened only by the substitution of shared suffering for the expected *Vereinsamung*.

Both *Im Korn* and its later relative *Aquis Submersus*, we may conclude, point to a tragedy of survival – (a condition or situation) – rather than to one of destruction (an event). For the one work Storm denies guilt in the lovers and stresses the social forces that conspire against them. For the other he speaks of guilt (in the parents), reminding us that the social difference between the *Gutsherr* and the schoolteacher's daughter contributes substantially to the catastrophe. And for both he uses the term tragic.

To move in our inverted chronology from *Im Korn* to *Auf der Universität* is to forsake the tenuous paths of speculation for the well-traveled way of analysis. For to call the former a tragedy, even in Storm's special context, and to include it among the tragic

Novellen of the earlier period is to commit a double (though perhaps pardonable) fault. *Im Korn* is of course not a Novelle but the mere skeleton of one, and Storm's insistence on including *Gemeinsamkeit* in the process of expiation raises more issues than can be readily accomodated even to the broad theory of tragedy. *Auf der Universität*, on the other hand, is a Novelle, and it offers in the death of its principal character at least one solid basis for calling the work tragic. Storm himself did not do so, but his description of Lenore Beauregard strongly suggests that he would have considered the term appropiate:

> Eine zarte, erregte Mädchennatur, mit dem eingebornen Drang nach schöner Gestaltung des Lebens, dessen Erfüllung die äußeren Verhältnisse versagen. So geht sie von Jugend auf traumwandelnd am Abgrund hin. Ein Hauch genügt, sie hinabzustürzen. So kommt es. Sie wirft sich einem Scheinbild in die Arme und wird sich dann bewußt, daß sie dadurch das ihr eingeborene Urbild der Schönheit so befleckt hat, daß nur das dunkle Wasser des Styx noch Hilfe bringen kann.[15]

A comparison of this statement with his defense of *Aquis Submersus* sets in sharp relief the similarities and dissimilarities of the two works. In *Aquis Submersus* the inimical force "eines Bruchteils der Gesellschaft" brings about the turn of events leading to catastrophe; in *Auf der Universität* "äußere Verhältnisse" play a similar role in preventing Lore from realizing her goal. In both stories the loss or failure to gain what is beautiful in life (its "schöne Gestaltung" and "das menschlich Schöne und Berechtigte") is identified with personal tragedy. But whereas Storm is at pains to reject guilt for Johannes and Katherina, his efforts to do so for Lore Beauregard are incomparably slighter. In her case he speaks of an "eingeborner Drang" and points out that she throws herself into the arms of a *Scheinbild* and only afterwards realizes her error. Finally, her own nature is such that she must forever move along the brink of disaster, needing but a *Hauch* to bring about her fall.

This difference between the two works as Storm judges them is a critical one. In his own explanation the heroine of *Auf der Universität* is more active than Johannes and Katherina in bringing about her downfall and is at the same time more conscious of her failings. In this connection it is significant that Storm felt *Auf der Universität* to be an inaccurate title. In the letter from which the above quote is taken he refers to the work as *Lore* and adds parenthetically "so müßte es nämlich heißen." One critic has commented that "Auf der Universität" sounded too definite (*bestimmt*) to Storm; "es wird umgetauft: 'Leonore.'"[16] Just the opposite is true. "Auf der Universität" is but one of several scenes in the Novelle; it scarcely relates to the child Lore, nor does it focus attention on what Storm himself calls the main concern of the Novelle, "die Charakterstellung der Heldin."[17] The title *Lore*, on the other hand, is a definite committal to what must first and last be considered the "point" of the entire narration.

Storm's suggestion of Lore's guilt, his emphasis on her as an individual, his insistence on keeping her absolutely central to the story and granting her generally a more decisive role in her own fate – these hold the promise of a severer concept of tragedy than *Aquis Submersus*, in which a luckless Johannes is victimized by the "Bruchteil der Gesellschaft" and by his own sins of omission (no larger but infinitely more fateful than Reinhard's in *Immensee*). In one respect at least the promise is fulfilled, but on the whole this Novelle faithfully reflects the determinism we have found to be basic to Storm's *Tragik*. Throughout most of the story Lore Beauregard does little or nothing. Her humiliation at the dancing lessons is scarcely more than a sensitive child's awareness that she is temporarily tolerated by the "gnädige Fräulein" and admired (for her beauty) by the narrator and his friend. Her rejection of the narrator's affections is summed up in her statement "Du heiratest doch einmal nur eine von den feinen Damen." Even her fateful act, the decision to spend her modest, hard-earned savings for finery and abandon herself to the riotous *Studentenleben*, is the result of a cruel error. When she learns of her mistake it is too late; her suicide is merely the physical or external equivalent of a death already experienced within.

It is admittedly difficult to see in Lore's fate more than an unfortunate, or pathetic, instance of social incongruity, of the vain struggle for something that lies outside one's own sphere. Criticism of this Novelle as tragedy and as a character study has perhaps for that reason been generally severe. Lore's "Drang nach schöner Gestaltung des Lebens" has been transformed to read "Hang zur Vornehmheit"[18] or a "leidenschaftliches Streben nach Standeserhöhung,"[19] or even a "leeres Ziel, weil es mit einer echten Erfüllung des Menschen nichts zu tun hat."[20] There is a good deal of truth in these appraisals. As far as individual character is concerned, Lore Beauregard is little more than a pretty girl born, unhappily, on the wrong side of town. Simply as character therefore she is hardly of sufficient proportions to become tragic. Moreover, her actions are neither fully necessary nor "great" enough to convince us of their purposiveness, of the inner inevitability that reduces the external forces of fate to mere circumstances. We may assume that Johannes Klein had just such objections in mind when he spoke of Lore as lacking in tragic personality:

> Sie ist nicht Persönlichkeit genug, um wirklich tragisch zu sein (ihr Ende ist theatralisch) und zu viel Persönlichkeit, um ein mittelmäßiges Leben zu führen. Ihr Schicksal ist sozial bedingt, und doch ist es kein soziales Schicksal.[21]

The distinction is an important one. Lacking both "character" and the inner necessity for action (*re*-acting to the false news that her fiancé will marry someone else is not the same as exercising the awful power of choice forced upon her by her tragic consciousness), she threatens to become pathetic, the plaything of social forces – and the *Raugraf*. Tragic action in any conventional sense must not be equated with blind coincidence or even shown as the direct result of it. Klein's objections are thus valid so long as we demand a character strong and complex enough to make free choice meaningful. Schütze expresses much the same misgivings:

> Jedenfalls lehnt man sich gegen den Zufall, dessen Laune hier ein junges Leben zum Opfer fällt – denn an dem Geschwätz des Schneidergesellen, der ihren Verlobten in der Fremde auf anderen Wegen gesehn haben will, hängt doch zuletzt die unglückliche Wendung – unwillkürlich auf.[22]

Both criticisms, however, fail to take into account Storm's limited and less conventional concept of tragedy. We have called his version the situation tragedy, thereby emphasizing its relatively static nature and its opposition to the accepted view of tragedy as a form of action. To defend Lore Beauregard as a tragic figure is to place the stress where Storm himself places it: on the cause for which she struggles and on the special way in which she is active. The first of these gives her dignity and raises her to a level worthy of the tragic outcome, the second represents a vivification of the inner life which both character portrayal and character action are here unable to show. In speaking of Lore's innate *Urbild* of beauty and placing her in the wrong (for her) social context Storm creates a potentially tragic situation. The contest is predictably unequal, to be sure, but not so heavily weighted in favor of the social sphere as to preclude a degree of personal tragedy.

As both work and author make clear, Lore Beauregard's cause is beauty, beauty as an innate quality and also as the deeper motivation for protesting against social incongruity. Her action as a tragic heroine is restricted, in terms of plot, to her early exposure to the "schöne Gestaltung des Lebens" and her subsequent renunciation of the sphere in which it resides (her refusal to see Philipp), then to yielding (the incidents beginning with the *Gelbfuchs* and the visits to the *Hexensabbat*), and finally to the renunciation of both spheres (her suicide). Beyond the level of plot Lore's action, however slight, is at once guilty and innocent. Because the slightest turn of events suffices to hurl her into the abyss her flaw may be said to be in the nature of things, in the kind of world, that is, into which she is born; and because she must live according to her innate urge and pursue her course because of what she is, she brings about her own fall. Lore's friend, the "lahme Marie," explains her dilemma this way:

> Es war vierzehn Tage vor Pfingsten; die Lore war schon lange unwirsch gewesen; ich dachte erst, weil der Tischler ihr noch immer nicht geschrieben hatte, mitunter aber kam's mir vor, als sei das ganze Verlöbnis ihr leid geworden, und als könne sie in sich selbst darüber nicht zurechte kommen. Sie scherte sich auch keinen Deut darum, ob sie mich oder eine von ihren vornehmen Herrschaften mit den

kurzen Worten vor den Kopf stieß; am schlimmsten war es aber, wenn sie gegenüber die Musik vom Ballhaus hörte; denn sie hatte dem Tischler doch versprechen müssen, nicht zu Tanze zu gehen.

Somewhat earlier, the narrator expressed a similar view: "Lore und Christoph! Ich konnte mir die beiden Menschen nicht zusammendenken," and the scenes at the *Ballhaus* make Lore's alternative equally impossible.

There are numerous hints in the story that Lore Beauregard clearly sees both alternatives with which she is faced. To remain in her own sphere would be a denial of the *Drang* which, for better or worse, determines her otherwise nebulous character; to follow those yearnings that force her into an alien sphere would be a sullying of the *Urbild* within. Yet in such a situation, not really of her own making, Storm's *Hauch*, the coincidence or *Laune des Schicksals* to which Schütze so strongly objected, assumes little importance. Lore chooses and acts, and however slight the action may be, it brings on the catastrophe. In the tradition of tragedy the outcome will be Lore's recognition of her deed. Her death is without question, and despite the work's social overtones, an act of will. Klein's condemnation of her death as being theatrical is off the mark, for it implies a failure to recognize one of the story's vital continuities, so vividly expressed in the child's dainty dance slippers and the bright *Tanzkleid* at the beginning, and at the end the death "in vollem Staat." We are reminded of a figure from an earlier Novelle: Anne Lene's anachronistic elegance represents the same "theatricality" and the same inability to conform to a world in which she lives but is out of place.

Auf der Universität offers a distinctly different possibility for tragedy and another kind of tragic figure from those of *Im Korn* and *Aquis Submersus*. These latter, we have seen, are tragedies of survival, one involving guilt, the other not.[23] Neither places stress on tragic action in any customary sense, although there are indications that Johannes and Katherina are actively involved in a struggle against overpowering social forces. Atonement takes two forms, the one solitary, the other shared suffering. In *Auf der*

Universität's similar context of an inimical social world the heroine is capable of limited action. The scant attention given to character portrayal – only in the last third of the story does Lore emerge as the truly central figure – and the absence of any direct statement about inner conflict (in keeping with the narrator's limited field of vision) make the task of reconciling Storm's view of Lore with Lore herself a difficult one. If we agree with Storm in granting her a measure of will, free choice and action, while admitting at the same time that character, the strength arising from inner necessity, is inadequately demonstrated, we must demand a new context for her, one, that is to say, which can be fitted into Storm's static tragedy and yet maintain its opposition to the pervasive determinism of her world.

The new context is given in two significant ways. The first is Storm's use of a few key scenes and events symbolically or as substitution for both overt statement about character and any direct (tragic) action by the characters. Lurking beneath the surface of Philipp's and Lore's world are strange and terrifying forces. Lore herself is of "fremdländischer Abkunft;" on her first appearance at the dancing class she is called "fremdartig;" her complexion and hair are dark,[24] and her general similarity to the *Harfenmädchen* with their "asiatischen Augen" (at the *Jahrmarkt*) is striking. In the *Mühlenteich* episode Philipp is able to approach Lore only through deception and, more important, at that isolated spot far out on the lake "über der Tiefe... denn der See soll hier ins Bodenlose gehen. Nur mitunter war es mir, als husche es dunkel unter uns dahin." The double effect of danger in union with Lore and of *Vereinsamung* is repeated in the episode called *Ein Spaziergang*. Lore's new world is a "halb verfallenes Haus" deep in the woods beside the sea. Its former owner had given it up because "es war ihm nicht gelungen, den großen Zug der Gäste in seine Einsamkeit hinauszulocken." Philipp finds the tavern *düster* and of course feels entirely out of place. Two additional details arrest our attention: the *Waldhaus* lies "im stillsten Sonnenschein," and dark *Schmetterlinge* flutter about the stone steps, symbols which reinforce the unity of the story by serving as submerged links to earlier and later episodes (Lore's body is taken from the sea; Philipp appears and is almost blinded by the "Sonnenschein, der im vollsten Glanze... gebreitet war." And in an earlier episode Philipp goes in quest of a *Brombeerfalter*. "Am Rande des Wassers sah ich Schmetterlinge fliegen; aber ich achtete nicht darauf... ich gedachte eines Bildes..." His picture, that of a young shepherd and a beautiful girl, whose dark eyes looked out into the "morgenhelle Einsamkeit," bears the inscription "Allein auf der Welt.")

As the examples make clear, the alien and terrifying aspects are intimately linked to Lore Beauregard; the intensifying of *Vereinsamung* – a movement from the uneasy little girl with the ill-fitting gloves to the regal (but still uneasy) figure on the horse, and lastly to the pale and aloof *Raugräfin* – is in precise parallel to Lore's steady march along the brink of social and personal disaster. These symbolic eruptions of alien forces into Philipp's ordered bourgeois world are expressions of inner forces unleashed at certain critical moments in the Novelle. They give Lore's character the depth and complexity denied her by more conventional means.

A second way in which Lore is given a tragic context may be seen in her reaction to the dilemma described by the "lahme Marie." If we do not concede that coincidence plays a major role in the story, we must grant Lore a degree of inner awareness not readily demonstrable in the actual description of her character. And this is what the ending, Lore's suicide, demands that we do. Faced with the two alternatives discussed earlier, Lore follows her natural bent and actively brings about the dissolution of her own character. This in itself may be merely pathetic, but her belated recognition that she has denied her real values (embodied in the unexciting figure of Christoph) or, in Storm's words, has sullied "das eingeborene Urbild der Schönheit," forces her to restore herself, to regain identity in a way that approaches true tragedy. The new context is given by the fact that Storm's situation tragedy, based as we have observed, on the unproblematic individual in contention with circumstances into which he chances to come, has had to accomodate a character possessed by a demonic force. Stuckert's claim: "Storm hat in der Gestalt Lore Beauregards zum erstenmal einen Menschen dargestellt, der von seinem Dämon geführt wird und unaufhaltsam seinem schicksalhaften Ende zutreibt"[25] is convincing in that it emphasizes the inner force that drives Lore. However, in *Auf der Universität* we are by no means at the point where it is correct to speak of a fully defined tragic hero such as we find him in the *Schimmelreiter*. Lore does not develop during her tragic experience. And even if we believe to discern her inner struggle, we are still unable to say that the whole personality is involved. Her spirit is not the major party in the struggle against social incongruity; it is rather an unordered series of emotions, merely a part of the whole person, that is, which must contend with forces bent on shaping or breaking.[26]

Auf der Universität is a tragedy of emotions in disorder. Its heroine is unable to escape her situation, to overcome the humiliating and dehumanizing power of a world that carefully preserves its social levels. But she does not retreat from the shambles of her life by living on with her defeat and her bitter memories. Her suffering is silent and solitary – *Vereinsamung* leads to, and is a part of, a tragedy which, in contrast to *Im Korn*, ends in death.

The unusual position this Novelle holds in respect to the other "tragedies" of the early period becomes apparent when we compare some of its main features with those of *Auf dem Staatshof*. In both works the heroine's death is preceded by growing isolation; her suffering is silent; belated help is offered by a suitor/friend, but in the face of a collapsing world – more social in the one, more personal in the other – it is refused; the refusal is affectionate, haughty, and necessary; finally, the "evaluation" of events offered by the narrator (in neither work is explicit statement the rule) betrays a most unambivalent stand: the heroine is granted fullest sympathy as one who has been the victim of life.

In contrast to Lore Beauregard, Anne Lene's death does not provide a tragic ending for the story. Aside from the ambiguous nature of her death, discussed in the preceding chapter, her role as representative of a decaying, will-less aristocracy (and her final acceptance of that role) makes her at best the victim of forces greater than, and outside of, herself or at worst an example of *Lebensuntüchtigkeit*, manifested at an alarmingly tender age. Moreover, Anne Lene's "differentness," a quality shared by Lore as well, results primarily from her refusal to act. Hers is a conscious renunciation of life, and while the failure to act may under certain conditions be as tragic as any sin of commission, the lack of a clearly willed act of self-destruction causes the stress to fall on situation rather than character flaw revealed through action.

In terms of tragedy, then, *Auf dem Staatshof* moves on a simpler level than *Auf der Universität*. There is one vital element less: the act of will, the force of personality which permits the heroine to act as a fully human being. Anne Lene's death, we have seen, is enigmatic to a degree, reflecting on the one hand the net result of an emotional but ineffective life, and on the other a choice, made by a character strong enough to refuse to join the opposition in its uninhibited merrymaking upon the ruins of a way of life – or weak enough to be unable to do so.

Posthuma represents the penultimate step backward from tragedy to the less complex and consequently less problematic character. As was true of *Im Korn*, it is difficult to make a convincing case for tragedy in this sketch or "novellistischer Keim" (Stuckert). There is too little to go on; and above all, the reader is granted only the briefest look into a situation depicted in remarkably objective fashion. The narrator has been dispensed with (or rather, Storm has not yet begun to employ him systematically) and thus there is no attempt to evaluate the characters from within the story and to enlist us in their cause. Yet in embryonic form at least the major elements comprising both kinds of Storm's situation tragedy are present.

As in *Im Korn*, *Posthuma*'s main character survives the catastrophe – here the death of the girl – and atones his guilt through *Vereinsamung* and long suffering. Social incongruity is present in both:

the situation in which guilt is incurred is the love affair between members of different classes. Certainly, there is little doubt but that Storm is making a clear case for guilt and is putting it in a social context that betrays the "Unzulänglichkeit des Ganzen" as a force stronger than individual will. As a potential tragedy of survival, then, *Posthuma* is a forerunner of *Im Korn* and the later representatives of the type.

Elements important to the tragedy of death are given a marginal position. The girl (nameless, as is the young man) is a delicate, will-less creature already marked for death; she is *lebensuntüchtig* in the manner of Anne Lene and, to a lesser degree, Lore Beauregard. An attempt at *Rettung*, although not clearly indicated, is suggested in the fact that the girl is given her due and the identity denied her in life is symbolically restored by the young man: not only is he forced to love her in death (motif of fate), he places a cross on her grave with her name engraved in it. His action is belated recognition both of his guilt-heavy emphasis on desire rather than love and of the girl herself as a human being endowed with dignity rather than as a mere plaything. The penalty for this belatedness overshadows the actual transgression, which is itself weakened by the pronounced atmosphere of death that pervades the story. By means of a set of contrasts – sunshine: shadow; middle class: poverty; life: death (and the black cross); flowers on most graves: weeds on this one (until the punishment of love is effected); the young man's retreat from public view and his attempt to pull the girl into the shadows with him: her acceptance of her position and of her lover's embarrassment – the central problem is given shape. Man's failure to act (in a potentially tragic situation) until it is too late is followed by renunciation and resignation.

The lover's suffering through recollection and renunciation of life is of course not unlike the fate of the protagonists in *Im Korn* or, if we disregard momentarily the question of death or survival, in *Auf der Universität* and *Auf dem Staatshof*. However, *Posthuma*'s closest correspondent is to be seen not in a tragic Novelle but in *Immensee*. To be sure, the latter lacks both a social problem and a catastrophe such as we find it in the four works under discussion; but in two critical respects they are alike: both involve the loss of something vital (love) due to the hero's failure to respond or react to a situation – and this is followed by the resigned acceptance of the loss; and both stress melancholy resignation at the expense of those elements indispensable to tragedy.

This is not to place *Posthuma* and *Immensee* at the same point on our tragic scale. In the former Storm has taken his first step away from *Resignationspoesie* toward greater guilt and harsher punishment than that which results from Reinhard's and Elisabeth's missed opportunity. But in *Immensee*, which lies just outside our tragic range, we reach the point at which heroic struggle dissipates itself in emotional reaction, retreat is without protest, and the climax reduced to an unwritten letter or an unspoken word.

The tragedies – or incipient tragedies, as they might better be called – examined in this chapter are based in varying degree on the loss of social status, on different social levels, on the inability to gain or preserve the order represented by family, home, etc., and finally on the alarmingly fragile tissue of human emotions torn and scattered by external events. By a series of subtractions we have arrived at Storm's well-known Novelle of resignation. Significantly enough, the line traced from *Im Korn* back to *Posthuma* (and ultimately to *Immensee*) is not a bold one nor the distance traversed very great in terms of the development of a tragic concept. While it may be said that some of the early Novellen are clearly more tragic than others – omitting from consideration the obviously "happy" ones – the criteria applied are of a highly limited nature and the term tragic necessarily relative. For this reason we have used Storm's own explanations and definition of tragedy as supporting evidence at various points in our discussion. As indicated earlier, author intent is rarely equatable with achievement, yet the discrepancy between the conventional view of tragedy and those of Storm's Novellen to which the appellation tragic is generally applied is so great as to force us to look for standards governing tragedy within Storm's own context if we are to continue using the term in any meaningful way.

In addition to the evidence offered above, a few general conclusions may be stated. It has been said that nowhere in Storm's works is death the major problem.[27] Considering that death occurs frequently in the Novellen and, as Coenen points out, in a variety of treatments,[28] the statement is undeniably startling. Yet if the works treated here are in any way typical, we may cite them as verification, for even where tragedy (or an approach to it) is involved, death is by no means a requirement. Two of our examples, *Posthuma* and *Im Korn* (as well as the later Novelle *Aquis Submersus*), choose survival, as we have seen; the other pair ends in death, but in only one of these is death an unambiguous, wilful self-destruction. More important, death cannot be called the issue or major problem in any of these. Storm's sense of tragedy, if he may be said to have one, consists in his realization that man cannot cope with those moments or situations in life in which he is beset by forces inimical to his own nature – and our examples make it clear that nature unfortunately does not necessarily involve the whole man, but rather his emotions. His reaction to the chaotic situation is variously depicted. Where there is some evidence of an active will and therefore a measure of guilt we find the approach to conventional tragedy clearest; *Im Korn* was surely for this reason to have been "tragischer." And where determinism appears strongest, e.g., in *Auf dem Staatshof*, tragedy becomes more problematic and we must resort to Storm's declared view of the mode for our justification of the term "tragic Novelle".

The incipient tragedies of Storm's early period represent a movement from almost total passivity and resignation to the kind of tragic guilt that arises from necessary action. At each stage we may observe the addition of, or an added stress on, some element which heightens the sense of conflict so vital to a tragic hero. Seen in this light, the "tragic" Novellen of the years before 1871 may be called preliminary steps toward full realization of man's "vergeblicher Kampf gegen... die Unzulänglichkeit des Ganzen."

If, as Bruch claims, the Novelle is *per se* incompatible with tragedy,[29] we may expect the later works to extend but not complete the movement. However, until a fully satisfactory case is made for refusing such works as *Ein Fest auf Haderslevhuus* and the *Schimmelreiter* admittance to the tragic sphere, we may insist on a gradual development toward tragedy, reflected most clearly in the shift of emphasis from *vergeblich* to *Kampf*.

CHAPTER FOUR

THREE THEMES IN *AQUIS SUBMERSUS*

I. Contrast and Continuity in the Frame

It has frequently been observed that the opening scenes of *Aquis Submersus* share certain features, notably locale and the bipartite form, with the *Innenerzählung* in such a way as to suggest an inner relationship of frame to story. However, investigations of this linkage have been for the most part either of a psychological nature – why such a connection, what were Storm's deeper reasons?[1] – or else have shown so great a reluctance in aesthetic analysis that they have failed to push beyond the immediately discernible fact that the frame of this Novelle achieves a *Spannungswirkung*[2] or lays "über das furchtbare Geschehen den lindernden Schleier der Zeit."[3]

Both notions, *Spannung* and *Milderung*, point to two widely different ways in which the frame effects contrast. But when applied to the historical Novellen this latter term is itself subjected to modification: according to Brecht, history was for Storm "perspektivische Verlängerung des eigenen Lebens in die Vergangenheit hinein." The device by which this is accomplished is the frame, and the major purpose served is the linking of past and present, "die Beziehung zwischen Einst und Jetzt, ihr ewig unausgetragener Prozeß."[4] This relation, says Brecht, is both an abyss and a connection between life and death. Thus it is suggested that continuity as well as contrast reside in the frame-story relationship of the *Chroniknovellen*. The following paragraphs will

99

endeavor to point out examples of both in *Aquis Submersus* and to evaluate their function in the structure of the Novelle.

As with so many of Storm's Novellen, *Aquis Submersus* begins with a childhood scene, drawn from the narrator's memory and offering a classic illustration of *Vergänglichkeitsideologie*. Typical too is the perspective from which the scene is viewed: the narrator recalls his *Vaterstadt* during his boyhood, turns his eyes northward to the nearby village with its grey church steeple, and then describes the large church meadow, "der Hauptschauplatz unserer Taten." The tone of these opening paragraphs is unmistakably idyllic and the recollection of *Jugendfreuden*, which centered on the *Priesterkoppel*, both vivid and nostalgic.

Even so, much of this pleasant landscape retains a pronounced quality of decay and destruction. The *Schloßgarten* is neglected (it has been this way, we are told, "seit Menschengedenken"), the hedges still bear some leaves *immerhin*, and the slight rise from which one can survey the countryside overlooks a dried-up fishpond. The heath over which the narrator and his school friend wandered is still extensive, but once it stretched in an unbroken expanse almost to the town on one side and the village on the other. The *Priesterkoppel* has a deep waterhole surrounded by willow stumps, and in the adjoining garden are two stunted appletrees.[5]

The illusory quality of this time-ravaged world, something that at once continues a past yet to be unraveled and warns against accepting life as the immediate force, is strengthened in a twofold way, by overt anticipation and by a covert or embryonic symbol: the *Wassergrube* in the meadow is called *gefährlich*, and the narrator adds, "wie ich jetzt meine;" secondly, the harmless fishpond opens a long series of symbols and symbolic references to water, one of the two primary destructive instruments in the Novelle.[6]

The second part of the narrator's youth is concerned with the village church as a center of interest and with the portrait and its enigmatic C.P.A.S. The introduction of an apparently insolvable mystery as a vivification of the past is of course the major purpose of this part of the frame, whose *Spannungswirkung* acts as an effective contrast to at least the first manuscript. But beyond the creation of suspense by means of the portrait (of an unknown subject by an unknown painter), there are a number of indications that the narrator is evaluating the scene in such a way as to deprive all the contrasted things of their "differentness". We have seen that the boy's idyllic landscape is in effect the consistent image of a world in which decay and the passage of time are dominant characteristics.[7] The interior of the church is *düster*, and the past looks in silence and with both pious and ominous eyes upon the living. The wild faces of the figures on the *Altarschrank* are contrasted to "das holde Antlitz der am Kreuz hingesunkenen Maria," a figure that would be capable of capturing the boy's heart had it not already committed itself to the portrait.

Especially significant in this emotional reaction to a scene overlaid with the past is the fact that amidst such things it is life itself, or the suggestion of it, which entrances the narrator. Not the grim, wild, or ugly but *das Holde* (as he sees it in the face, "das holde Antlitz," of the Virgin Mary) has for him a special appeal. Storm tells us that he was seized by a "phantastisches Verlangen" to learn more about the child, and in describing its portrait he uses the word *unschuldig*, repeats the adjective *hold*, and says, finally, that he felt an irresistable compassion for it. The implications of his reaction are made clear by the words "aus dem zarten Antlitz sprach neben dem Grauen des Todes, wie hilfeflehend, noch eine letzte holde Spur des Lebens." Despite the apparent contrast, the real issue is death *and* life, is at bottom a continuity, for both to the narrator of *Aquis Submersus* and to Storm in general the past is meaningful because it can be, and inevitably is, rescued into the present.

Contrast, then, as it is used in the frame, is to emphasize the passing of human life but in the special sense that the movement of life, from past to present, is far more important than either life or death *in statu*. "Auf dem Rahmen lasen wir die Jahreszahl 1666; das war lange her" says the narrator. But necessarily the past will not remain buried or dead: the aesthetic justification for the manuscript fiction – and indeed for all of Storm's often highly elaborate frames – lies in this vital connection to, and interdependence of, past and present. One of the frequent conscious contrasts in the frame is the remark made by the narrator as he enjoys tea at the sexton's house: "es war alles helle, freundliche Gegenwart. Nur eines Abends – wir waren derzeit schon Sekundaner – kam mir der Gedanke, welch eine Vergangenheit an diesen Räumen hafte, ob nicht gar jener tote Knabe einst mit frischen Wangen hier leibhaftig umhergesprungen sei." The "helle, freundliche Gegenwart" has its specific characteristics: the sexton's house suffers from *Altersschwäche*, the pictures on the walls were cut from *Reformationsalmanachen*, and the sofa is simply *alt*. One might of course object that Storm's idea of "freundliche Gegenwart" was primarily *Geselligkeit* – we have seen elsewhere that this lay close to the author's heart[8] – but even so, we are unable to separate present sociability from a past that intrudes (in this instance not only in the physical surroundings, but in the narrator's own thoughts) at virtually every moment into the present. We may recall in this connection that the portrait fills the church (*jetzt!*) with its presence, not physically of course, but spiritually, "wie mit einer wehmütig holden Sage." *Hold* thus occurs for the third time in a startingly similar context: the Virgin Mary, the hint of life in the dead child's portrait, and here as a saga that lives in the present and dominates the church interior.

Less demonstrable but equally suggestive of continuity is the manner in which the first inscription is treated. Although it might seem a violation of realism to have the young narrator hit upon the true meaning of C.P.A.S. and thus outsmart his elders, the twin virtues of imagination and intuition are as plausible in the boy (who has, besides, a distinct advantage by virtue of his *Vergänglichkeitsgefühl*) as in the others. Moreover, the gradual accumulation of evidence through discovery and the partial rather than total accuracy of the guess – the pastor is not the true father, as the reader learns – rescue the passage from any reproach of improbability. However, it seems important to have part of the mystery solved, especially by one whose reaction to the past is explained as a kind of mysterious bond; the compassion for the dead child and the only partially erroneous evaluation of the "finsterer Prediger" suggest such a connection. By leaving a considerable residue of mystery an important principle of narrative technique is served; but conversely, by having some of the past explained by the present *before* it explains itself Storm's law of organic continuity is clearly illustrated and the gap between life and death narrowed.

The second part of this long introductory frame likewise affords abundant examples of continuity in contrast. Since it would not be to our purpose to list all of them here, we may choose only those which suggest the most significant ways of linking past and present. The first of these might be called coincidence, for there is something almost illogically fortuitous in the discovery of the two manuscrips. Despite a certain heavy-handedness on Storm's part, the reader accepts this discovery as a matter of course. This is doubtless due to the fact that while it may seem forced *per se*, it represents the last link in a chain of otherwise plausible coincidences. Knowledge of the portrait in the village church is of course perfectly logical, as is the discovery of a second painting in a house (whose inscription could entice anyone to enter) in the narrator's native town. The mention of other *Siebensachen* is a stroke of good fortune and also in no way a violation of the story's realistic tone. But from this point on the reader's credulity may become somewhat strained. The house owner quickly points to the little engraved chest, and the narrator picks it up: "Als ich sie... herunternahm, fiel der Deckel zurück, und es zeigten sich mir als Inhalt einige stark vergilbte Papierblätter mit sehr alten Schriftzügen." It would be pointless to carp at this bit of luck, but the eagerness with which the yellowed and forgotten pages make themselves known does come alarmingly close to animation.

Though we may object to technique here, we must admire the deeper purpose. An insistent past, whose continued existence in the present is visible at every turn and whose "mysteries" manage to liberate themselves – by rare coincidence as well as "naturally" – from oblivion, conspires with an insistent present in the form of a youthful narrator whose interest and empathy are directed backwards to create a continuous line. Such a linear effect, it may be objected, is common to the passage of time altogether and therefore does not throw additional light on Storm's treatment of it here. Yet when we consider the elaborate attempts in *Aquis Submersus* to return to "das sichere Land der Vergangenheit," it is no less than astonishing that the present should figure so largely.

A second example of the weaving of past and present into a continuous line is supplied by the formal outline of the frame itself, made meaningful only by the frame's second part. If for convenience we consider the frame as representing the present and the *Innererzählung* the past, we may superimpose the former on the latter and examine their chief points of coincidence. As observed earlier, both frame and story are bipartite. Between the two parts of each there is an interval of several years which serves for a change of scenery, as it were. Moreover, the interval represents a natural caesura for tone and tempo on the one hand and story or plot on the other. Despite the brevity of the frame in comparison with the story it encloses, one is able to speak of the first part's *Stimmung*, its seemingly more eventful contents, and its sense of greater urgency and drama. Possibly all three are much the same here, but the point is that we are engaged in the meager events in a way that is not true of the frame's second, shorter part. Similar proportions hold for the *Innererzählung*, whose first part is, as Stuckert says, "frisch, farbig... dramatisch bewegt," while the second suggests a "dunkle Mollmelodie" and possesses a "viel flacher verlaufende Spannungskurve."[9]

On the side of plot we must also grant the first part a greater degree of richness, a fact that is reflected in the length. Of the eight pages (Böhme edition) comprising the frame – this does not include the brief intrusions between the two manuscript halves or the closing paragraph of the Novelle – six belong to the first part and only two to the second. Ernst Feise lists three major functions of the frame: description of the "örtlicher Hintergrund," "Frage nach Bild und Inschrift," and "Auffindung des Manuskripts,"[10] two of which are found in the first part. Similarly, all the major happenings of the *Innenerzählung*, barring the last one, occur in the first part.

A further similarity lies in the resolution of mystery. In the frame the narrator solves a riddle and uncovers the tale in two stages; in the story Johannes relates his tragic fate and in a similar way uncovers the mystery for the reader in two major steps. The intensification of mystery evident in the closing lines of the frame's first part, "und so blieb denn der eigentliche Sinn der Inschrift nach wie vor ein Geheimnis der Vergangenheit..." is repeated at the end of the first manuscript:

> Was ich von nun an alles und immer doch vergebens unternommen, um Katherinen oder auch nur eine Spur von ihr zu finden, das soll hier nicht verzeichnet werden... Zuletzt bin ich zu längerem Verbleiben nach Hamburg gegangen, von wo ich ohne Anstand und mit größerer Umsicht meine Nachforschungen zu betreiben gedachte. Es ist alles doch umsonst gewesen.

A final instance of the fusing of *jetzt* and *einst* may be seen in the interval between the two manuscript halves and in the closing paragraph of the Novelle, lines which return us to the original narrator and hence close the frame as well. The locale of the second manuscript part is, as has been pointed out, the same as in the frame. The "einsame Kammer" in which the frame narrator discovers and reads the manuscripts is in fact the room in which they were written. Thus it is more than a "museum;" besides preserving the past in its original setting (*Stimmung*), it makes us aware of a series of time levels centered on a fixed point. The first part of the *Innenerzählung* ends its account with "es ist alles doch umsonst gewesen." Then comes a brief intrusion into the (manuscript narrator's) present, i.e., an interruption of the narrative past within the manuscript past: a future christening is mentioned which the frame narrator hopes will be "frische Gegenwart" – and we are told that the narrator will have to pass the woods behind Gerhard's estate. This last is dismissed, in a sense, with the words, "aber das alles gehört ja der Vergangenheit."

Storm's reader should have no difficulty in keeping the time levels straight; indeed, it is unlikely that he will be aware of the multiple shifts that take place in the few lines of text that close one manuscript and open the other. The technique is common to many of Storm's Novellen and its inconspicuousness here merely attests to successful narration. Still, the combination is an arresting one: the MS narrator closes (temporarily) his account of the past, returns to his present and in doing so speaks of the future, which forces him to recall the past. Immediately thereafter the frame narrator inserts his comment, "hier schließt das erste Heft der Handschrift," wishes the manuscript author a gay christening, and poses the second of the two questions the manuscript is to answer.

The closing paragraph of the Novelle begins with the words "hier endete die Handschrift." It is interesting to observe the tense, especially in the light of the frame narrator's information and the *schließt* of the earlier intrusion. It is as though a considerable distance had been put between the frame narrator (as well as his reader) and the manuscript narrator, as though the line between past and present had suddenly been drawn clearly and finally. The frame narrator's message bears this out: both Johannes and his painting of Lazarus have disappeared, the puzzle posed in the frame finally solved, his participation as reader (and ours as later readers) ended, and all stages of time except the impersonal present moment pushed into the "es war einmal" region.

However, if we inquire more closely into the nature and effect of the time jumble described above, we see that the series of interruptions, jumps in time, etc., are designed not merely to show the contrasts between Johannes' happy past and his lamentable present, between the idyllic childhood of the frame narrator and the stark tragedy that transpired in the same place nearly two centuries before, but to stress the intimate relationship of one to the other and their part in a greater whole. When Johannes says, "aber das alles gehört ja der Vergangenheit," or when the frame narrator speaks of Johannes and his *Lazarusbild* as *verschollen*, we must understand them as partial truths, as fragments of the "ewig unausgetragener Prozeß." For not only do the several levels of past and present interweave in both frame and *Innenerzählung*, they offer mutual support and thus guarantee permanency to each other. Such, for example, is the effect if not the intent of the present tense in the insertion at the end of the first manuscript: until the full tale is told we are not to relegate it to the past. And such is the effect of the identical locale in frame and story: coincidence and a *wesensverwandte* narrator must conspire to rescue events from oblivion. Storm is at pains to establish sufficiently strong links between past and present to effect this rescue, not so much by means of "perspektivische Verlängerung des eigenen Lebens in die Vergangenheit hinein," as Brecht explains it, but rather through just the reverse process. It is *Vergangenheit* that protrudes into the present, and precisely where it appears to contrast most sharply with the present we discover the inner continuity. In this sense *Aquis Submersus* disproves its final words, *aquis submersus*.

II. The Witch Episode and the Problem of Fate

To many of Storm's critics the episode dealing with the burning of a young woman accused of witchery represents at best a somewhat superfluous insertion and at worst an utterly irrelevant and disturbing interruption at a critical moment in the story. Although Storm himself was not unwilling to heed criticisms of the Novelle – he admits, for instance, that Katherina could have been made to act more forcefully in the scene depicting little Johannes' death – his reaction to Emil Kuh's censure of this "schrecklicher Zwischenfall" is emphatically negative. He suggests that Kuh's objections may stem from "subjektiven oder zufälligen Umständen" and rejects any notion that the plot is retarded by the episode. Rather it is, Storm explains,

> das Movens, das ihn [Johannes] aus der Stadt und den Prediger aus seinem Hause treibt, und dann – der Johannes geht ja wie durch eine Seitendekoration durch die Geschichte hindurch. Es ist ja in der Tat auch nur ein kulturgeschichtlicher, wie Sie wollen, Seiten- oder Hintergrund; denn da die Hexe schon bei ihrer Erwähnung tot ist, so kann doch – wo nicht unberechenbare Umstände im Inneren des Lesers hinzukommen – das Interesse desselben nicht wohl vom Geschick der Haupt-

personen abgelenkt werden. Auch hat sich in der Tat bis jetzt niemand daran gestoßen, obgleich ich nach Empfang Ihres Briefes specielle Examina angestellt habe.[11]

One is tempted to read a measure of uneasiness in Storm's opinion poll. Certainly, the justification he gives has something concessive about it, for the episode's function as *Seitendekoration* or *Hintergrund* fails to weaken the reproach of plot retardation.

It is admittedly idle to wish that Storm and Kuh had continued their discussion (the letter from which we quote above was the last Kuh was to receive before his sudden death; and it was not their habit, moreover, to extend their criticisms and arguments over several letters), but a more adequate defense of the witch episode, as well as an explanation as to why it need not be dismissed as a "schrecklicher Zwischenfall," coming as it does amidst a greater and in some ways more violent tragedy, could well serve to define more clearly the position this scene holds in the tragic events of the second part. With an idea to arguing the case for the *Hexenverbrennung*, the following paragraphs will attempt to continue Storm's and Kuh's unfinished debate and to show the role this episode plays in the overall structure of *Aquis Submersus*.

To review briefly the events that open the second manuscript: Johannes has come to a town on the North Sea where he has been commissioned to paint the raising of Lazarus from the dead and a portrait of the burgomaster. Soon after his arrival the pastor of a nearby village appears and arranges to have his portrait done for the church. On his daily visits to the village Johannes sees a pale boy, also called Johannes, who is constantly at the side of the "finsterer Prediger." He is stirred by the boy's eyes and the sorrow ("kein froher Zug") in his expression; he often feels the urge to hold the child in his arms, but of course cannot explain why. His curiosity about the child's mother remains unsatisfied, for he learns only that the "schlanke, jugendliche Gestalt" which he has seen from a distance and which suggests to him that the mother may be one of the *Vornehmeren* is scarcely ever seen by the villagers themselves.

On an evening shortly before completing the pastor's portrait, Johannes is sitting with his brother in their town lodgings. His thoughts turn to Katherina, and

> da, gleich einem Stein aus unsichtbaren Höhen, fiel es mir jählings in die Brust: Die Augen des schönen blassen Knaben, es waren ja ihre Augen! Wo hatte ich meine Sinne denn gehabt!–Aber dann, wenn sie es war, wenn ich sie selber schon gesehen! – Welch schreckbare Gedanken stürmten auf mich ein!

At this point Johannes' brother calls his attention to the marketplace, which is filled with the noise and gaiety of a *Hochzeitsschmaus*. As the party passes beneath their window Johannes hears a voice say

> Ei freilich, das hat der Teufel uns verpurret! Hatte mich leblang darauf gespitzet, einmal eine richtige Hex so in der Flammen singen zu hören!

There follows now a description, some four paragraphs in length, of the affair insofar as Johannes is acquainted with it and the reaction both brothers have to the *Hexenwesen*. In order to avoid having to witness the spectacle, Johannes, who had agreed to resume painting on the day following the *Verbrennung*, is persuaded to spend the next day in the village instead.

The walk to the village is an uncertain wandering, accompanied by Johannes' account of the throng of villagers pressing toward the town to see the witch burned. When he arrives at the sacristy and begins painting, the sacristan's old servant starts her "lang Gespinst von der Hex und ihrer Sippschaft hier im Dorfe," speaks of *Vorspuksehen*, the *Leichlaken* that were seen above the pastor's house, and the human frailty of the pastor's wife "bei all ihrer Vornehmheit." Johannes is an unwilling listener; he leaves his work, wanders in a circle about the sacristy, and finally ends up at the *Priesterkoppel*, where he finds Katherina.

Doubtless it is the epic breadth of this scene – admittedly not appropiate in a Novelle – which prompted Stuckert and others to call the entire second part of *Aquis Submersus* less dramatic and colorful. The introduction of the witch burning does indeed come at a moment in the story when our attention ought to be focused exclusively on Johannes' and Katherina's long awaited confrontation. We have given Storm's own explanation for the interruption, but we cannot on that basis alone accept the episode as necessary to the Novelle. Rather, we must inquire further into the relationship between this *Seitendekoration* and the lovers' tragedy.

Part of the dramatic impact of the first part may be attributed to Johannes' own forcefulness, to the fact that he and Katherina are actively involved in a struggle against external forces. His journey to Preest, his quarrel in the tavern with Wulf and von der Risch, his reaction to the bit of cloth that Dietrich shows him, and his final fight with Wulf are at bottom impotent protests but they do at least show the luckless Johannes in a more active role. When we compare these events with the chain of circumstances running through the second manuscript, we are forced to concede that a different spirit reigns. On one occasion only does Johannes react with the forcefulness he showed at times in the first part: "Da wurde ich meiner schier unmächtig; ich riß sie jäh an meine Brust, ich hielt sie wie mit Eisenklammern und hatte sie endlich, endlich wieder!" For the rest he is as though completely resigned to his fate. To be sure, the realization that Katherina is the child's mother awakens a violent reaction ("welch schreckbare Gedanken stürmten auf mich ein!"), but it can scarcely be said that Johannes is the *movens* here, either linguistically or in fact. At this point the witch theme is introduced, appropriately replacing any action on Johannes' part. And, as indicated earlier, it is not Johannes himself but his brother who decides that escape to the village should be made the next day.

From this point in the Novelle until Johannes learns of his son's death, two strands of plot, the witch story and the lovers' fate, move in close proximity to one another. The parallelism is underscored by a number of contrasts and connections common to both and occurring with such striking regularity as to suggest a quasi-allegorical function on the part of the witch story. This latter is introduced in a roundabout, if not paradoxical, way: the marriage celebration with its "lustigen Leuten" is coupled with the impending witch burning, and the complaint is heard that the devil has robbed the audience of a live victim. Immediately prior to this, we recall, is Johannes' "discovery" of Katherina in the young boy; this is coupled with his fear, his "schreckbare Gedanken," and the perhaps subconscious realization that the end of his long search will mean not a joyous resumption but the end – death in its figurative sense – of his and Katherina's relationship.

The reveler's remark which Johannes overhears reminds him of the "grausam Spektakul" to be held the following day: a young woman has confessed her pact with the devil and is to be burned. That same morning, however, she was found dead in her cell, "aber dem todten Leibe mußte gleichwohl sein peinlich Recht geschehen." Johannes' brother expresses the contrast eloquently: "den trübet, was mich tröstet!" A similar coupling may be seen in the confrontation scene.

> "Bleib doch", sagte ich, "es spielet ja fröhlich dort mit seinem Moose."
> Sie war an den Rand des Gebüsches getreten und horchete hinaus. Die goldene Herbstsonne schien so warm hernieder, nur leichter Hauch kam von der See herauf. Da höreten wir von jenseit durch die Weiden das Stimmlein unseres Kindes singen:
>> "Zwei Englein, die mich decken,
>> Zwei Englein, die mich strecken,
>> Und zweie, so mich weisen
>> In das himmlische Paradeisen."

Katherina has been found, it is true, but this tranquil scene is a chimera: for Johannes she is dead. Her eyes are *geisterhaft* and her words "auf Nimmerwiedersehen hier auf Erden" reëmphasize the ill-concealed warning contained in her child's song. Her anguished cry, "O wehe, mein arm entweihter Leib!"[12] is reminiscent of the dead witch, whose "todten Leib" must get its "peinlich Recht."

The comparison is surely neither unlikely nor forced, for the response to her cry "O, Jesu Christ, vergib mir diese Stunde!" is in effect the carrying out of "peinlich Recht." The question of guilt need not concern us here. As the *Hexe* is innocent, so too must Katherina be presumed innocent of the drowning of her son (already marked for death, as indicated in the verses above).[13]

Immediately after Katherina leaves in answer to the pastor's call, Johannes goes to the sacristy, only to hear the sacristan give his account of the witch's *Justifikation*. At this precise moment ("Ich hatte nicht die Zeit zur Antwort," says Johannes) Katherina's scream is heard. Her dead child is at once the fruit and the symbol of Johannes' and Katherina's love; his death coincides with their awareness of the death of their union. There is nothing more for them to share but the sense of guilt for their child's death. And so the parallel is extended to the moment of greatest pathos in the Novelle. Both the "witch" and Katherina are dead, one in a literal, the other in a figurative sense; their *Justifikation* is ex post facto: the witch is burned, and Katherina is finally and irrevocably condemned through the death of little Johannes.

Storm's refusal to attribute guilt to the lovers lends support to the parallel outlined above. The "peinlich Recht" that must be meted out to the corpse of the "witch" is apparently *Unrecht*. The narrator – and through him Storm himself – leaves no doubt in the reader's mind but that pure superstition is at work here. Guilt is therefore impossible, as both Johannes and his brother realize. Similarly, the *Sünderin*, as Katherina calls herself, is for Storm free of guilt to the degree that forces outside herself conspired to bring about the tragedy. In this sense she too is the victim of an unenlightened age.

Yet the line separating superstition and enlightenment is in at least one instance precariously thin. If the young "witch" is no more than the victim of an ignorant society it seems odd indeed that Katherina's fate, and through her that of Johannes as well – should be clearly foreseen by the same forces which practice witch-hunting with such enthusiasm! The pastor's wife, a "blasse und schwächliche Creatur," is linked to the *Hexenwesen* and *Hexenverbrennung* by the same superstition that Johannes and his brother condemn. Mutter Siebenzig has seen the death shrouds flying above the parsonage. This is part of the *Geschwätz* Johannes is unwilling to listen to; he leaves the house and wanders aimlessly. Turning to the west, he views the sea, where in a single night "des höchsten Hand" had taken the lives of thousands. He ends the subject with the thought, "wir sehen nicht, wie seine Wege führen!" The answer to the implied question is of course the reunion with Katherina. We shall comment presently on the religious tone of the episode; meanwhile, a further instance of Katherina's connection to *Vorspuksehen* may be cited. Johannes is told of his son's death by the old woman who had mentioned the *Leichlaken*. Her explanation is that the shrouds have fallen "auf des Pastors Dach;" only when Johannes fails to comprehend her words does she add, "das soll heißen, daß sie des Pastors kleinen Johannes soeben aus dem Wasser ziehen." Later, when Johannes returns to his quarters, he finds his brother in bed; the "abscheuliches Spectakul" in which he had to assist is the cause of his condition. Ironically, Johannes himself has just assisted in a similar spectacle.

The three shrouds are presumably the three deaths of which we learn in the course of the Novelle. Gerhard dies, the child drowns, and Junker Wulf is killed by a dog. The sequence is fraught with irony. Wulf's death, Johannes believes, could have meant life for himself and Katherina. Had it happened earlier – such is the implication – none of the real tragedy would have transpired. As we have seen, Storm's emphasis on fate in the form of external forces appears to lend the news of Wulf's accidental death a substantial measure of tragic irony. But the greater irony surely lies in the very fact that Johannes fails to see the true meaning of the events, whose sequence is based on deeper necessity. Gerhard's death shortly before Johannes' return is the first critical blow to the lovers' future. The "homecoming" and first reunion with Katherina, although superficially happy events, are an early and necessary part of the catastrophe. Katherina is therefore lost to Johannes before the second manuscript begins. His discovery of her in the village is necessarily ironic and part of the tragic rather than happy chain of incidents; the discovery that Johannes is his son is followed by the drowning, another instance of the potentially happy event being in reality a continuation of the tragic line. And Wulf's death, finally, the potentially happy event that is in effect "nur ein Entsetzen zu den andern," is an irony surpassed only by Johannes' failure to see that it could not have influenced the course of events once they had begun.

It is a function of the witch episode to reflect and prophesy the tragic course of action. By momentarily disguising calamity with gaiety, by warning of future catastrophe (in the same way that Johannes was warned when he inadvertently walked into the *Binsensumpf* after leaving Katherina's room), by combining elements of religion with the darker forces of the supernatural, and by suggesting a parallel to Katherina's "double death," this *Zwischenfall* clearly summarizes both the tragedy and its source.

If the *Hexenepisode* offers a parallel to Katherina's symbolic death, it may be said to reflect a change in Johannes as well. We have said that he is less dynamic and forceful throughout the second part of the Novelle. As the pastor sends (*treibt!*) his parishioners to the witch burning, so is Johannes urged by his brother and his own turbulent emotions to go to the village. His piety, much less apparent in the first part, becomes so pronounced as to find expression on virtually any occasion: on seeing the sea as it catches the sun's early rays ("O Herr, mein Gott und Christ/ Sei gnädig mit uns allen"); on preparing to paint his dead son ("Ich fiel an meines Kindes Leiche und sprach ein brünstiglich Gebet"); or on learning that the 'witch' had died before her *Justifikation* ("und freute mich, daß unser Herrgott – denn der war es doch wohl gewesen – das arme Mensch so gnädiglich in seinen Schoß genommen hatte"). In two examples particularly the artistic intent is apparent, and it is worth observing that both occur twice in a similar context. The first takes us back to the fateful evening at Gerhard's *Hof*. Johannes' adversaries have unwittingly driven him into Katherina's arms.

Der Mondschein war am Himmel ausgethan, ein schwüler Ruch von Blumen hauchte durch das Fenster und dorten überm Walde spielte die Nacht in stummen Blitzen. – O Hüter, Hüter, war dein Ruf so fern?

– Wohl weiß ich noch, daß vom Hofe her plötzlich scharf die Hähne krähten, und daß ich ein blaß und weinend Weib in meinen Armen hielt, die mich nicht lassen wollte, unachtend, daß überm Garten der Morgen dämmerte und rothen Schein in unsre Kammer warf.

And when Johannes receives the news of Junker Wulf's death from the bite of a rabid dog, he says

> Mir war's bei dieser Schreckenspost, als sprängen des Paradieses Pforten vor mir auf; aber schon sahe ich am Eingange den Engel mit dem Feuerschwerte stehen, und aus meinem Herzen schrie es wieder: O Hüter, Hüter, war dein Ruf so fern!

Unmistakable reminiscences of the *Tagelied* in the one, religious imagery in the other. The use of the word *wieder* is clear indication that Storm intended to relate the two scenes. A less obvious but equally valid connection is little Johannes; he was conceived on the night when Wulf was attempting to separate the lovers, his very existence is, we have seen, the symbol not only of Johannes' and Katherina's union but of the unbreachable barrier between them (their own creation!) as well, and *his* death, not Junker Wulf's, erases any possibility for reunion.

The question arises as to the identity of the *Hüter* in the two passages. In the former we have only the barest suggestion that Johannes is referring to God; until then his actions, meager though they be, were more or less his own, and the entire scene as quoted above cannot be said to bring out Johannes' piety in any way. The allusion to the "heidnische Venus," which begins the scene, points rather to the pagan spirit of the passage. In the latter we have a most unambiguous context: in addition to the reference to paradise, etc. (an echo of little Johannes' song), we are told immediately afterward that Johannes "schaute in die ewigen Gestirne" and that it seemed to him "als sei der Kirchthurm drüben meinem Fenster nah gerückt."

Before evaluating the question of religion and its relation to the witch episode (and ultimately to the entire story), we may cite the second example. Early in the second part Johannes is watching the bustling market scene from his window. He cannot enjoy it because

> die Schwere meines Gemütes machte das bunte Bild mir trübe. Doch war es keine Reu, wie ich vorhin an mir erfahren hatte; ein sehnend Leid kam immer gewaltiger über mich; es zerfleischte mich mit wilden Krallen und sah mich gleichwohl mit holden Augen an.

In one of the most effective passages in the Novelle, Johannes succumbs to his agony at a vanished past:

> Drunten lag der helle Mittag auf dem wimmelnden Markte; vor meinen Augen aber dämmerte silberne Mondnacht, wie Schatten stiegen ein paar Zackengiebel auf, ein Fenster klirrte, und gleich wie aus Träumen schlugen leis und fern die Nachtigallen. O du mein Gott und mein Erlöser, der du die Barmherzigkeit bist, wo war sie in dieser Stunde, wo hatte meine Seele sie zu suchen? –

The reply is immediate. The pastor appears beneath Johannes' window, calls his name ("mit einer harten Stimme"), and thus introduces the events leading to the lovers' reunion. This latter, which for a brief moment shows us the old Johannes, ends with Katherina's words: "Es ist ein langes, banges Leben! O, Jesu Christ, vergib mir diese Stunde!" which are answered by the pastor, who calls her name ("Es war die harte Stimme jenes Mannes").

We may turn finally to the larger question of fate in *Aquis Submersus*. What specific form is it given, how are the themes of religion and superstition interwoven and made to contribute to the concept of fate, and to what degree is the second of these themes, superstition as illustrated primarily in the witch episode, an integral part of the whole?

It is necessary to review briefly the major illustrations of Johannes' and Katherina's "love story" insofar as this latter represents one long attempt at union. During their childhood play an incident brings them together and makes them "gute Gesellen:" Johannes shoots the *Buhz*, an obvious symbol of von der Risch as a threatening force. But just as the *Buhz* (cobold) is in reality nothing more than an owl, so is von der Risch, as later events show, not the destructive element in their relationship. Symbolically, therefore, Johannes' action is without point. Later, when Johannes and Katherina confess their love, it is Bas' Ursel who, through her emphasis on *Stand* and her suspicion, acts as a hindrance. And here too the threat is more imagined than real, for suspicion and disapproval can conspire to do no more than delay the union. The major incident in the first part, the night on which Johannes is forced by Wulf's dog into Katherina's arms, closes with his early morning flight from Katherina's room.

> Nahezu erschrocken aber wurd ich, da meine Augen bei einem Rückblick aus dem Gartensteig von ungefähr die unteren Fenster neben dem Thurme streiften; denn mir war, als sähe hinter einem derselbigen ich gleichfalls eine Hand; aber sie drohete nach mir mit aufgehobenem Finger und schien mir farblos und knöchern gleich der Hand des Todes.

Although he dismisses the incident as a product of his "aufgestörten Sinne," it marks the turning point in his fortunes, the beginning of the dissolution of their union. Significantly, he connects the *Hausgespenste* with the *Binsensumpfe* but believes to have escaped its power when he is able to extract his foot and continue on his way.

The remainder of the first manuscript and a considerable part of the second deal with Johannes' futile search for Katherina. Not until a further external power enters the story does his quest take a meaningful direction. On giving in to his anguish and crying out "wo hatte meine Seele sie zu suchen?" he is put back on the right track by the pastor. Shortly thereafter, and accompanying the further search and gradual discovery of Katherina, the witch episode is introduced, culminating, as we have seen, in the deaths of the witch, little Johannes, Junker Wulf, and, in a symbolic sense, of Katherina. We have observed that the tone of the second manuscript is incomparably more religious and at the same time more resigned than the first.

Seen schematically, the sequence offers a combination of supernatural forces which combine to force Johannes onto a circular path (symptomatically, the same circle can be seen in his indecisive wandering about the *Koppel*, at whose center is Katherina, and in the use of paintings, to be discussed in the following section).

His first "Hüter, Hüter, war dein Ruf so fern!" is followed by a *Todeshand* and the *Binsensumpf*; and his cry by the appearance of the pastor, who offers Johannes a twofold possibility of finding Katherina: by taking him to her home and by absenting himself on the critical day to witness the witch's execution; Katherina's cry, "O, Jesu Christ, vergib mir diese Stunde!," is answered by the pastor and followed by the news of the *Justifikation*; and Johannes' second "Hüter, Hüter..." is encircled by the religious image and the news of Wulf's death.

Fate, we may conclude, intrudes into the happenings only when Johannes has actively brought about his union with Katherina. From this point on the supernatural accompanies him until the reunion dissolves the lovers' bonds totally. Earlier hints of supernatural forces were, we have seen, without true influence or meaning. The appearance of the hand on the morning after the love tryst is a warning, the other supernatural manifestations a substitute for Johannes' actions. Without that warning, we maintain, both the *Hexenverbrennung* incident with its numerous examples of superstitions and prophecies that come true and the religious aspects would appear truly superfluous and Kuh's accusation against Storm justifiable.

There remains, finally, the role of the pastor. If we are to use Johannes' and his brother's enlightened piety as a touchstone, there is little doubt but that the militantly fanatic clergyman is not the true voice of religion in this story. His character, as has often been remarked, is not fully drawn, and Storm himself despaired of making him more complete and comprehensible without radically altering the story. Thus we are confronted with an intriguing, highly problematic figure whose generally important role in the second part is highlighted by his two appearances on the occasions when Johannes and Katherina turn directly to God. One may say that despite Johannes' show of piety religion represents a force in *Aquis Submersus* entirely counter to the conventional; it is joined to the pagan supernatural and plays a role very similar to that played by superstition, spookery, witchery, etc.

Storm, we recall, refers to the witch episode as the *movens* which removed the pastor from the village and thus enabled later events to take their course. It must be added that in terms of the story itself the pastor's unsympathetic religion and the role he is made to play are scarcely different from the series of supernatural events and prophecies that invade the first and second manuscripts. Rather than opposing one another, these dual forces work together to usurp the action and, once the fateful union has been consummated, to determine the destiny of the lovers. The witch episode, in addition to offering a symbolic parallel to the lovers' fate and a prophecy that will be fulfilled, contains both pastor *and* prophecy, religion and superstition. Its ultimate importance lies in the fact that here, in this large segment of the second manuscript, Johannes and Katherina are prepared for their final tragedy and are made to see it clearly for the first time.

III. Death and the Symbol of Painting

Of the large number of Storm's Novellen to employ symbols consistently as an integral part of structure, i.e., in a primarily non-decorative way, *Aquis Submersus* is perhaps the most successful. Certainly it would be difficult to name a second work in which symbols are as lavishly yet unobtrusively employed. The "classic" Storm symbols – Hauke's *Schimmel*, Agnes' and Harre's swallows, Tendler's Kasperle, John Glückstadt's *Brunnen*, etc. – stand out principally because as major symbols they enjoy a virtual monopoly (that is, they rarely compete with more than one or two other important symbols in the story) or because they tend to be univalent: obviously apt at but one level, they are manifestly dependent on the particular object, emotion, or action they are intended to signify. Reinhard's waterlily may serve as an obvious and typical example. It stands for the unattainable (happiness, Elisabeth – the two are scarcely separable in *Immensee*), is white (pure), near and yet just beyond reach, is protected by a web of things that hinder free movement toward it, is seen most clearly and wanted most ardently when the possibility of attaining it has already been removed, etc. To be sure, *Immensee* contains other symbols – the heather, the canary, the gypsy girl – but none is so striking and memorable as this. More important, they offer in their sum no essential chain by which the story is held together; while they are more than merely decorative, they nevertheless cannot claim to be indispensable. Finally, their real function is invariably slighter than their symbolic function; they are there to vivify, to concretize and thus place special stress on some characterizing detail. The waterlily, and of course the immediate details surrounding it, have no point in the story except that of standing for something else. By virtue of this single function we may call such a symbol simple.

Several simple symbols occur in *Aquis Submersus* and contribute substantially to the vividness of the Novelle. *Buhz, Hunde, Singvögel, Urahne*, for example, all offer a pictorial commentary on death as a central theme, and all are referred to more than once in the story. However, with the possible exception of the dogs, none can be said to possess both real and symbolic value. In at least two instances (*Buhz, Singvögel*) even this latter is weakened by overt explanation or reference within the work itself.

This brief and necessarily inadequate discussion of what we call a simple symbol is intended only to stress the difference between this common (but highly useful) device of poetic equation and the kind which most closely resembles a leitmotif, the complex symbol.[14] One such symbol occurs in *Aquis Submersus* in such a way as to justify the claim that it at once mirrors the death theme and contributes to its very creation. As our examples will show, it possesses both real and symbolic value; it is in the former that its special nature is most apparent.

With admirable consistency, and unlike a number of other protagonists in Storm's Novellen, Johannes is allowed to work at his profession throughout the story and thereby keep painting – as object and action – in the foreground of events. The three paintings mentioned in the frame are all from the hand of Johannes and depict in anticipatory fashion the three major events in his life. Little Johannes, we have seen, is the symbolic death of Johannes' bond with Katherina and in his own right a source of real (though not developed) tragedy; the pastor is instrumental in bringing about the reunion with Katherina and therefore also the death of the child; Gerhard is both Johannes' protector and the object of unfailing admiration, affection and loyalty. In this last painting Johannes puts his dead son in Gerhard's arms, thus closing the family line and uniting beginning and end of the tragedy.

As the frame is at pains to demonstrate, the discovery of the three paintings is in the nature of coincidence. One of the more important effects of such discovery is that the death theme is introduced and placed in a central position before the actual finding and reading of the manuscripts. The question of chronology or arrangement, however, is less simple. Why are the paintings, and through them three principal characters, introduced in this particular order? It would be difficult to make a convincing case for the order of importance of these characters in the Novelle; nor is it entirely satisfactory to claim that the reader's interest is captured first by the boy and the initials, then held by the mystery of later, less important or less intriguing characters. A third possibility, that of inner symmetry, suggests itself: not the child itself, but its death is the last major event for Johannes (Wulf's death, which evidently occurred earlier, does not touch him in the same way, as we have seen). The appearance of the pastor in Johannes' life and the portrait of him that is subsequently painted are next to last, and Gerhard of course first.

It is not so much a question of the need for establishing which painting, or the person depicted, comes first but rather of recognizing that, having been given a series of paintings which remain unexplained for a good portion of the story, the order of introduction should be chronologically in precise reverse. And such a sequence seems especially appropiate to the frame, for just as this latter leads into the story proper from a later point in time, so do the three paintings continue the reverse order, beginning with the end of the MSS and ending with the opening of the tragedy, with the dead Gerhard. Placing the child Johannes in his arms has the effect of creating a circle or closing the ring.

It has been remarked that the ring technique is apparent in several places in *Aquis Submersus*. As in *Immensee*, so here too the most striking illustration of this technique is the *Bild*, from which the story proceeds and to which it returns. That it is not the same picture points to more than a minor difference: it is again the relation of the simple device (that permits the "flashback") in *Immensee* to the elaborate one here that tells its own story and itself plays a role in the events. The frame, then, uses paintings to lead into the story through a series of backward steps; and it employs the ring technique, beginning with a picture (or three pictures) and closing with the Resurrection of Lazarus.

Similarly, the first MS opens with Johannes painting – or rather sketching – the features of the lifeless Gerhard. The second MS ends when Johannes completes the portrait of his dead son. Between these two are a series of paintings executed or seen by Johannes and representing a series of steps toward tragedy. In both senses they may be said to serve as the autobiography of the artist himself. We may follow these steps through the two manuscripts and indicate the task or tasks each painting fulfills in the Novelle.

Johannes' return from Holland requires no less than six pages of text, for the "liebliche Erinnerung" of his earlier life at Gerhard's *Hof* accompanies him on his walk through the "maigrünen Buchenwald." From this insertion we learn of his idyllic childhood, the mutual affection of the children, and his enmity to von der Risch. On this morning Johannes is "aller Sorge quitt;" in his thoughts he sees Gerhard,

> meinen edlen großgünstigen Protector, wie er von der Schwelle seines Zimmers mir die Hände würd' entgegenstrecken, mit seinem milden Gruße: "So segne Gott deinen Eingang, mein Johannes!"

Thus nature, recollection, and anticipation unite to create a joyous beginning of Johannes' adult life. It is unnecessary to recount the "homecoming" in detail. Johannes' last words before entering the gate are "seitdem waren fast fünf Jahre dahingegangen. – Wie würd' ich heute alles wiederfinden?" Despite the appropiateness of the question, we are struck by the slightly ominous overtone, for the vision of a welcoming Gerhard (immediately before the "flashback") and its tranquil setting give no cause for anxiety.[15] But the question is a warning, and it is supported by the mention of "die grausamen Stapfen des Krieges" that have devastated the countryside. This combination of idyllic and potentially tragic, already observed in the witch episode, is especially noteworthy because it occurs in virtually identical form wherever paintings are mentioned in the story.

Johannes' first attempt to paint, we have said, takes place at Gerhard's coffin. Significantly, he does not paint his protector at all – as was his intention: "an seinem lebenden Bilde ihm mit meiner Kunst zu danken" – but merely sketches his features. We shall indicate the importance of this distinction in another place; what is important here is to note that death introduced Johannes to us, and Johannes to his future fate. The meeting with Katherina (a reunion if we take the inserted childhood scene into account) also occurs at Gerhard's coffin. Her first words, "ach, Ihr seid zu spät gekommen!," are accompanied by a gesture heavy with implication: "Und über dem Sarge hatten unsere Hände sich zum Gruß gefaßt." As Johannes' return lies in the shadow of death, so does the rejoining of the future lovers take place over the dead body of their sole supporter in an inimical world.

In the brief conversation with Junker Wulf shortly afterward, Johannes is told to paint a portrait of Katherina, for "wenn eine adelige Tochter das Haus verläßt, so muß ihr Bild darin zurückbleiben." This early threat of renewed separation and the hours spent together while Katherina's portrait is painted bring them closer together. Thus the painting, which is intended as a mark of farewell (Katherina is to marry von der Risch as soon as possible), becomes instead one of the instruments of their union. The dogs,

Bas' Ursel's suspicious nature, her reference to the garden ("Draußen aber passire eben nichts") and the gardener who cleans the hedges, von der Risch's open hatred, Dieterich's "dummes Wort" about class distinction – these are hindrances and warnings that remain unheeded or unrecognized until it is too late.

But the most evident and prophetic warning is given by a painting. In the family portrait gallery two portraits in particular arouse Johannes' interest. The one is of Gerhard in earlier years; Johannes attempts a second time to paint him – "ich suchte nun mit meinem Pinsel die Züge meines edlen Beschützers nachzuschaffen" – but does not finish the work. The other represents "eine Edelfrau von etwa vierzig Jahren... die kleinen grauen Augen sahen kalt und stechend aus dem harten Antlitz." From this ancestor, Johannes realizes, Wulf has inherited his evil nature. "Nicht vor dem Sohn des edlen Gerhardus; vor dieser hier und ihres Blutes nachgeborenem Sprößling soll ich Katherinen schützen." In one of the most ironic scenes in the Novelle Katherina tells Johannes of the Edelfrau: "sie soll ihr einzig Kind verfluchet haben; am andern Morgen aber hat man das blasse Fräulein aus einem Gartenteich gezogen, der nachmals zugedämmt ist." When Johannes questions her further he learns that "sie wollte den Vetter ihrer Mutter nicht zum Ehgemahl... es heißt, sie hab einen andern liebgehabt; der war nicht ihres Standes." Just as part of Wulf appears to be a direct inheritance from the *Edelfrau*, so are certain events passed on to a later time – "dann, längst vergessen, taucht es plötzlich wieder auf, den Lebenden zum Unheil." Not the curse in this case, but its cause; and not the suicide, but an "accidental" drowning. Even the *Gartenteich*, we have seen, plays its role in the present.[16] These warnings and anticipations give the painting its symbolic value. But just as important to the story is what we have called the real value of an object or action. The parallel between past and present is so close that Katherina is brought to confess her love.

> Fest umschlossen standen wir vor dem Bild der Ahnfrau,
> die kalt und feindlich auf uns niederschauete.

In direct defiance of the past with its lesson (yet Katherina does say "Laß uns nicht trotzen, mein Johannes!"), they thus take one further step toward the catastrophe.

Johannes' next attempt to paint need not detain us long. As with Gerhard's portrait, here too only the preliminaries are made: while waiting for Katherina in the *Tannenwalde*, Johannes sketches her *Vaterhaus*, which she will not see again once she is with him in Holland. And as before, the sketch is to serve as model for a later "farbig Schilderei." The half-truth (Katherina is not to see her home again) in Johannes' mind underlines the importance of his art as an activity which both accompanies and mirrors death.

A little noticed but highly important incident is the painting of the merchant's daughter while Johannes is in Holland. This welcome commission is finally to give him the means to return to Germany and bring Katherina back with him. But the task of painting proves too much; already weakened by the wound inflicted by Junker Wulf, he is unable to leave when he had planned but must first await the coming of spring. The chronology is significant:

> Eben wurden zum Weihnachtsfeste auf allen Straßenplätzen die Waffelbuden aufgeschlagen, da begann mein Siechtum.

When he finally arrives in Gerhard's village, he learns that Katherina has disappeared,

> Seit Neujahr ist das Fräulein im Schloß nicht mehr gesehen worden.

His prolonged absence has thus proven fateful. The painting of the portrait, intended to hasten the reunion, prevents it instead, for had Johannes been able to leave as planned, he would have been in time to find Katherina. As a result, one more hope for happiness is destroyed and the death of little Johannes given additional motivation.

It is tempting to find a good deal of irony in the subject of Johannes' next painting, which brings him to the North Sea town near Katherina's new home.[17] A distiller's widow commissions him to depict the raising of Lazarus from the dead. Johannes refuses to give his subject the features of the deceased distiller; instead he paints – "zu eigener Verwunderung" – those of Gerhard. One wonders at Storm's choice of subjects. Is there any special appropiateness to Lazarus? Who in *Aquis Submersus* is raised from the dead, and in what sense? Johannes in that he is to find Katherina again and for a brief moment "resurrect" their past; Katherina in that she too lives again briefly and passionately in the reunion scene. Or one may say that the spectre of Johannes' and Katherina's ill-fated union is raised here symbolically and as ironic illusion. None is demonstrably right or wrong, and all are to a degree applicable. Since our immediate association to the Lazarus story is the idea of miracle, it can perhaps be said that the subject's appropiateness – aside from its religious quality in a section of the story strongly religious in tone – lies in the fact that the reuniting of the lovers appears to reside in considerable part in the region of the irrational or supernatural. Our explanation of the witch episode in general would support this explanation.

In any case, the raising of Lazarus is in its application here a *Scheinleben* and therefore ironic; the tragic events come rapidly thereafter, and so Johannes is again painting death rather than life. Giving the Lazarus Gerhard's features, we may note in passing, reinforces the association with death. Also, this is Johannes' third attempt to the "do justice" to his former protector, an indication that the role this *Leitsymbol* plays in the story is not yet over.

The pastor's portrait, one of the external or plot circumstances that brings the lovers together again, is painted simultaneously with the Lazarus.

> An den Tagen, wo ich nicht da draußen war, hatte ich auch die Arbeit an meinem Lazarus wieder aufgenommen, so daß nach einiger Zeit diese Bilder miteinander nahezu vollendet waren.

Immediately after this brief statement, the witch episode is introduced. It is worthwhile to recall a particular detail of the transition. Johannes and his brother are sitting together one evening; their thoughts turn to the past, and both remember their dead sister, who "seit lange schon mit Vater und Mutter seiner fröhlichen Auferstehung entgegenharrete." After a short silence, Johannes thinks of Katherina and makes the "discovery" to which we referred in the analysis of the *Hexen* scene.[18] This additional instance of a "liebliche Erinnerung" just prior to depicting the harsher world of the present contains both a linguistic and an ironic reminder of Lazarus in the *Auferstehung*. The pastor's role is such that the parallel to Lazarus – as we see it in the "nahezu vollendete Bilder" and in the justification for Johannes' presence in the town near Katherina – points directly to prophecy, for just as Johannes paints a resurrection that is symbolically his own and/or Katherina's, so is the pastor the means for introducing the lovers' *Scheinleben* that ends in death. And as Lazarus is *verschollen* in the end, so may Johannes' and Katherina's union be said to be *verschollen*.

The painting of little Johannes, anticlimactic in a sense and hence basically undramatic, places Johannes in the ambiguous position of chronicling what he himself has helped to bring about; for what he must now do is turn his art to the very thing his art has made possible. Pausing briefly in his "schweres Werk," he enters the room opposite him in order to eat something.

> Indem ich aber eintrat, wäre ich vor Überraschung bald zurückgewichen; denn Katherina stund mir gegenuber, zwar in schwarzen Trauerkleidern, und doch in all dem Zauberschein, so Glück und Liebe in eines Weibes Antlitz wirken mögen.

He soon discovers the deception; it is not Katherina but "nur ihr Bildniß, das ich selber einst gemalet." Yet this further instance of a *Scheinleben* is particularly effective in the manuscript's final scene, for Johannes' earlier work – the portrait of a mourning Katherina – returns him to the beginning and closes the circle. And as the mourning, the presence of Katherina (who is pictorially *and* physically there – in the adjoining room) is fitting, so is the deception. Painting throughout the Novelle was primarily for the future life and happiness of the lovers; in reality, however, paintings depict, express, or ultimately cause death and tragedy. Not merely as a symbol, therefore, but as a combination of symbol and *movens*, an inseparable unity that deserves the name of complex symbol, paintings play their role in telling and creating the events.

It has been remarked that while Johannes' technical ability remains with him, his real creative power is broken in the personal catastrophe, "und so bleiben Name und Werk des Malers für die Nachwelt verschollen."[19] This is no doubt the point of the Novelle's final statement, which mentions the disappearance of the Lazarus painting. For the artist Johannes, that is to say, the words *aquis submersus* are just; but for the man himself a somewhat different meaning must be sought. The frame, we recall, mentions three paintings that depict major events in Johannes' life. Two of these we have encountered in our summary of the tragic events, that of the child and of the pastor; the third remains only a project throughout the story. Unknown to him, Johannes' fate, his entire future, is bound up with Gerhard. His artistic attempts to "recapture" his protector, as it were, to repay him with "lebender Kunst," remain unsuccessful until the very end – or more exactly, until after the manuscripts have told Johannes' story. It may seem strange that this one subject should defy completion while the incomparably more tragic one of little Johannes should be completed so quickly – and the letters C.P.A.S. added just as quickly. Of course the painting of Gerhard is finally finished too; both the frame and the manuscript itself tell us as much. Yet the delay and the multiple attempts mentioned in the MSS indicate a special purpose in keeping Gerhard until last. We may say that symbolically this represents Johannes' inability to come to terms with the reality of his own situation at the beginning of the tale. For do not Johannes' actions (and therefore his paintings) betray a growing alienation from the spirit of Gerhard? And is not his tragedy the tragedy of Gerhard's family as well? We may assume that a number of years pass before Johannes finally brings himself to paint Gerhard and to place the dead child in his arms. Here surely is Johannes' final recognition – incomparably more meaningful than the hasty C.P.A.S. – of the circle he has described and of the intimate relation this first and last death bear both to each other and to himself as accomplice to tragedy.[20]

Significantly, the portrait of Gerhard and the child is the only painting outside the story proper; it is therefore the only clear indication of the story's connection as a part of the past to the future, i.e., the reader's present. For the Lazarus is "verschleudert und verschollen," and the other two pictures mentioned in the frame are preserved and discovered by strictly fortuitous circumstances. In a symbolic sense, therefore, it may be said that we are given the inheritance not of the artist but of the man, and to be sure in its most meaningful form. The struggle to repay Gerhard with art ends in the obliteration of art and in the symbolic recapitulation of a life which led from Gerhard through death and tragedy and back to Gerhard and death.

CHAPTER FIVE

HINZELMEIER: "NACHDENKLICHE GESCHICHTE"
AS PROBLEMATIC *KUNSTMÄRCHEN*

I

Apart from the youthful *Hans Bär* (1837), a dramatized fairy tale scene (*Schneewittchen*, 1845), and a number of *Döntjes* for Biernatzki's *Volksbuch*, Storm's contribution to the German *Kunstmärchen* consists of a scant half-dozen tales. One of these, *Das Märchen von den drei Spinnfrauen* (1840), is a reworking of the well-known *Drei Spinnerinnen* as we know it from the Grimm and Müllenhoff collections.[1] The other five are original Storm stories, written at two different periods of his life and generally ranked among the best German fairy tales produced since the Romantics.[2] *Der kleine Häwelmann* and *Hinzelmeier* were written in 1849 and 1850 and first published by Biernatzki; *Bulemanns Haus, Die Regentrude*, and *Der Spiegel des Cyprianus* belong to the years 1863-64, to that brief period in which, as Storm says, "eine ganze Saat der schönsten Märchenmotive in mir aufkeimte."[3]

Storm's own view of his fairy tales, while decidedly not as acute or elaborate as much of his other self-criticism, nevertheless corresponds rather closely to our critical assessment today. In a letter to Emil Kuh (Dec. 22, 1872) he has particular praise for *Bulemann, Regentrude*, and *Cyprianus*:

> Ich lege einigen Wert auf diese Märchen, da nach meiner Ansicht das Märchen als poetische Kunstform in unserer Literatur äußerst schwach vertreten ist und überdies die drei Sachen so recht aus dem Vollen geschrieben sind; sie entsprangen alle drei fast zugleich in meiner Phantasie.[4]

And to Brinkmann he writes (Jan. 18, 1864):

> Ich glaube, daß das, was ich bisher geschrieben, von besonderer Güte ist, und daß ich mit diesen Märchen einen ganz besonderen Treffer gezogen.

The projected *Märchensammlung*, he goes on to say, has "kein einziges verbrauchtes Motiv darin; wenigstens in den drei ersten (i.e., the later tales: *Bulemann*, *Regentrude*, and *Cyprianus*) ist alles rein aus meiner Phantasie herausgewachsen." And his final judgement, also expressed in a letter to Brinkmann (Jan. 10, 1866), is that

> sie sind nicht allein mit das Beste, was ich geschrieben habe, sondern ungefähr das Beste, was in dieser Art in deutscher Zunge existiert... diese Märchen werden in der deutschen Poesie lange leben.

Despite their undeniable quality, none of Storm's fairy tales ever achieved the popularity of *Immensee* nor did they become in any real sense *volkstümlich*. Whether this latter is even possible for a *Kunstmärchen* may of course be debated. Storm himself was aware of certain difficulties. "Mit dem Kunstmärchen ist es freilich eine heikle Sache; wir haben kaum ein Dutzend, die in Betracht kommen," he writes to Heinrich Seidel (Sept. 6, 1873),[5] and on another occasion he complains of the "Antipathie des Publikums gegen das Wort Märchen"[6] and the dilettantism prevalent among fairy tale writers of his age.[7]

But whatever the reasons, historical or stylistic, for the failure of these poetic-realistic (and, in contrast to Mörike's, plot-weak) fairy tales to achieve broad popularity, they continue to stand as major achievements of "der letzte, bedeutende Dichter, der Kunstmärchen geschrieben hat."[8]

The "heikle Sache" of which Storm speaks points to another difficulty. Are these tales really *Märchen* at all? In his Storm biography Stuckert uses the term sparingly. *Häwelmann* is a *Kindermärchen* in the manner of Hans Christian Andersen, *Hans Bär* follows the Grimm tradition, *Hinzelmeier* is a *Märchen* containing strong reminiscences of Romanticism, especially of Hoffmann and Novalis, and appears to Stuckert to be one of the "seltsamsten, geistig widerspruchvollsten und stilistisch uneinheitlichsten" of all

Storm's prose works. Of the three later tales he finds that only the *Regentrude* qualifies as a *Märchen* ("das Gepräge eines Märchens trägt eigentlich nur *Die Regentrude*"[10]); the others are presumably *Erzählungen* ("Noch weniger als auf *Bulemanns Haus* paßt die Bezeichnung Märchen auf die Erzählung *Der Spiegel des Cyprianus*"[11]), and to support his view Stuckert quotes Storm's own admission in the preface to the *Drei Märchen* (1866) that one should not take his use of the term *Märchen* "zu genau."[12]

It is worthwhile to pursue this question of terminology further. During the period of his greatest fairy tale activity Storm writes (to Brinkmann, Jan, 18, 1864) that he uses the word "im weiteren Sinne, wie auch Hauff es tat." Yet when he has occasion to speak in any critical way of the individual fairy tales he is careful to qualify.

> Wie ich in der Vorrede der drei Märchen sagte, trägt der Cyprianus den vornehmen Ton der Sage, während Bulemann auch eine "seltsame Historie" genannt werden könnte (to Kuh, Dec. 22, 1872).
>
> Bulemanns Haus werde ich der Gartenlaube anbieten; es ist Schwarzbrot darin, mit derben Strichen gezeichnet; grenzt mehr an die Sage oder Spukgeschichte; es grotesk-phantastisch (to Brinkmann, Jan. 18, 1864).
>
> Das kleine Märchen Häwelmann ist doch nur ein Einfall, und Hinzelmeier mehr eine phantastisch-allegorische Dichtung (to Kuh, Dec. 22, 1872).

Storm is often ready to give this or that work another, more precise label, but he inevitably returns to the broader and less restricting term *Märchen*. For on the whole it is, as he once confesses to Brinkmann, a point not worth debating: "Jedes dieser drei Märchen – ich will über das Wort nicht streiten – ...hat den Ton, der aus dem Stoff erwächst" (Jan. 10, 1866).

What, then, are the criteria by which Storm judges his fairy tales? Originality, we have seen, is a primary demand; his not infrequent references to the fact that the subject (*Stoff*) is "völlig von mir erfunden" (to Kuh, Dec. 22, 1872) or that the tales arose "in meiner Phantasie" stress the pride he feels in the creative side of his demonic "Märchendrang:" "doch hätte niemand als Th. St.

der Verfasser dieser Sachen sein können" (to Brinkmann, Jan. 10, 1866). A second requirement is what might be termed spontaneity and the impression of simplicity such as we feel it in the *Am Kamin* tales. It is, in Storm's words, an error, a "quantitative" departure from the poetic "wenn man einen Begriff, der *poëtice* immer nur szenisch dargestellt werden darf, durch eine Sache darstellen will." The consequences of such a departure are a reduction of interest "an dem unmittelbar Dargestellten."[13] A final requirement is that a fairy tale be free from allegory or *Tendenz*. In his defense of the *Drei Märchen* against Brinkmann's criticism, he accuses his friend of having regarded these "von den holdseligsten Phantasien belebte Märchen" from an allegorical or tendentious standpoint. "Wie darfst Du denn das? Wo es gelesen ist, von Männern, Weibern oder Kindern, hat es Entzücken erregt..." (to Brinkmann, Jan 10, 1866).

In illustrating the high regard in which Storm held his fairy tales we have quoted liberally from the correspondence that deals primarily with the *Drei Märchen*, i.e., with *Regentrude*, *Bulemann*, and *Cyprianus*. It is neither coincidence nor a wilful one-sidedness in our selection of quotations which causes the stress to fall on these particular tales at the expense of the earlier ones. Storm simply felt that they were better, were closer to his ideal *Märchen*. The first of the "neglected" tales, the *Häwelmann*, is in a sense dismissed with the words quoted earlier: "das kleine Märchen... ist doch nur ein Einfall" – and one wonders if Storm meant "klein" to refer only to length. As for the second, *Hinzelmeier* does not come in for extensive criticism anywhere in Storm's correspondence. Isolated references to it generally take the form of comparisons or illustrations of sins of commission.

The earliest reference to *Hinzelmeier*, or rather to its 1850 version *Stein und Rose*, is a four-verse dedication which Storm penned in the copy sent to his parents:

> Von mir auch bringt's ein seltsam Stück,
> Das ist aus Träumen ganz gesponnen.
> Das hab' ich in der Sommerzeit
> Beim warmen Sonnenschein ersonnen.[14]

The second line contains a familiar thought: originality and *Phantasie*, we have seen, are of prime importance to Storm. The "seltsam Stück" of line one is the first of several such descriptions he gives the tale. In a letter to his father (Jan. 24, 1856) he speaks of Hinzelmeier als "eine wirklich anmutige Arbeit jetzt" (the "jetzt" refers to the new version in contrast to *Stein und Rose*!). A letter written to Mörike a few weeks earlier (Dec. 2, 1855) contains this reference to the work:

> Das Märchen, oder wie es jetzt überschrieben ist, "Hinzelmeier. Eine nachdenkliche Geschichte," habe ich jetzt – es ist zuerst 1850 geschrieben – umgearbeitet, und zweifle ich nicht daran, daß es Ihnen besser gefallen wird als die Angelika.[16]

Some three months before (Aug. 27, 1855) Storm had confessed to Mörike, "Mir ist, als hätte ich die 'Angelika' nicht sollen drucken, sondern als Studie ruhig im Pult liegen lassen," and so the praise of Hinzelmeier is at best slightly tainted. In the letter to Brinkmann in which he speaks of the error of presenting an idea (*Begriff*) by means of a thing (*Sache*) Storm cites his *Hinzelmeier* as an example, "wie dies in meiner Geschichte durch die Rose und die Brille geschehen," and warns of the danger of weakening the poetic impression by trying to find "hinter diesen Dingen noch etwas anderes, als was sie sich geben." And finally, to his friend Eggers (who had reviewed the *Hinzelmeier* in his *Literaturblatt des deutschen Kunstblattes* and expressed displeasure above all of the sixth chapter) Storm concedes that the work has "gewiße Mängel und Dunkelheiten." He answers his friend's criticism of the devil chapter by yielding entirely:

> Ich gebe Ihnen das ganze sechste Kapitel preis, mehr können Sie von einem Autor nicht verlangen... Aber nicht wahr, Freund Eggers, Sie stehen mir bei? Es sind doch hübsche Bilder in der Geschichte, sogar kleine Menzelchen, möchte ich behaupten (letter of Dec. 20, 1856).

The positive remarks in the quotations above do not offset the uneasy, defensive attitude Storm has to *Hinzelmeier*. Only by taking a wider view of the fairy tale, and this generally in the perspective of time (such as the comment of later years to Heinrich

Seidel, "ich bilde mir in der Tat ein wenig darauf ein, daß ich viele Jahre nach dem Hinzelmeier noch Bulemanns Haus, den Cyprianusspiegel, und die Regentrude zu schreiben vermochte," Sept. 6, 1873[17]), or by defending specific things in it can he accept the work as one of those which will live long "in deutscher Poesie." This ambivalent situation is reflected both in the subtitle, "Eine nachdenkliche Geschichte," and his realization that he had in a sense betrayed his artistic principles in the composition of the tale. In referring to it as a "phantastisch-allegorische Dichtung" he praises and damns it in the same word, for while the phantastic may be desirable, the notion of allegory certainly was not. Moreover, he says that he did not tell this fairy tale (*Geschichte!*) "mit vollem Glauben" but stood "halb reflektierend daneben."

This ambivalent view of Hinzelmeier has been perpetuated by its critics. Stuckert, while calling the work "widerspruchsvoll, uneinheitlich," etc., nevertheless finds in this "Versuch" evidence of "den ganzen Zauber seiner Stimmungskunst," simple and straightforeward language ("aber viel körniger und gegenständlicher als in den vorhergehenden Novellen"), and "den sicheren Griff des Epikers."[18] J. Wedde, at the other extreme, calls *Hinzelmeier* the most nearly perfect of all Storm's Novellen and a "hochklassisches Stück deutscher Literatur."[19] Others, e.g., Biese, Jehle, and Botzong, grant the tale a measure of quality but place it below those written a decade earlier.[20]

It is by virtue of this problematic position *Hinzelmeier* holds among the *Märchen* that we find a closer examination of it rewarding. For just as Storm made certain demands on the fairy tale as genre and found them unrealized in *Hinzelmeier*, so may we say that this tale demands a certain kind of reading, a special examination of its "differentness," and our consideration as one of the important examples of Storm's early novellistic production. The following pages will therefore direct themselves to the task of re-interpretation, an examination of alleged influences, the question of *Hinzelmeier* as *Märchen*, and its position among Storm's early Novellen.

II

The plot, as both versions have it, concerns young Hinzelmeier's quest for the philosopher's stone. Woven into the tale as a counterforce are the secret of the rose and Hinzelmeier's parallel quest to enter the rose garden. From his eternally youthful parents he learns that he is one of the *Rosenherren* and has but to fetch the rose destined for him – and with it its *Pflegerin*, the *Rosenjungfrau* – to secure lasting youth and beauty. On learning his family secret Hinzelmeier goes out into the world to learn a trade (*Kunst*); but it must be a great art, he insists, one that nobody has yet been able to learn. After spending a year with a wise master, Hinzelmeier decides that his "große Kunst" will be to seek the philosopher's stone, and he vows not to return until he has found it. A year later he is sent on his way with a *Wanderspruch*, a bottle of elixir, and a raven (*Rabe*) which the master has made from a black hair plucked from his beard. The raven is to accompany Hinzelmeier on his adventures: "Wege sollst du weisen / Krahirius sollst du heißen." Krahirius is equipped with a pair of green spectacles that perch on his beak.

At three critical moments in the story Krahirius drops the spectacles upon Hinzelmeier's nose, causing the scene before his eyes to change. The first occurs as he is about to enter the *Rosengarten*, the second just as he finds the *Rosenjungfrau* after nine years of wandering, and the third, after nine further years, when his mother appears in his dreams and warns him not to forget the rose. On two occasions the glasses fall or are removed from his nose, and each time Hinzelmeier is granted a brief moment of "sight:" he identifies Kasperle's *Stein der Weisen*, and just before his death he sees the *Rosenjungfrau* approaching him. Both moments of recognition prove to be fruitless, and so Hinzelmeier dies without having fulfilled either quest. After hurling the raven into the sky and planting a rose at Hinzelmeier's head, the rose maiden returns to the garden to eternal captivity.

As Storm himself was uncomfortably aware, this "phantastisch-allegorische Dichtung" does not support a straight reading but invites interpretation in at least three places. *Stein und Rose*, the title of the first version, makes this clear enough, as does the subtitle of the standard version, "Eine nachdenkliche Geschichte." Moreover, even while lamenting his treatment of rose and spectacles in the story, Storm is careful to grant the importance of idea ("ein bestimmter Gedanke... dessen Gültigkeit über die in casu dargestellten Fakta hinausgeht")[21] in a fairy tale. Among critics, Stuckert reflects this dilemma in his statement,

> die symbolisierende Anlage dieses Märchens hat die Leser immer wieder veranlaßt, in dem, was doch nur absichtslos spielende Phantasie von stärkster Anziehungskraft war, einen geheimen "Sinn" zu geben.[22]

Yet he himself speaks of the *Idee* behind the tale as a conflict between knowledge and life, and he explains (or interprets):

> In dem unendlichen Drang nach letzter Erkenntnis und Leben – von Storm im Stein der Weisen symbolisiert – wird das unmittelbare Glück des Lebens versäumt.[23]

Two earlier critics of *Hinzelmeier* are less reluctant to interpret. Botzong finds the meaning of the tale to be similar to that in Storm's other early Novellen:

> Eine Seite der Idee des Märchens ist echt Stormisch: Sehnsucht nach Glück und vergebliches Hoffen. Sie kehrt wieder in allen Novellen... Das Märchen von "Hinzelmeier" ist wohl nicht zuletzt eine Art Glaubensbekenntnis, das Leben zu fassen, so lange es Zeit ist: "O Jugend, o schöne Rosenzeit", lautet der Anfang des alten Liedes, dessen sehnsuchtsvoller Klang Storms Novelle "Späte Rosen" durchzittert. – Die Idee des Märchens will weiter besagen, wie leicht der Mensch sein bestes Glück im Leben verscherzt, wenn der nachdenkliche Verstand ihm das unmittelbar frische Empfinden und Zugreifen tötet und ihm nur Mittel und Wege weist, um glücklich zu werden, nie aber um glücklich zu sein... Hinzelmeier gehört zu den jung alten Menschen, er ist kein Lebenskünstler, denn er spekuliert zu viel über das Leben[!][24]

And Jehle offers specific equivalents for some of the story's more important symbols:

> Hinzelmeier hat zu wenig auf die Poesie geachtet, weil die grüne Brille der Alltäglichkeit ihm immer das Wunderland verwandelte. In seinem Suchen nach

Weisheit hat er die höchste Weisheit vergessen. Bis zum Schluß verharrt er in seinem Irrtum und so stirbt er einsam und unter Qualen... Ohne Zweifel handelt es sich im Hinzelmeier um ein romantisches Problem. Poesie und Alltag sind auch hier einander gegenübergestellt, wie bei E. T. A. Hoffmann, auf den Todsen hinweist [*Über die Entwicklung des romantischen Kunstmärchens*, Diss. Berlin, 1906, p. 117]. Der Ausgang ist aber ein völlig anderer. Bei Hoffmann siegt am Schluß immer die Poesie, ebenso wie Novalis' Hyazinth auf seiner Suche sein Rosenblütchen findet. Todsen erwähnt zwar diesen Unterschied, führt aber nicht aus, welche Umwälzung diese Verschiedenheit anzeigt. So stark ist die Nüchternheit geworden, daß selbst der zur Poesie vorherbestimmte Hinzelmeier nicht mehr den rechten Weg finden kann. Daß die Rosenjungfrau die Liebe verkörpert, zugleich aber die Poesie und der Inbegriff des Höchsten ist, zeigt am stärksten Storms Verbundenheit mit der Romantik. Wedde nennt Storms Einstellung der Liebe gegenüber den "rückhaltlosen Kultus einer mit dem Geiste versöhnten schönen Sinnlichkeit" [J. Wedde, *Theodor Storm*, Hamburg, 1888, p. 29]. Dies ist genau das, was die Romantiker anstrebten.

Wedde sieht in Hinzelmeier vor allem denjenigen, der diese sinnlich-übersinnliche Liebe immer vergißt über der Suche nach dem "Stein," der Verkörperung des toten Gedankens; "den Teufel sprengt er zur Welt hinaus – der Verstand zerstört die alten Formen des Wahns, die bisher das Leben hemmten – aber des Übels Kern beseitigt er nicht." [p. 29] Diese geistreiche Deutung ist etwas einseitig und mir scheint, daß sie mit der andern, der Gegenüberstellung von Poesie und Nüchternheit verbunden werden müßte. Schütze's Auslegung, daß "unendliches Verlangen nach Glück, aber Unvermögen, es zu erreichen, in Hinzelmeier märchenhaft symbolisch gestaltet" sei [P. Schütze, *Theodor Storm*, Berlin, 1911, p. 162], ist doch wohl zu oberflächlich.[25]

These criticisms reveal notable differences in the emphasis given to the tale's major symbols. Schütze's infinite "Verlangen nach Glück" becomes in Stuckert's interpretation an infinite "Drang nach letzter Erkenntnis und Leben;" Botzong's "nachdenklicher Verstand" is for Jehle "Alltäglichkeit" and "Nüchternheit" and for Wedde "die Verkörperung des toten Gedankens." And "Poesie," finally, is "das unmittelbare Glück des Lebens" or simply "Liebe" or, in Wedde's words, a "schöne Sinnlichkeit." The variations, it should be repeated, arise for the most part from the different order of importance the interpretations give the symbols. Without insisting on the absolute validity of one reading at the expense of the others, we shall attempt to suggest a satisfactory explanation for *Hinzelmeier*'s symbols and indicate where necessary the untenability of some of the statements above.

Schütze's explanation, which Jehle finds too superficial, ought rather to be criticised for placing the stress where the reader might want it rather than where Hinzelmeier himself puts it. For his encounters with the *Rosenjungfrau* are not only fortuitous but strictly secondary so far as he is consciously aware. His goal is his "große Kunst," is the philosopher's stone, and he is never fully clear as to the significance of his mother's words "mitunter auch durchs Fenster" or the relation his rose maiden may have to the other quest. Wedde's theory of "Sinnlichkeit" may be dismissed for lack of evidence in the story itself. Jehle's equivalents for stone and rose, *Alltag* and *Poesie*, offer an interesting reversal of values. Not the stone or Hinzelmeier's quest for it, but love and poetry represent the highest wisdom. One can accept the importance of love in the tale – and of course its embodiment in the rose maiden – but it is difficult to see poetry in quite the same way. It appears almost as though Jehle bases her interpretation on the earlier version of the fairy tale, for there we are introduced to what at least passes for art.

The rose garden chapter of *Stein und Rose* contains most of the evidence that art is an issue in the work. When Hinzelmeier's mother reveals their family history she speaks of an "unscheinbare weiße Mauer" which surrounds the rose garden. Its portal

> ist beständig von einer jungen Schaar belagert, welche sich den Eingang mit Gesang und Liedern zu erkaufen strebt. Auf diese Weise wird die größte Zahl der Jungfrauen aus ihrer Gefangenschaft erlöst.[26]

On his wanderings Hinzelmeier comes upon the garden. His companion during this part of his journey is a young fop who carries a fiddle on his back. When Hinzelmeier is asked where he is going, he replies, "Ich reise auf meine Kunst," whereupon his companion remarks on the absence of an instrument. The noise and confusion before the rose garden are such that Hinzelmeier at first takes it for a *Narrenhaus* and is tempted to turn back, "denn das leidet meine Kunst nicht." Among the crowd of people and tents is a group of young men carrying musical instruments: harp, drum, barrel-organ, fiddle, chimes, flute, etc. Hinzelmeier realizes that each person must play "seine eigene Melodie" and sing "sein eignes Lied nach seiner eignen Weise." When he inquires about harmony he is told that there is none.

> Hier gibt es nichts als Dilettanten, hier gilt unumschränkte Notenfreiheit, hier sucht Jeder seinen eignen Ton, und wenn er ihn gefunden hat, dann springen die Pforten des Rosengartens auf. Dieses ist das Punktum und besser als alle Harmonie![27]

As Hinzelmeier and his companion approach the garden's "unscheinbare weiße Mauer" a blue hair band is seen to flutter over it. At once all the cavaliers drop their instruments and try vainly to catch it; Hinzelmeier's companion hurls his cap into the air, captures the ribbon, then binds it to his fiddle and steps before the gate. A zither player "von mädchenhaftem Äußern" attempts to gain entry with a song he renders "mit zarter Stimme." A rosy light shines from within the walls and the mighty gate groans on its hinges; but it does not open, and the singer steps back into the crowd. An older man, a clarinet player, tries next, playing a "stürmische Marschmelodie, dreimal von vorne nach hinten." Hinzelmeier is told that he has played so long before the gate that his beard has grown to his boots – "und noch immer hat er seinen Ton nicht treffen können."

Hinzelmeier's companion is now ready to try his luck. Handing Hinzelmeier a Jew's-harp, he tells him, "wer zuerst seinen Ton trifft, bestellt für den Andern Quartier." He steps up to the gate and sings,

> und immer klingender strich er die Saiten und immer silberner sang er:
> > Nun will ich die Welt bezwingen
> > In seligem Müssigang...
>
> Und kaum war der letzte Ton heraus, so flogen die Pforten tönend auseinander, und ein Strom von Rosenduft quoll auf den grünen Plan heraus. Der Geigenspieler aber drehte sich auf dem Absatz und rief: "Seht ihr, Herr Vetter, das heißt gepfiffen!" und seine Geige schwenkend verschwand er in den Rosengarten, dessen Tore sich rauschend hinter ihm schlossen.[28]

When Hinzelmeier hears the sound of "Rinke, ranke, Rosenschein!" he throws his Jew's-harp over the wall and is about to join in the song. But suddenly Krahirius drops the glasses upon his nose and the rose garden disappears from view.

In this fifth chapter, which represents the major difference between the two versions of the fairy tale, art is both romanticized and mocked. In the *Stein und Rose* version Hinzelmeier speaks of his *Kunst*, to be sure, but there is no real indication that he is referring either to poesy or song. When asked where his *Spielwerk* is, Hinzelmeier does not reply – ostensibly because he and his companion are interrupted by the appearance of a rider, but in actuality because Storm has not thought to give him one. The borrowed Jew's-harp, needless to say, is not used and there is absolutely no suggestion as to what would have happened if Hinzelmeier's companion had not struck his "tone." Certainly the explanation given earlier that only dilettantes who seek their own tone and, upon finding it, enter the garden cannot be taken to include the kind of agreement the fop makes with Hinzelmeier. Unless, that is to say, the whole episode is to be seen as a kind of romantic fantasy (such as we see it in the *Taugenichts* or the *Marmorbild*, which are, however, by no means devoid of symbolic meaning) with an ample portion of satire included.

Another difficulty arises when we consider Hinzelmeier's two earlier remarks concerning his art. He is traveling, he says, "auf meine Kunst," and the possibility that he has come upon a madhouse causes him to say that his art cannot endure that. At worst the remarks may be meaningless – Stuckert doubtless would have it this way – and at best they suggest that a close connection exists between the "große Kunst," the *Wanderspruch* given to Hinzelmeier by the master, and art in this fifth chapter, especially as it is practiced so successfully by the fop. To Hinzelmeier, "große Kunst" means to seek the philosopher's stone; according to the words of the *Spruch*, "Finden und schaffen zugleich / Das ist die Kunst!;" and to the fop it is "Bezwingung der Welt in seligem Müssigang." But the connection is by no means clear, and a systematic interpretation of this chapter breaks down on the lack of consistent symbolization. This is surely a part of Storm's reason for subjecting the chapter to such extensive revision. However, on the evidence at our disposal we may say, in criticism of Jehle, that *Poesie* does not emerge as one of the two important meanings in the story; to judge from the *Rosengarten* episode, *Poesie* in the wider sense of music and poetry is not a meaning at all but is itself symbolic of something else, of what is called one's own tone. And Jehle's other force, *Nüchternheit* or *Alltag* (one questions the wisdom of equating the two in Storm), cannot possibly be placed in diametrical opposition to *Poesie*. This is made clear by the results of the revision.

In its new form the chapter is called "Der Eingang zum Rosengarten," which faithfully reflects the shift in emphasis. To accommodate the renovated garden in the story Storm drops all mention of the "unscheinbare weiße Mauer" and the crowd of artists from the mother's explanation to young Hinzelmeier. She tells him instead that it is a question of finding the right way,

> denn der Eingänge sind viele, und oft verwunderliche. Hier führt es durch einen dicht verwachsenen Zaun [cf. the "weiße Mauer, über welche sich ein dichtes Flechtwerk von immer grünen Linden erhebt" in the first version], dort durch ein schmales Winkelpförtchen [cf. the "gewaltige Pforte," the "verhängnisvolle Pforte," or "eine hohe künstlich geschnitzte Pforte"], mitunter...mitunter auch durchs Fenster!

Hinzelmeier's way takes him to a large farmhouse, where he sees pancakes fly from the chimney, turn slowly in the sunshine, and fall back down the chimney. He enters and is given something to eat and drink. The wine makes him so gay

> daß er ganz wie von selber zu singen anhub. "Er ist ja ein lustiger Mensch!" rief die Alte von ihrem Herde hinüber. Hinzelmeier nickte; ihm fielen auf einmal alle Lieder wieder ein, die er vorzeiten im elterlichen Hause von seiner schönen Mutter gehört hatte. Nun sang er sie, eines nach dem andern:
>
> > Das macht, es hat die Nachtigall
> > Die ganze Nacht gesungen...
>
> Da wurde in der Wand, dem Herde gegenüber, unter den Reihen der blanken

Zinnteller ein Schiebfensterchen zurückgezogen, und ein schönes blondes Mädchen, es mochte des Hauswirts Tochter sein, steckte neugierig den Kopf in die Küche.

This turns out to be the entrance to the rose garden, and the girl is of course the *Rosenjungfrau*. The brief encounter between Hinzelmeier and the farmer's daughter has, however, little fairy tale magic in it. A spring breeze blows a blue ribbon from the girl's bonnet, and Hinzelmeier catches it with his hat (thus effecting the rescue of an anacreontic device into Biedermeier by way of Romanticism). In returning it, Hinzelmeier bumps heads with the girl and it is apparently love at first sight. Hinzelmeier asks the way into the room and hears his mother's voice, "mitunter auch durchs Fenster." But as he is about to climb through the window, the green spectacles fall upon his nose and cause the scene to change.

Despite the acrobatic pancakes and the green glasses this scene represents a kind of disenchantment in the standard version. Those requisites of German Romanticism, the musicians and their gay encampment before the walls of the mysterious rose garden, have disappeared and in their place we are given one of the most *hausbacken* settings possible. Behind, amongst, and above the pots and pans of a *Bauernküche* the rose maiden appears – and Hinzelmeier's surmise that she is probably the farmer's daughter is, if not poetic, at least highly reasonable. Behind her is the rose garden; to gain access Hinzelmeier would have to go through the window, through the pots and pans. Jehle's only comment on this unusual state of affairs is

Es ist sehr interessant, daß der Dichter Hinzelmeiers erste Begegnung mit der Rosenjungfrau in eine ganz wirkliche Bauernstube verlegt... Erst allmählich kommt das Märchenhafte wieder zum Vorschein,

and her conclusion is that Storm has made great progress beyond the *Stein und Rose* by means of "Ausübung eines stärkeren Realismus."[29]

As to art in general or the polarity of *Poesie* and *Alltag*, the revised fifth chapter offers even less to go on than *Stein und Rose*.

The entire issue of *Kunst*, of one's own tone, has disappeared; moreover, *Alltag* (not *Nüchternheit!*) has come so close to what could pass as the poetry of life that we may see in this accomodation Storm's intention to fuse the two entirely. Common to both versions, for example, is the scene in chapter two ("Der Zipfel") in which young Hinzelmeier slips through the wall as he had seen his mother do and finds himself "wohin er am wenigsten zu gelangen dachte – auf dem Hausboden." We may follow his actions in detail:

> "Sonderbar!" sagte Hinzelmeier, "warum ging die Mutter denn doch immer durch die Wand?" Da er indessen außer den bekannten Gegenständen nichts bemerken konnte, so wollte er durch die Bodentür wieder ins Haus hinabgehen. Allein die Tür war nicht da. Er stutzte einen Augenblick und meinte anfänglich sich nur geirrt zu haben, *weil er von einer anderen Seite, als gewöhnlich, hinaufgelangt war.* Er wandte sich daher und ging zwischen die Mäntel durch nach dem alten Schranke, um sich von hier aus zurechtzufinden; und richtig, dort gegenüber war die Tür; er begriff nicht, wie er sie hatte übersehen können. Als er aber darauf zuging, erschien ihm plötzlich wieder alles so fremd, daß er zu zweifeln begann, ob er auch vor der rechten Tür stehe. Allein so viel er wußte, gab es hier keine andere.
> [italics mine]

The kitchen scene is a variation of this earlier adventure in Hinzelmeier's attic: behind or amidst the familiar everyday things is the ideal one seeks. It is but a question of seeing them in just the right way, of approaching them in the manner appropiate to the individual. Thus the "eigener Ton" is rescued in less obvious form into the new version of the story, and the mother's warning – or perhaps hint – that "der rechte Weg" is but one of many possibilities is given added importance by these later events.

We are never told what the "eigener Ton" is, but the episodes that follow Hinzelmeier's first encounter with the rose maiden make it relatively easy to identify. Hinzelmeier's conscious goal, we recall, is the *Stein der Weisen*, the symbol of "letzte Erkenntnis." His quest for it is, he believes, his "große Kunst," and this is never actually denied in the story. What proves illusory is not so much the stone, therefore, as the right way to it. Demonstrably false, for example, are the advice and learning given him by the master (who remains an *Altgesell* and never finds the stone either) in the form of the elixir – which Storm promptly forgets – and the bespectacled bird. For when the latter drops the glasses upon Hinzelmeier's nose, both the worthlessness and inappropiateness of Hinzelmeier's learning are exposed. Hinzelmeier's father has already made this clear. When he hears that his son has chosen to search for the philosopher's stone as his *Kunst*, he consoles his wife with the words,

> Er mußte seinen Weg gehen. Ich wollte auch einmal den Stein der Weisen suchen und habe statt dessen die Rose gefunden.

We recall that Hinzelmeier belongs to a special race; Frau Abel speaks of a "Gnade der Geburt" that separates the *Rosenherren* from "gewöhnliche Menschheit." Is not this an indication that one's true way is not *angelernt* but a part of one's own destiny, is in other words the tone that represents a person's truest identity? That Storm places the goal in such proximity to everyday life and, in his revision of the story, removes the "artists" altogether is our best evidence that he was not thinking of art or *Poesie* in the narrower sense.

Father Hinzelmeier's conscious goal was the same foolish quest as his son's. His achievement therefore has something fortuitous about it, especially in view of the fact that birthright alone is not enough. To discover what he did right (which is of course not told us; we learn merely that Frau Abel waited sixteen years!), we need to inquire further into what Hinzelmeier did wrong. His failures and their cause may be found in the six trials which he undergoes, beginning with the first encounter in the kitchen and ending with his death. Hinselmeier brings about the meeting with the *Rosenjungfrau* by his singing, and we may take this to be the crucial test. But contrary to the *Stein und Rose* version there is no conscious attempt to display one's art; "ihm fielen auf einmal alle Lieder ein, die er vorzeiten... gehört hatte," and Hinzelmeier himself explains that "es kam mir nur so. Ich singe sonst gar nicht." Yet his spontaneity and naturalness bring him within reach of the rose, and only the green glasses rob him of final success. With the spectacles on his nose Hinzelmeier sees the devil, whom he takes to be the *Stein des Anstoßes*. He removes him by blowing him into another planetary system, but his reappearance – Kasperle insists that he met the devil just two days before Hinzelmeier appears – suggests that the *Meisterschuß* was pointless. The *Stein des Anstoßes* is thus falsely identified, the trouble lies within Hinzelmeier himself.

His second meeting with the rose maiden is also happenstance. Stopping at a *Wirtshaus*, Hinzelmeier learns that someone has been inquiring after him. He is told to look on a street corner, but the *Blumenmädchen* he sees are wearing "plumpe Schnallenschuhe... das waren keine Rosenjungfrauen." He discovers her finally in an old house:

> Er erkannte mit einemmal das Mädchen aus der Bauernküche; nur trug sie heute nicht das bunte Mieder, und das Rot auf ihren Wangen war nur der Abglanz von dem Rosenlichte.

She reproaches him for having wandered about in the world for so long. Frau Abel had already expressed concern at this possible danger and had compared her son with the luckless Kasperle. But it is not yet too late. Shortly before, Hinzelmeier had seen his reflection in a copper pan: his features were old and worn. Now he sees his image in the eyes of the rose maiden, "ein Gesicht, so jung und frisch und lustig, daß er laut aufjauchzen mußte." This time the townspeople separate the pair, the raven drops the glasses upon Hinzelmeier's nose, and the entire town vanishes.

With the glasses on his nose again Hinzelmeier sees Kasperle, who claims to have found the philosopher's stone. But Kasperle too is wearing spectacles and hence cannot see the obvious:

> Und kaum hatte Hinzelmeier seine Brille abgenommen, so ließ er sie vor Erstaunen ins Gras fallen und rief: Ich habe es! Herr Kollege, man muß ihn essen.

Kasperle also removes his glasses, but he must study the stone for a time before identifying it as a *Lederkäse*, thus indicating that he is a less fortunate exemplar of Hinzelmeier. The rose maiden, incidentally, had discovered this earlier: "Der Kaspar singt auch schön... aber so schön wie Er macht er's doch nicht." The scene ends with Hinzelmeier's statement that he feels as though he had come appreciably closer to the stone.

The last chapter, entitled "Der Stein der Weisen," brings two episodes. Hinzelmeier again stops at a *Wirtshaus* and hears that an "arme Dirne" has been searching for him.

"Es schien ein Blumenmädchen zu sein", sagte der Wirt, "wenn Ihr sie sprechen wollt, Ihr werdet sie leicht an den Straßenecken finden können."

But Hinzelmeier is not ready for the final encounter. He must sleep first, and when the cock crows he will continue his search. In his dreams he hears his mother's admonition, "vergiß die Rose nicht!" but the raven drops the glasses on his nose and his dreams change. The final episode depicts Hinzelmeier's toilsome journey across a wide, desolate field. At the farther end is a hill and on its top a flat gray stone. "'Das ist der Stein der Weisen!' sagte Hinzelmeier zu sich selber. 'Endlich, endlich wird er dennoch mein werden!'" When he at last reaches it he collapses and his head sinks onto the stone. At this moment the glasses fall from his nose and in the distance he perceives the figure of the rose maiden. She arrives too late, for Hinzelmeier has died of old age.

In reviewing these six adventures one is forced to reject Stuckert's assertion that the story is "nur absichtslos spielende Phantasie." There is, first of all, too consistent a structure and too logical a progression through the various adventures for us to accept haphazardness as a primary characteristic of composition. For example, the three encounters with the rose maiden – a magic number in fairy tales, as Storm certainly knew – use consistently the prosaic reality of *Bauernhof* and *Wirtshaus* for their setting. As Hinzelmeier grows older the rose maiden becomes gradually poorer and more forlorn, indicating that the goal is moving farther away. Moreover, the three encounters are terminated by three stages in Hinzelmeier's quest for the stone. We have said that the *Stein des Anstoßes* was incorrectly identified; this was the case with the *Stein der Weisen*, i.e., the *Lederkäse*, as well. And Hinzelmeier's last journey – across the desolate landscape to the stone on the hill – brings him not to the philosopher's stone, at least not in any meaningful sense, but to his gravestone.

Each positive encounter is terminated by the green glasses, and each time they are removed from Hinzelmeier's nose he gains a new view of reality and appears, if only temporarily, to come closer to it. To view life through the glasses is thus to see it in distortion, and so it may be said that the raven is the master's heritage, his learning, and the spectacles Hinzelmeier's use of it. Since to see the world through the eyes of the philosopher is not to see it truly, we may assume that Hinzelmeier's true vision ought to lie in the simple recognition of the rose garden's importance.

If we inquire further into the uses to which the rose motif is put in the story, we discover with some surprise that love is not the primary one. Frau Abel specifically states that the special qualities with which the possessor of the rose is endowed are youth and beauty. One of the most effective symbolic actions in the fairy tale is Hinzelmeier's backward look just before he dies:

> doch in demselben Augenblick fiel auch die Brille von seiner Nase. Da sah er tief am Horizonte, am Rande der öden Ebene, die er durchwandert hatte, die weiße Gestalt der Rosenjungfrau.

Hinzelmeier's unobstructed view reveals to him symbolically the landscape through which he has spent, or wasted, his life wandering – and at whose farther edge is the ideal he has failed to attain. The glasses are off, and we know that he sees truly. But his look is backward; youth, beauty, love, and above all fulfillment are beyond his grasp. One is reminded here of Reinhard's *Wasserrose*: its unattainability is surely the more obvious and final because it comes at the end of the quest, that is to say after the object of the search is already a part of the past! We have no reason to reject or emend Frau Abel's words; eternal youth and beauty await the possessor of the rose. But Hinzelmeier has already lost both, fulfillment is by virtue of his mistaken quest impossible. To be sure, the *Rosenjungfrau* may represent love among her other attributes, but the ideal of fulfillment is paramount. Thus the fairy tale's meaning would appear to be that the *Stein der Weisen* (knowledge, intellect, the synthesis of things that represent wisdom in contrast to simplicity, spontaneity, the unspoiled but ever threatened innocence of childhood – as Storm never tires of depicting it) as *Lebensideal* is an illusion, is in fact a gravestone. One thinks of Tolstoy's *How Much Land Does a Man Need?*, to which the foolish peasant supplies his own answer: the six-foot plot for his grave. For attainment, the synthesis of the two spheres of *Leben* and *Erkenntnis*, comes only with death – and in the process of attaining, so Storm feels, one passes by the life one was destined to live. Frau Abel's admonition not to waste one's heritage poses as an alternative the age and decay of ordinary man. This latter has little to do with the heroes of Storm's Novellen.

We may comment finally on the meaning of the burghal setting. The drastic revision of the *Rosengarten* chapter makes it apparent that Storm is consciously endeavoring to remove some of the romantic other-worldliness from his story and to place it more nearly toward the center of nineteenth century realism. Perhaps nowhere in Storm's writings are we closer to the ideal of German Biedermeier than here, for Hinzelmeier's world is almost completely that of Storm's own landscape (cf. the spring morning at the beginning of chapter five); and his ideal, we have observed, is in closest proximity to the *Alltag*. But it is a partially enchanted landscape, an enhanced *Alltag* (we are to some degree still within the domain of the *Märchen*). The moderate poeticizing of reality was enough for Storm and certainly more in keeping with Hinzelmeier's quest than, for example, Novalis' *Poesie* as the essence of life. Hinzelmeier's own "tone" therefore has that mixed quality about it which we observe in Storm's other early Novellen: "der Inbegriff des Höchsten," to use Jehle's term, is indeed youth, happiness, is Botzong's "schöne Rosenzeit." But it is as elusive as Storm's Biedermeier heroes are fragile. Its enemy is time, is *Vergänglichkeit*, and to this Hinzelmeier succumbed.

III

To return to Storm's own view of *Hinzelmeier*: we recall the apologetic explanation that he did not narrate "mit vollem Glauben" but took a semi-reflective position outside the tale. His dissatisfaction with the work derives from its failure to meet his general requirements for a *Märchen*. We have summarized these latter as originality, spontaneity and the impression of simplicity, and the freedom from allegorizing and *Tendenz*. But even if we grant that *Hinzelmeier* somehow fails in these three areas, we are not justified in applying them as absolute criteria to determine the degree of success of the story. Originality, for example, cannot possibly be as important as Storm would have it. Among the fairy tales we need only to cite the *Drei Spinnfrauen* as an example of successful adaption; and among the Novellen proper *Ein Bekenntnis* comes to mind as a striking example of the manner in which Storm proceeds from an a priori question. Heyse's Novelle *Auf Leben und Tod*, published two years before *Ein Bekenntnis*, had dealt with the problem "ob man einem Unheilbaren zum Tode helfen dürfe." But this was, as Storm explains to Heyse, "nicht das meine. Ich wollte darstellen: 'Wie kommt einer dahin, sein Geliebtestes zu töten?' und 'Was wird aus ihm, wenn er das getan hat?'"[30] Allegory and *Tendenz*, finally, may be taken as post facto explanations for what appeared to Storm to be *Hinzelmeier*'s compositional failure. We shall have occasion later to question this more fully.

Stuckert explains the "problem" of Hinzelmeier by pointing out Storm's unusual *Kunstübung*. It is, he says, an "ungewöhnlicher Fall,

> daß der Dichter aus bewußter Absicht, aus literarischer Tradition und einer bestimmten Idee heraus versucht hat, ein Märchen zu schreiben... Eine 'Idee' zum Ausgangspunkt einer Erzählung zu wählen, entspricht in keiner Weise Storms Kunstübung."[31]

It is difficult to concur in this judgement, as the exceptions noted above make clear. We are left therefore with Storm's open dissatisfaction with *Hinzelmeier qua Märchen* and with the critical assertion that the work is a departure from Storm's usual method of composition and consequently one of his strangest, most disjointed works. Before attempting to explain in greater detail how and why the tale fails to remain within the limits of the *Märchen* as Storm understood it, and consequently why Hinzelmeier strikes Storm's most recent biographer as an unsuccessful fusion of form and content ("So kommen Inhalt und Form in keiner Weise zur Deckung"[32]), we may comment on the question of literary influence.

All accounts of *Hinzelmeier*'s sources with which I am familiar deal only cursorily with the purported models and stimuli. Stuckert writes:

> Als Anregung liegt zugrunde das Märchen "Schnapupu" von Ferdinand Röse, das dieser dem jungen Storm in Kiel vorgelesen hatte, was später zwischen den beiden Männern zu einer lebhaften Korrespondenz Veranlassung gab. Einige Jahre danach ist es dann von Röse unter dem Titel "Das Sonnenkind" in dem Volkskalender "Der deutsche Pilger durch die Welt auf das Jahr 1845" in Stuttgart veröffentlicht worden. In beiden Märchen handelt es sich um den Gegensatz von Erkenntnis und Leben... Es ist also ein typisch romantisches Thema, das Storm sich hier gestellt hat, und so sind denn auch die Beziehungen zur Romantik, vor allem zu E.T.A. Hoffmann und Novalis, im "Hinzelmeier" stärker als irgendwo sonst in seinem Prosawerk.[33]

As his authority Stuckert cites Böhme's commentary to his Storm edition and the studies by Todsen and Jehle. Strangely enough, there is virtually no overlapping among the accounts given by these three critics. Böhme mentions only Röse and, more generally, the Geibel-Röse group as influences:

> Storm ist im "Hinzelmeier" unstreitig beeinflußt von einem 1841 geschriebenen Märchen seines Jugendfreundes Ferdinand Röse "Das Sonnenkind", das dieser in dem von ihm redigierten Volkskalender "Der deutsche Pilger durch die Welt auf das Jahr 1845" (Stuttgart, Hallberger), S. 57-89, veröffentlichte und zu dem Geibel und Storm Lieder lieferten... Schärer, der Biograph Ferdinand Röses, schreibt in seinem, in der Berliner Staatsbibliothek in Handschrift aufbewahrten "Leben von Ferd. Röse", S. 41: "In Kiel hatte er seinem Studiengenossen Theodor Storm sein Märchen 'Schnapupu' (aus dem später 'Das Sonnenkind' wurde) vorgelesen, was

> in der Folge zu einer eifrigen Korrespondenz über dessen Idee Veranlassung gab; nach einer Notiz Röses an mich soll aus diesem Austausch später Storms Märchen entstanden sein." Noch frühere Einflüsse des Geibel-Röse-Kreises in Lübeck scheinen vorzuliegen durch eine dort 1834 von einigen dieses Kreises geschaffene Dichtung 'Heringssalat', in der auch schon die Gestalt des Retla Aipok (bei Storm: der Meister) und märchenhafte Verwandlungen vorkommen."[84]

Jehle is more cautious in her mention of influences. Certain parts or aspects of Hinzelmeier remind her of passages from other works, e.g., "unwillkürlich erinnert der außergewöhnlich stimmungsvolle Schluß an Eichendorffs Schilderung von Ottos Ende in 'Dichter und ihre Gesellen;' " the description of the *Rosenschrein* and the Kasperle scene are reminiscences of E. T. A. Hoffmann, as is the contrast between *Poesie* and *Alltag* altogether. Todsen, too, is struck by the similarity to Hoffmann, especially in a more general way.[86]

Botzong's study of Storm's fairy tales – which Stuckert's otherwise comprehensive bibliography strangely fails to include – devotes rather more space to the question of influences, but here again we get the impression that too little careful investigation has been made. There is, for instance, no mention whatever of Röse's *Sonnenkind*. Considering Röse's total disappearance from literary histories on the period, and more particularly in view of the fact that Böhme's commentary volume appeared the same year as Botzong's dissertation (1935), such an omission would be understandable were it not for that fact that Storm himself mentions the *Sonnenkind* (with place and date of publication!) no less than three times in his *Erinnerungen*. The *Erinnerungen...an Ferdinand Röse*, for example, contain this reference:

> Röse klagte, daß ihm das Talent der schönen Formgebung fehle, das, nach seiner Ansicht, Geibel in vollem Maße besaß; daher denn auch, wo er in seiner Prosa Lieder bedurfte, seinen Mangel gern aus dessen Reichtum deckte, wie in seinem Märchen "Das Sonnenkind", das im "Pilger durch die Welt" 1845 erschien.

He begins his *Erinnerungen an die letzten Kieler Semester* with a reference to Röse's "tiefsinniges Märchen 'Das Sonnenkind'," which his friend read to him. In the same *Recollection* he addresses these words to Röse:

> Armer Magister Wanst! Wo sind jetzt deine Märchen! Wo dein großes Drama "Ahasver"... Keine deiner Saaten ist aufgegangen, selbst dein Sonnenkind ist in dem "Pilger durch die Welt" pr. 1845 nur verkrüppelt an das Tageslicht getreten. . Damals aber, an jenem Sommernachmittag im Walde, warst du noch so hoffnungsreich und im Vollgefühl einer großen Lebensaufgabe; und mit Behagen hattest du neben ernsteren Studien auch jenes Märchen hingeschrieben. Nur für den Liederbedarf des Hans Fideldum, den du allein nicht zu decken wußtest, wurde die Beisteuer der Freunde in Anspruch genommen.

Before commenting further on the *Sonnenkind* and Storm's references to it, we should point out that Botzong's failure to mention this work, although somewhat puzzling, ought not to be heavily stressed, for her list of possible influences is at once plausible and original. There is an unmistakable similarity, she says, between *Hinzelmeier* and Novalis' *Hyazinth und Rosenblütchen*. The master in Storm's tale presumably goes back to E. T. A. Hoffmann's Pepser in *Das fremde Kind*, who in turn is a descendent of the Schreiber in *Heinrich von Ofterdingen*.[37] More important, Botzong calls our attention to Hans Christian Andersen's *Snow Queen*, in which certain key figures and objects clearly forshadow those in *Hinzelmeier*.

The total number of "influences" and similarities might at first suggest that Storm had the cento quality of *Hinzelmeier* in mind when he refused the work unqualified praise and, what is worse, tacitly admitted that it lacked spontaneity and simplicity. Certainly, he makes no outright claims for originality other than in the verse dedication quoted earlier, which was not the case with *Cyprianus*, *Bulemann* and the *Regentrude*. In claiming complete originality for the first two, he is careful to document certain minor exceptions:

> nur daß im "Spiegel des Cyprianus" (ich habe den Namen des alten nordischen Zauberers gebraucht) bei dem Gespräch des Oberst Hager mit dem Kuno, ehe er ihn tötet, die Volksballade von der Gräfin von Orlamünde hineinspielt, aus der ich auch den Namen "Hager" benutzt habe... "Bulemanns Haus" entstand aus der Anschauung der Schiefertafelbilder zu deutschen "Kinderliedern" ohne Jahreszahl vor vielleicht fünfundzwanzig Jahren erschienen.[38]

Such painstaking fidelity is in striking contrast to the vagueness with which *Hinzelmeier* is treated. Is this simply because the latter is accorded such slight treatment altogether? Or, to repeat our initial statement, is it because Storm secretly held it to be a cento? Such questions unfortunately cannot be answered with finality any more than the entire problem of literary influences admits of final assertions.

However, several things speak against influences of the kind that can be established beyond reasonable doubt. There is first of all Storm's assertion that he never worked (intentionally!) from literary models.

> Es ist dies alles unwillkürlich bei mir gewesen. Über die Bücher, welche, aber erst auf der Lübecker Schule, meine Lieblinge waren und entschiedenen Einfluß übten, ist die Pietschsche Biographie zu vergleichen. Es waren vorzugsweise Heines "Buch der Lieder" und Goethes "Faust"; auch Eichendorffs "Dichter und ihre Gesellen", später auch die übrigen Werke Eichendorffs und Mörikes Gedichte. Einen besonderen Einfluß hatte auf der Lübecker Schule auf mich mein unglücklicher Ferdinand Röse, dessen ich in den "Zerstreuten Kapiteln" unter seinem Beinamen Doktor Antonio Wanst gedacht habe; später Theodor Mommsen, mit dem ich in den letzten Jahren meines Studentenlebens zusammenlebte in Kiel.[39]

One is struck both by Storm's firm and forthright denial that he ever employed literary models and by the reference to Röse. For when we consider the company his Lübecker friend keeps here – Heine, Goethe, Eichendorff, Mörike – and the fact that Storm himself mentions elsewhere the two works that make up virtually all of Röse's literary production, the *Märchen Sonnenkind* and a drama, we are obliged to admit the possibility that Röse's fairy tale may have exerted the sort of influence on *Hinzelmeier* which Böhme claims – without Storm having been aware of it.

Another objection to accepting the theory of literary influence is the fact that the *Märchen von den drei Spinnfrauen* is never mentioned in Storm's discussions of his fairy tales. The reason would appear to be obvious. Although it is no slighter a tale than, for example, *Häwelmann*, its authorship was, to Storm's mind, doubly dubious. The fictional narrator of the *Geschichten aus der Tonne*, Claas Räuber, was also a childhood friend; moreover, the tale is a literary *Nacherzählung* whose model is known and variants of which may be found in Grimm et al. And originality, we have shown, is so important to Storm that he feels called upon to stress it repeatedly in his comments on the fairy tales and even to point out inconsequential borrowings from other writers. His failure to do either for *Hinzelmeier* leaves us at the mercy of those who have established, *unstreitig* or otherwise, influences without offering at the same time the analysis so necessary to critical conjecture. It is unfortunate that Storm had so little to say about *Hinzelmeier* and that the *Sonnenkind* is available only in "verkrüppelter" form; but we should not for this reason permit ourselves the luxury of speculation based on inadequate or missing evidence. We may attempt here briefly a verification of Böhme's assertion and Botzong's supposition by examining Röse's *Sonnenkind* and Andersen's *Schneekönigin*.

The first of these, which has been deservedly forgotten, relates the various adventures of the dwarf Aipok in his attempt to break the spell cast on him by an evil spirit and to win the *Sonnenkind*. We may note some points of similarity to *Hinzelmeier*. There is the *Märchen* hero's goal: to win a spirit (i.e., not merely earthly) creature by performing certain tasks. Jakob Vielanz, alias Dr. Retla Aipok, is told that it is a "schwere, gefährliche Prüfung für einen Menschen, sich einem Sonnenkinde zu verbinden – so haben höhere Mächte es doch so gefügt."[40] He may remain with the *Sonnenkind* seven times seven minutes, but then he must go out into the world and return only when he has found the two most important things "zum Heil der Menschheit" (p. 60). Additionally, he must wander seven times seven months through the world "ohne Deinem Sonnenkinde in Gedanken, Worten und Werken untreu zu werden!" (p. 61)

> Die Dinge, welche Jakob auffinden soll, sind das Traumtyp und die Niesmaschine. Wenn ein Mensch beide besitzt und die Sonne küßt, so kann er die Welt glücklich machen (p. 61).

This three-fold task is of course more in keeping with the European fairy tale than Hinzelmeier's half-conscious quest to find the *Rosenjungfrau* or his fruitless search for the philosopher's stone. But the tedious description of Aipok's adventures, the numerous irrelevant asides (in the form of episodes and the author's excursions into contemporary satire), and the complex plot remove the tale from the region of either *Volks-* or *Kunstmärchen* and place it within the continuing tradition of 17th and 18th century *Schelmen-* and *Barockromane*.

A second point of similarity may be said to lie in the idea behind both tales. Eternal youth and beauty, and behind these the attainment of happiness, are the heritage which Hinzelmeier has but to deserve, that is, to earn anew. Jakob's reward depends on a rigidly gradated series of steps or tasks.

> Wenn er diese [die Sonne] küßt, ist die schwierigste Aufgabe der Bannlösung vollbracht, und wird er seine eigenthümliche Gestalt wieder erhalten, und das Sonnenkind wird sich ihm auf Erden nähern. Eigentlich sollte er aber die andere Aufgabe der Bannlösung vorher vollbringen, welche darin besteht, ein wahrer Magister der Weltweisheit zu werden, d.h., im Besitz des Traumtyps, und der Niesmaschine zugleich zu sein. Versteht er, mit der einen die Träume der Menschen zu fixiren, und mit der andern, ihnen ihre Irrthümer zu nehmen, so kann, und wird ihm keine Universitas Literaria das Diplom verweigern. Die Niesmaschine sichert nämlich, indem sie die Irrthümer beseitigt, das irdische Glück. – Das Ewige, Jenseitige, lebt jetzt leider ja nur als Traum in so Vielen. – Nur wenn Beide in Einer Hand sind, können sie dem Menschen frommen, dann typt das Traumtyp auch Wachgedanken. Hat Jemand Eine von Beiden allein, so verliert er sich entweder so weit auf die Irrthümerjagd, bis ihm die Wahrheit selbst zum Irrthume wird, oder er wird ganz von dem Traum des Ewigen befangen, bis er die Erde nicht mehr beachtet, und dann auch Träume, welche durch Irdisches eingegeben sind, für Bilder des Ewigen hält, bis er endlich nur Irdisches träumt (p.p. 76-77).

What emerges from this interminable and contrived account is that Röse's hero is searching for the golden mean, the happy balance between *Geist* and *Leben*. But it is precisely here, where the point of the tale is explained, that Storm departs from the supposed model. The master's learning, the green spectacles, and altogether the quest for the philosopher's stone are of no avail; indeed, they represent in symbolic form the real impediment to human happiness and self-fulfillment. To Aipok, on the other hand, the instruments of happiness are so vital that they are made into specific stages or tasks on the way to fulfillment and are explicitly explained as such. Earlier in the tale the master explains to Jakob why he has been favored by the powers despite the fact that the *Sonnenkind* had already been promised to Krepander, "der Geist der Dämmerung:"

> Den Meister Tannhäuser hatte Krepander für seine Verbindung mit dem Sonnenkinde gewonnen, weil allerdings Sonnenkinder nur in der Ehe mit andern Sonnen- oder auch Feen-Kindern beständiges Glück haben.Diese, beiderseits Geister-Ehen, sind aber eben so langweilig und fruchtlos, wie überhaupt alles nur Geistige und alles *ununterbrochene* Glück auf Erden (p. 62).

Nothing could be further from the spirit of *Hinzelmeier* than this commitment to a kind of Voltairian rationalism, for whereas Hinzelmeier's parents are a perfect example of "ununterbrochenes Glück auf Erden," Jakob is given his chance to win the *Sonnenkind* because of that very danger. Thus the "Gegensatz von Erkenntnis und Leben," as Stuckert would have it, is common to both tales only insofar as the one offers an illustration of *Gegensatz* and the other a refutation of it. When Stuckert goes on to say of *Das Sonnenkind* that "das unmittelbare Glück des Lebens versäumt [wird],"[41] it becomes difficult to believe that he was directly acquainted with the tale.

Other reminiscences of the *Sonnenkind* in *Hinzelmeier* might be seen in the role the devil plays (although Krepander is not actually the devil but, as the spirit of darkness, a mere relative), the prominent position of the *Wirtshaus* in both stories, the early encounter with the heroine and the long quest that follows, the role of the pretty *Wirtstochter*, and the wise master. At bottom, however, these do not add up to a convincing argument for borrowing; and the differences are both too numerous and too fundamental to be overlooked in the search for similarities. The hero of the *Sonnenkind* is a misshapen dwarf who must regain his true form before winning Eveline; Hinzelmeier has only the problem (a graver one, admittedly, but much less *märchenhaft*) of finding his true identity. Aipok, furthermore, is a simple *Erdenkind* who can be wedded to a spirit being and thus form, symbolically, a union based on the eternal and the earthly; Hinzelmeier is one of the chosen race who has but to recognize his true function – and this in no way involves a reconciliation and fusion of *Geist* and *Leben*. Aipok, finally, is successful in his quest while Hinzelmeier fails and condemns himself to death and his *Rosenjungfrau* to eternal captivity.

One more character should be mentioned as a possible *Anreger* for Hinzelmeier. Hans Fideldum, with whom the tale opens, is a happy-go-lucky musician who discovers Aipok and persuades him to tell his story. As the fairy tale progresses, he becomes involved in some of the adventures, helps bring about the happy ending, and wins for himself the innkeeper's daughter. He is in no way problematic, however, and basically the *Sonnenkind* is not his story but Aipok's. His resemblance to Hinzelmeier is hence a superficial one at best.

The similarities we have been able to establish do not in our estimation merit serious consideration as literary influences. And if it cannot be said that any of the persons or events in Röse's fairy tale affected *Hinzelmeier* in any deeper sense, the other major "influence," Andersen's *Die Schneekönigin*, must be regarded as an even less likely candidate. In this well-known and more accessible fairy tale, two things in particular strike one as possible forebears to events and objects in *Hinzelmeier*. As Botzong says, the *Spiegelsplitter*, especially the one that flew into Kay's eye, may have been the source of Storm's *Brille*.[42] Also, Kay's "Eisspiel des Verstandes" in the Snow Queen's palace is a general analogue to the quest for the philosopher's stone. But here too it is difficult to speak of direct influence. Beyond these two examples, one a rather arresting parallel and the other a faint echo, we must look rather hard for eligible sources. There is, for example, the inserted *Märchen* which the *Winde* tells Gerda and in which a certain resemblance may be seen to the rose garden in *Stein und Rose*:

> Hinaus über den schmalen Feldweg hängt eine alte Ritterburg. Dichtes Immergrün rankt sich um die alten roten Mauern in die Höhe, Blatt an Blatt, über den Altan hin, und auf demselben steht ein schönes Mädchen. Sie beugt sich über das Geländer und schaut auf den Weg hinunter.[43]

But this is, after all, another variant to the widespread fairy tale motif of the "Rettungswerk des Helden"[44] and the imprisoned heroine (cf. *Waberlohe, Dornhecke, Turm, Schloß*, etc.) and hence may result from broad familiarity with the *Volksmärchen* rather than direct borrowing. Other minor resemblances – a crow or raven, the devil, the roses and their connection to the heroine, the bankruptcy of intellect (the glass splinters in Kay's eye and heart made him *verständig*) – do not diminish the fundamental difference either in the point of the two fairy tales or in Storm's highly personal and un-fairy tale ending. It seems fair to conclude from these examples that neither of Hinzelmeier's alleged *Anreger* offers convincing evidence that Storm's literary debt is any but the slightest. Doubtless he was as well acquainted with Andersen's fairy tale as with *Das Sonnenkind*, but familiarity alone was apparently not enough to counteract the forces which shaped Hinzelmeier. We may return to the question of Storm's failure to remain within the general limits of the fairy tale – a failure which, we have seen, prompted both author and his critics to regard the work as highly problematic.

IV

Reduced to a general formula, the European fairy tale is the "geschlossene Bewältigung der Welt in erzählerischer Weise,"[45] a description that fits both "novellenartige" and magic fairy tales, and both *Volks-* and *Kunstmärchen*. Common to most of its types is the element of the marvelous ("das Märchen stellt sich also einer Welt der 'Wirklichkeit' gegenüber"[46]) and a basic structure which is followed with striking consistency. The first of these, "das Wunderbare," usually excludes the figure of the hero – that is to say, he moves in and out of marvelous episodes (sometimes reacting to them with the astonishment of ordinary mortals) without altering his identity as a non-magical being. The episodes themselves depict an initial difficulty or difficulties and the struggle to overcome them. Thus one may speak of an unhappy beginning and a happy ending, with a series of forward steps and "tragische Hemmungen" in between.[47]

While it cannot be said that a fairy tale's "authenticity" is measurable solely by the degree to which it holds to general characteristics of the genre as a whole, we may nevertheless demand that a *Märchen* give us what Andrè Jolles calls a "moralische Befriedigung."[48] The happy ending is thus an ethical conclusion ("ethischer Schluß"), which cannot be violated without destroying the basic premises on which the fairy tale rests. Using Cinderella as an example, Jolles explains that the actual evil in the antagonists (stepmother and sisters) is given less importance than our feeling of injustice at Cinderella's situation. Our satisfaction, he goes on to say, arises

> nicht so sehr dadurch, daß ein fleißiges, gehorsames, geduldiges Mädchen belohnt wird, als daraus, daß das ganze Geschehen der Erwartung und den Anforderungen, die wir an einen gerechten Lauf der Welt stellen, entspricht.
> Diese Erwartung, wie es eigentlich in der Welt zugehen müßte, scheint uns nun für die Form Märchen maßgebend zu sein.[49]

Since reality or the world outside the fairy tale rarely satisfies our sense of justice or corresponds to the "Ethik des Geschehens," it is rejected as being tragic. Jolles' definition of tragedy as it applies to the *Märchen* may be quoted here:

> Tragisch... ist: wenn sein muß, was nicht sein kann, oder: wenn nicht sein kann, was sein muß. Tragisch, so können wir sagen, ist der Widerstand zwischen einer naiv unmoralisch empfundenen Welt und unsren naiv ethischen Anforderungen an das Geschehen.[50]

It is scarcely necessary to search through fairy tale collections for exceptions to Jolles' *Märchen* as "einfache Form." They exist in considerable number, especially among the *Kunstmärchen*, but the point is that such exceptions ought to be regarded as violations and, to this degree, hybrid forms that deserve a special designation. This is true of *Hinzelmeier*, in contrast to its predecessors (*Sonnenkind, Schneekönigin, Hyazinth und Rosenblüth*, etc.) or, indeed, to most of Storm's other fairy tales. It has been pointed out that of the

Drei Märchen only the *Regentrude* bears the "Gepräge eines Märchens," while the others are more properly classified as *Erzählungen*. Thus it might be appropiate to ask which of Storm's fairy tales really qualify as such. From a formal standpoint, only *Regentrude* and *Hans Bär* can be called true fairy tales; the others represent varying degrees of departure from the convention (whereby we take the stand that despite its complexity the *Märchen* is a more rigid and hence more readily definable form than, for example, the Novelle).

If we test these faulty fairy tales as to general structure and ethical outcome (i.e., the achievement of the reader's "moralische Befriedigung"), we discover that only *Hinzelmeier* violates both conditions. *Bulemann*, for example, has neither a hero nor the task-resolution sequence. In fact, except for the monstrous cats there is little in the tale to remind us of *Märchenwelt*. Yet it resolves its central problem (greed) in fairy tale fashion and in a manner thoroughly satisfactory to our moral sense of what must be: "So sitzt er noch jetzt ["seit Menschengedenken" or even longer] und erwartet die Barmherzigkeit Gottes." And *Cyprianus*, another study in evil, owes its happy ending to the proper use – and "proper" involves here the human virtue of love – of the tale's sole bit of magic, the mirror.

Hinzelmeier, on the other hand, cannot give us this one satisfaction. Though it shows a greater number of fairy tale characteristics, its premises are basically anti-*Märchen* and its hero marked for failure. A comparison of some of its incidents with those in Storm's "genuine" fairy tales should illustrate the point more clearly. *Hans Bär* is stolen from his poor parents and brought up in captivity by a large bear. The beautiful *Dienstmädchen* in the *Märchen von den drei Spinnfrauen* can sew and knit but she cannot weave – and her rich young suitor happens to be "gewaltig aufs Spinnrad versessen." The Wiesenbauer's daughter cannot marry Andrees unless they can make it rain within twenty-four hours. (This is but half the problem; the other is the catastrophic drought that is ruining the crops). *Hinzelmeier*, on the other hand, enjoys an idyllic childhood, spends two years with a wise man, and never suffers a setback until the story is well over half told.

Hans Bär escapes his prison cave, returns to his parents, spends some time as *Holzknecht* (his master attempts to have him killed), fights a giant, wins a princess and a kingdom, and reigns "noch viele Jahre mit seiner schönen Gemahlin glücklich und in Frieden." The *Dienstmädchen* solves her increasingly difficult tasks of presenting her suitor with woven cloth by calling on the old *Spinnfrauen* for help. The old women appear at the wedding; when the groom asks them about their ugliness (long nose, obesity, broad lips) they attribute it to too much weaving, whereupon the groom secretly destroys the spinning wheel. "Als die Hochzeit vorüber war, lebten sie ohne Spinnrad in Glück und Frieden..." Young Andrees outwits the *Feuermann* and the young couple is able to find the *Regentrude*, whose rain ends the drought and makes the wedding possible. But Hinzelmeier is not only unable to make use of the help given him to perform his task; the aid itself proves to be a negative force and the (external) cause for his failure. His death represents the defeat of an ideal and of the good power in the tale.

Hinzelmeier is thus a total reversal of the success story common to these other fairy tales. The typical sequence of *Notlage-Aufgaben-Bewältigung* or, in Jolles' formulation, "tragischer Anfang, Fortschreiten in der Richtung der Gerechtigkeit, tragische Hemmungen, ethischer Schluß"[51] is made to read: successful (idyllic) beginning, progression away from "gerechtes Geschehen," tragicomic retardation, tragic ending. The implications of this reversal offer us the best clue as to why *Hinzelmeier* is problematic whereas *Bulemann*, for example, is not. Except for the magic of metamorphosis and Bulemann's longevity, the latter tale does not take place in a fairy tale world at all. The moral satisfaction we derive from Bulemann's fate is an extension of our judgement from reality into the alleged irreality of the fairy tale world. The effect of such an extension is the loss of the latter's validity, for if we have no need to "rescue" our opinion of Bulemann and our verdict on his fate by granting them a place in the anti-reality of the fairy tale world we admit that reality and fairy tale are not separate and hence not in conflict with each other. We simply have no cause to remove a villain from reality in order to have him meet his just deserts in a *Märchen*.

But Hinzelmeier is neither a Bulemann nor a non-hero; we should therefore expect him to experience a different fate from what would surely be his lot in reality. His failure to act according to the principles of the fairy tale brings about a rearrangement of the *Märchenstruktur* as illustrated above. Or, to put it another way, the norms by which he is judged are borrowed from a sphere inimical to the fairy tale. When the forces of evil (raven and glasses must be regarded as such) vanquish the forces of good (Hinzelmeier's heritage and the rose maiden) and bring about tragedy, grave doubts are raised as to the validity of Hinzelmeier's world. In a word, Storm has inadvertently rejected the fairy tale while continuing to use it. For if the problem of man's quest for true identity (his "eigener Ton") and happiness can be solved at all, it must be solved positively or else given another form. In 1850 Storm was apparently unable to see the utter incompatibility – though he certainly sensed it, as his correspondence shows – between the form and the content of his subject.

We are well acquainted with Hinzelmeier's character from our examination of other works of the period. For example, we need to stretch the point only slightly to see in Hinzelmeier a disguised exemplar of Reinhard. Both lives move from the idyllic to the tragic; both incur a kind of guilt through omission and a degree of passivity; both fail to perform their real task. It is no coincidence that both heroes see their error in the end: Reinhard (who is but the first of many such figures in Storm's Novellen) must look back into the past. "Hinter jenen blauen Bergen liegt unsere Jugend. Wo ist sie geblieben?" And Hinzelmeier sees his *Rosenjungfrau* on the distant edge of the bleak plain he has just crossed. We have commented on the partial disenchantment of Hinzelmeier's world. When we recall the way in which "das Wunderbare" is treated – the stone is a cheese, the devil a naive fool who affords a comic interlude, the flying pancakes irrelevant, and Hinzelmeier's heritage a magical remnant that possesses power only when earned in a mortal way –, we are tempted to call *Hinzelmeier* a Biedermeier *Erzählung* in an unfortunate disguise. If tragedy is found where that which cannot be must be, then *Hinzelmeier* belongs to that group of Novellen we have called incipient tragedies. In the form of the fairy tale it contradicts the principles of that genre and thus deserves the problematic view its author had of it. As an early Novelle or *Erzählung* it deserves no such criticism.

NOTES

PREFACE

[1] Fritz Martini, *Deutsche Literatur im bürgerlichen Realismus. 1848-1898* (Stuttgart, 1962), p. 637.
[2] Th. Storm, *Eine zurückgezogene Vorrede aus dem Jahre 1881.* Reprinted in *Theodor Storm. Werke. Gesamtausgabe in drei Bänden*, hrsg. u. eingel. v. Hermann Engelhard, (Stuttgart, 1959), Vol. III, p. 524.

CHAPTER ONE

[1] *Marthe und ihre Uhr* (1847), *Im Saal* (1848), *Posthuma* (1849), and *Immensee* (1849). Of these works, only *Posthuma* was not published first in the *Volksbuch*.
[2] Reprinted in *Theodor Storm. Werke. Gesamtausgabe in drei Bänden*, hrsg. u. eingel. v. Hermann Engelhard, (Stuttgart, 1959). Vol. III, pp. 499-500.
[3] *Theodor Storm, Briefe an seine Freunde* (hrsg. Gertrud Storm), Braunschweig, 1917), p. 5.
[4] A frequently cited remark by Storm to Emil Kuh, "Ich arbeite übrigens meist auf Lappen und schreibe danach das Ganze zusammen," has supplied some critics with a kind of *apologia* for Storm's numerous partitions. Eichentopf, for example, concludes from this "eine derartige Arbeitsweise konnte nicht ohne Einfluß auf die Komposition der Handlung bleiben; sie gibt für die... eigentümliche Technik der Aneinanderreihung eine neue, befriedigende Erklärung," thereby disregarding both the stress Storm himself consciously placed on *einzelne Momente* and the fact that preliminary and hence piecemeal segments of a work do not in themselves explain literary technique in the finished work. Eichentopf himself remarks elsewhere that Storm subjected a number of his works to intensive revision! (Hans Eichentopf, *Th. Storms Erzählungskunst in ihrer Entwicklung*, Diss. Marburg, 1908. Also printed in *Beiträge zur dt. Lit.-Wissenschaft*, No. 11.; see pp. 43-46).
[5] "Lyrische Novellen," perhaps the earliest and most common of these labels, is retained by Johannes Klein (*Gesch. der dt. Novelle*, 4th Ed., Wiesbaden, 1960, p. 266 *et seq.*); the less common "Novellen der Liebesbeziehung" is used by Fritz Lockemann, (*Gestalt und Wandlungen der deutschen Novelle*, München, 1957, p. 154 *et seq.*) The other terms may be found in virtually all of the literary histories or essays dealing with this writer. Erich Schmidt, for example, calls Storm's early Novellen "Resignationspoesie" (*Charakteristiken* I, Berlin, 1902, p. 407).
[6] Franz Stuckert, *Theodor Storm* (Bremen, 1955), p. 240.
[7] Cf. Paul Kluckhohn's comment on the Biedermeier Novelle: "Bevorzugte Er-

zählungsform ist ganz allgemein die Novelle, die man geradezu die Modegattung jener Zeit nennen kann... Nun entspricht freilich nur ein Teil der Biedermeiernovellen den Forderungen der reinen Novellenform. Die meisten sind mehr Zustandsnovellen als Darstellungen unerhörter Begebenheiten, oder auch 'Studien,' wie Stifter seine bekanntesten Erzählungsbände genannt hat." ("Biedermeier als literarische Epochenbezeichnung," *Deutsche Vierteljahrschrift* 13 (1935), p. 28).

[8] Cf. Fritz Böhme, "Nach einem im Nachlaß Storms befindlichen Heft mit der Aufschrift: Immensee. Der erste Druck nebst der Umarbeitung für die 'Sommergeschichten und Lieder' hat Tycho Mommsen sie mit sehr scharfen Glossen versehen: 'Lebende Bilder,' 'tote Kunst,' 'Die Katze, die der Jäger schoß, macht nie der Koch zum Hasen' und neben den Schlußabsatz 'Da haben wir des Pudels Kern, eitel Prosa!'" (*Storms Werke*, Leipzig, 1935, vol. 9, p. 183).

[9] Biernatzki's *Volksbuch auf das Jahr 1850 für die Herzogthümer Schleswig, Holstein und Lauenburg*, pp. 56-86. I am indebted to the Dartmouth College Library for procuring for me a microfilm of the complete Biernatzki version.

[10] Both the Böhme edition of Storm's works and the Morgan-Wooley textbook edition of *Immensee* (1927 edition) do, however, give the major variants discussed in this chapter. See Böhme, vol. 9, pp. 185-90; Morgan-Wooley, pp. 130-39.

[11] The *Häuschen* in an earlier chapter (*Die Kinder*) serves the same end. We note that Elizabeth will go to India with Reinhard only if her mother permits. Also, the idyll is interrupted when the parents call them home. Both actions are symbolic of the children's inability to act for themselves and to withstand the pressure exerted on them from outside.

[12] Lockeman, p. 157.

[13] Cf. Eichentopf, *op. cit.*, p. 45: "Aber der Verfasser ist in dem Bestreben, nur die Hauptsituationen vorzutragen, zu weit gegangen, was für manchen Leser ein Stein des Anstoßes geworden ist. Der Sprung von dem Kapitel 'Im Walde' zu dem nächsten 'Da stand das Kind am Wege' ist zu unvermittelt."

[14] The standard version offers this addition to the *Immensee* chapter: "Er hatte seit Jahren, wo er deren habhaft werden konnte, die im Volke lebenden Reime und Lieder gesammelt, und ging nun daran, seinen Schatz zu ordnen und wo möglich mit neuen Aufzeichnungen aus der Umgegend zu vermehren." (Engelhard, vol. 1, p. 271; Böhme 1, 269).

[15] For a detailed discussion of lyric insertions in Storm's prose, see Rolf Lenhartz, *Die lyrische Einlage bei Theodor Storm*, Mnemosyne 14 (1933). Cf. esp. pp. 98-99: "Die Gedichte in 'Immensee' sind so sehr in das Geschehen verwoben, daß sie allein, in ihrer Reihenfolge betrachtet, die ganze Novelle wiedergeben können.

    Hier an der Bergeshalde
    Heute, nur heute bin ich so schön
    Er wäre fast verirrt
    Meine Mutter hat's gewollt
    Sterben, ach sterben soll ich allein

sind die lyrischen, aber novellenwichtigen Zentren des Geschehens, alle gruppiert um das Hauptlied 'Meine Mutter hat's gewollt'."

[16] A recent study sees this entire scene as sexual imagery. "The night is 'schwül' when Reinhard feels the irresistible urge to swim out to the white water-lily. He throws off his clothes and wades into the water. Suddenly he is engulfed ('Die Wasser quirlten über ihm zusammen'). The atmosphere hints at all the sinful, sensual thoughts that hang unspoken about *Immensee*. The whole description of the attempt to reach the water-lily suggests enmeshment in a dark web of sin:

> Zugleich aber fühlte er sich wie in einem Netz verstrickt; die glatten Stengel langten vom Grunde herauf und rankten sich an seine nackten Glieder. Das unbekannte Wasser lag so schwarz um ihn her...; es wurde ihm plötzlich so unheimlich in dem fremden Element.

When he manages to tear himself free, he looks back from the shore at the inaccessible white lily, still – 'wie zuvor fein und einsam über der dunklen Tiefe.' But though he has escaped from the weeds he has not escaped from the dangers which they represent, for it is again 'schwarz' and 'schwül' when he is alone with Elizabeth in the boat later and the atmosphere is electric." M. A. McHaffie and J. M. Ritchie, "Bee's Lake, Or the Curse of Silence. A Study of Theodor Storm's *Immensee*," *German Life and Letters* New Series XVI (1962), no. 1, pp. 36-48. As the authors rightly admit, such an interpretation places us on highly problematic ground. Perhaps it is safer to speak, as we do, of Reinhard's inability to grasp happiness. But there is nothing in the story which would deny validity to this more arresting and original view.

Another very recent study of *Immensee* (Robert Ulshöfer, "Epische Situation und symbolisches Ereignis in der Prosadichtung. Dargestellt an Storms "Immensee'," *Der Deutschunterricht* (1956) H. 3, pp. 37-45) offers the more conventional view of this scene: "Reinhards ganzes Leben stellt sich dar in dem vergeblichen Bemühen um die Wasserlilie. Bis in die Satzkonstruktion und Wortwahl hinein ist diese Schilderung von symbolischer Bedeutung:

> Dann war es plötzlich unter ihm weg, die Wasser quirlten über ihm zusammen... Er gab indes sein Unternehmen nicht auf... zugleich aber fühlte er sich wie in einem Netze verstrickt... Als er von hier auf den See zurückblickte, lag die Lilie wie zuvor fern und einsam über der dunklen Tiefe.

Früher war Elisabeth Waldeskönigin, jetzt ist die Wasserlilie, unerreichbar, fern, einsam, unberührt" (p. 44).

[17] *Charakteristiken* I, p. 406.

[18] Cf. F. Stuckert, "Theodor Storms Novellistische Form," *Germanisch-Romanische Monatsschrift* 27 (1939), p. 26.

[19] Cf. E. Max Bräm, *Geschichte der dt. Literatur* (Bern, 1943), vol. III, p. 46.

[20] Klein, *op. cit.*, p. 266.

CHAPTER TWO

[1] Cf. Franz Stuckert, *Theodor Storm* (Bremen, 1955), p. 230.
[2] Theodor Fontane, "Der Tunnel über der Spree. Aus dem Berliner literarischen Leben der vierziger und fünfziger Jahre," *Deutsche Rundschau* LXXXVII (1896), p. 223.
[3] *Storms Werke* 9, p. 155-56.
[4] Th. Storm, *Briefe an seine Kinder* (published as vol. 11 in Th. Storm's *Sämtliche Werke*, ed. by Gertrud Storm; Braunschweig, 1916), p. 104. The letter is dated January 17, 1870. Cf. also Stuckert, *op. cit.* p. 479 (note 13).
[5] R. M. Browning, "Association and Disassociation in Storm's Novellen," *PMLA* XLVI (1951), p. 387: "In its protoform this story is related in the collection of ghost-stories called *Am Kamin* as is proved by many details of significant correspondence with *Auf dem Staatshof*."
[6] Stuckert, *op. cit.* p. 235.
[7] Cf. Gertrud Storm, *Theodor Storm. Ein Bild seines Lebens* (Berlin, 1913), p. 69.
[8] Stuckert is of a different opinion. Referring to the "typische Haltung des historischen Erzählers," he explains "nur scheinbar gleicht diese Darstellungsform der Technik der früheren Erinnerungsnovellen" (*op. cit.*, p. 261).
[9] Browning's study (*op. cit.*) represents the best and most recent attempt to evaluate the question of Storm's relation to his works through devices that concern narrative point of view.
[10] Johannes Klein, *Geschichte der deutschen Novelle* (Wiesbaden, 1954), p. 273.
[11] Fritz Lockemann, *Gestalt und Wandlungen der deutschen Novelle* (München, 1957), p. 159.
[12] Klein, *op. cit.*, p. 273.
[13] Cf. Walter Reitz, *Die Landschaft in Storms Novellen* (Diss. Bern, 1913), p. 43.
[14] With the exception of the five-line opening, which is so separated. But these lines, we have seen, apply to the entire story and may be regarded as its prologue.
[15] Cf. pp. 68 & 73 above.

CHAPTER THREE

[1] "Alle diese Resignationsnovellen von 'Immensee' bis zur 'Halligfahrt' (1870) [1871] hin stammen ihrer inneren Haltung nach aus der "windstillen" Zeit des Vormärz, man könnte mit einem neu eingeführten literarischen Begriff auch sagen, des "Biedermeier", dem Storm seine entscheidenden Jugendeindrücke und seine Bildung verdankte." Franz Stuckert, "Idyllik und Tragik in der Dichtung Theodor Storms," *Deutsche Vierteljahrsschrift* 15 (1937), p. 518.
[2] The list of 29 includes both the *Erstlingswerk Hans Bär* (1837) and the *Märchen*. For a complete list of Storm's prose fiction see page viii. The fact that only three stories are directly concerned with death becomes all the more striking when we consider that "death or the dead appear in forty-two of the fifty-eight Novellen

contained in Albert Köster's edition of Storm's works." Frederic E. Coenen, "Death in Theodor Storm's Novellen," PMLA, 64 (1949), p. 341. See also p. 97 above.
3 Th. Storm, *Briefe an seine Frau*, ed. by Gertrud Storm, Braunschweig 1915, p. 124f. For a discussion of *Im Korn*, see Fritz Böhme, "Ein unbekannter Novellenplan Theodor Storms," *Lit. Echo* 18 (1915/16), pp. 644-47; also F. Stuckert, *Theodor Storm* (Bremen, 1955), p. 277, and Thea Müller, *Theodor Storms Erzählung "Aquis Submersus"* (Beiträge zur dt. Literaturwissenschaft 26, Marburg, 1925), p. 24ff.
4 *Briefe an seine Frau*, June 28, 1862 (p. 124f.)
5 *Op. cit.* p. 126.
6 *Böhme*, p. 647.
7 F. Stuckert, *Theodor Storm*, p. 277.
8 Gertrud Storm, *Th. Storm. Ein Bild seines Lebens* (Berlin, 1913), vol. 2, p. 81.
9 Stuckert, *op. cit.* p. 481.
10 *Briefe an seine Frau*, p. 125.
11 Gertrud Storm, *op. cit.* vol. 2, p. 176.
12 *Ibid.* p. 175-76.
13 F. Stuckert, *Idyllik und Tragik...* p. 512.
14 *Ibid.* p. 536ff.
15 Th. Storm, *Briefe an seine Freunde*, ed. by Gertrud Storm, Braunschweig, 1917, p. 98 (Letter to Hartmuth Brinkmann dated Easter 1863).
16 R. M. Meyer, *Die dt. Litteratur des Neunzehnten Jahrhunderts* (Berlin, 1900), p. 488.
17 *Briefe an seine Freunde*, p. 99.
18 Paul Schütze, *Theodor Storm. Sein Leben und seine Dichtung* (Berlin, 1907), p. 155.
19 Fritz Lockemann, *Gestalt und Wandlungen der deutschen Novelle* (München, 1957), p. 160.
20 Johannes Klein, *Geschichte der deutschen Novelle* (Wiesbaden, 1960), p. 274.
21 *Ibid.* p. 233.
22 Schütze, *op. cit.* p. 155-56.
23 To Storm at least this is true. As indicated above, however, (p. 82) Storm's emphasis on social forces at the expense of guilt is not a totally satisfactory explanation of the tragic outcome.
24 It would be interesting to trace in greater detail the gradual change in Lore's 'color' as it is revealed in Storm's adjectives. On seeing Lore again after a number of years, Philipp notes that "unter den braunen Wangen schimmerte das Rot der vollsten Jungfräulichkeit," and as she sits on the *Raugraf*'s horse she becomes "blaß... wie der Tod." When Lore hears the false report about her fiancé, she turns "kreideweiß," and when Philipp sees her at the *Waldhaus* he is shocked to see that "kein Rot schimmerte mehr durch diese zarten blassen Wangen." Finally, her face in death is "das bleiche Gesichtchen." Its pallor seems a symbolic equation to the "blasser vornehmer Student" whose victim she had become and to the world of the *Waldhaus* with its "blasser Kellner," its "milchbärtiger Junge," etc.
25 *Theodor Storm*, p. 275.

[26] For the distinction between the tragedy of feelings or emotions and the tragedy of spirit I am indebted to Erich Heller's essay on "Goethe and the Avoidance of Tragedy," published in the collection *The Disinherited Mind* (Cambridge, 1952). See esp. p. 47f. In this essay Heller speaks of "emotions in disarray."
[27] Coenen, *op. cit.* p. 349. See also footnote 2 above.
[28] P. 349.
[29] Bernhard Bruch, "Novelle und Tragödie: Zwei Kunstformen und Weltanschauungen," *Zeitschrift für Ästhetik und allgemeine Kunstwissenschaft* 22 (1928), pp. 292-330. See esp. pp. 301-313.

CHAPTER FOUR

[1] Cf. R. M. Browning, "Association and Disassociation in Storm's Novellen," *PMLA*, 66 (1951), p. 400. Also, Rudolf Buck ("Theodor Storm: 'Aquis Submersus'," *Der Deutschunterricht* (1953) H. 1, pp. 92-107), considers the frame's relation to the story. In a short section of his study entitled "Sinn und Symbolik des Rahmens" he reviews the locale of the frame and arrives at this conclusion: "Schauernd blickt der Dichter, und das ist neben der Erregung der Spannung der hauptsächliche Sinn der Rahmenhandlung, in die Vergangenheit, die stufenweise immer weitere, eisigere Räume öffnet; er muß mit ansehen, wie das eigene Leben unaufhaltsam und unwiederbringlich in dieses Verrinnen hineingeschlungen wird. Jede noch so schöne Gegenwart ist in sich schon bedroht. Es handelt sich hier um ein Grunderlebnis Storms. Der ganz persönliche und lokale Ausgangspunkt der Rahmenhandlung vom Dichter aus wird uns damit klar. Erst durch diesen persönlichen Bezug bekommt der zeitliche Ablauf seine Bitterkeit, erst dadurch wird er aber auch anschaulich und dichterisch gestaltbar" (p. 94).
[2] Hans Bracher, *Rahmenerzählung und Verwandtes bei G. Keller, C. F. Meyer und Th. Storm*, (Hássel, 1909), p. 122.
[3] Ernst Feise, "Theodor Storms *Aquis Submersus*," in *Xenien: Essays in the History of German Literature* (Baltimore, 1950), p. 226.
[4] Walter Brecht, "Storm und die Geschichte," *Deutsche Vierteljahrschrift* III (1925), pp. 446-47.
[5] To this list Feise (*op. cit.*, p. 227) adds the "bemooste Strohdach" and a number of expressions such as "Vergangenheit," "die Jahre gingen hin," etc.
[6] The other is the series of paintings, discussed in part three of this chapter. It would be worthwhile to examine closely the numerous references to water in the Novelle and attempt to determine whether a meaningful pattern exists, and above all if a role similar to that assigned to paintings may be given to this element as well. A preliminary listing of occurrences strongly suggests such a role:
(a) "das ausgetrocknete Bett des Fischteiches (in the *Schloßgarten* of the narrator's home town;

(b) the *Priesterkoppel* ("Hauptschauplatz unserer Taten"), which holds the "gefährliche Wassergrube";
(c) the CPAS portrait of the boy holding the waterlily;
(d) daughter of the *Edelfrau* drowned in the Gartenteich ("es wachsen noch Schachtelhalm und Binsen aus dem Boden");
(e) Johannes stumbles into the same *Binsensumpf*;
(f) Johannes sees the *Meeresstrand* and is told of the destructive flood;
(g) the reunion on the *Priesterkoppel* near the pond (Johannes had seen Katherina earlier; and shortly before their confrontation he suspects the presence of a *Wassergrube* on the *Koppel*;
(h) Johannes' reason for painting the waterlily;
(i) his own sense of *Schuld*: "sie hat uns alle in die schwarze Flut hinabgerissen;"
(j) "die tosende Brandung... tönte aquis submersus."

[7] Feise (*op. cit.*, p. 227) remarks that the word *alt* occurs no less than 18 times in the eight-page frame.
[8] Cf. chapter two, pp. 48ff.
[9] Franz Stuckert, *Theodor Storm* (Bremen, 1955), p. 336.
[10] Feise, p. 227.
[11] Letter to Emil Kuh, dated August 24, 1876. In: Paul R. Kuh, "Briefwechsel zwischen Theodor Storm und Emil Kuh," *Westermanns Monatshefte* 67 (1889-90), pp. 552-53.
[12] Stuckert (*op. cit.*, p. 333) sees in this cry Katherina's desperation at being married to an unloved man. Such a reading strikes me as improbable because her earlier reference to herself as *Sünderin* surely has to do only with her former union with Johannes. Moreover, her attempts to keep Johannes (whom she had recognized as her lover even before they had seen each other again) at arm's length and to defend the pastor as one who took in the sinner and loved a child not his own hardly suggest that she feels her body to be *entweiht* through marriage to the pastor. In a word, the sentiment as Stuckert sees it may not be entirely inaccurate, but it is unlikely that she means it in this way.
[13] For a discussion of guilt in *Aquis Submersus*, see chapter three, pp. 82ff.
[14] Despite evident points of similarity, leitmotif and the complex symbol (which may include action as well as object) are distinguishable in one critical respect: the former is itself a kind of structure (*Formgebilde*), it recurs in approximately identical form and is not necessarily restricted to an object; while the latter, although contributing to structure, is first and foremost an object or a complex of actions and objects centering on an object.
[15] Johannes' thoughts or wish-dreams are to betray him again later. As he leaves Katherina's room, escapes from the *Binsensumpf* and wanders toward the village, he envisions the future:

Schon sahe ich uns auf einem fröhlichen Barkschiff die Wellen des grünen Zuidersees befahren, schon hörete ich das Glockenspiel vom Rathhausthurme

Amsterdams und sah am Hafen meine Freunde aus dem Gewühl hervorbrechen und mich und meine schöne Frau mit hellem Zuruf grüßen und im Triumph nach unserem kleinen, aber trauten Heim geleiten.

The incident is a further illustration of the close proximity of happiness and tragedy in the Novelle, and of Johannes' inability to see the dangers before it is too late. One may say, however, that Johannes' optimistic version of the future is often accompanied by self-admonition that keeps him and the story in constant touch with the broad realistic base on which Storm's works are built. A few lines before the passage quoted above Johannes warns himself to face facts:

Ein Häuflein Rehe stund nicht fern im silbergrauen Thau, und über mir vom Himmel scholl das Tageslied der Lerche. Da schüttelte ich all müßig Träumen von mir ab; im selbigen Augenblick stieg aber auch wie heiße Noth die Frage mir ins Hirn: "Was weiter nun, Johannes? Du hast ein theures Leben an dich rissen..."

[16] See p. 117 above.
[17] Johannes is also to paint the burgomaster's portrait, but since it does not merit mention again in the manuscript, we may consider it purely background detail.
[18] See p. 109 above.
[19] Stuckert, p. 333.
[20] Rudolf Buck discusses paintings in his study of *Aquis Submersus* (see note 1 above) but is so concerned with the work's *Grundstimmung* – a result, he feels, of Storm's *Grunderlebnis* – that he is unwilling to go beyond a few generalities. Gerhard's portrait, for example, is the means to create a "Verbindung über die halbe Novelle hinweg," Katherina's portrait "bereitet die Trennung vor" and represents also the *Frist* granted the lovers before separation. Buck concludes:

Wenn wir einen Gesamtblick auf die Gemälde werfen, die in der Novelle von Bedeutung sind, so muß uns auffallen, daß sie fast ausnahmslos in ihren Vorwürfen den Gegensatz von Leben und Tod zum Thema haben. Die Darstellung der Toten überwiegt, und auch auf dem Bilde der Geliebten hebt sich der sinnliche Zauber höchster Weibesschönheit ab von der Folie der Trauer. Die Gemälde und ihre verschiedenartigen Funktionen im Werk sind letzten Endes also auch Sinnbilder für die Grundstimmung, welche in der ganzen Novelle und in Storms Dichtung überhaupt waltet (p. 101).

CHAPTER FIVE

[1] No. 14 in the *Kinder- und Hausmärchen*, no. 409 in Müllenhoff's *Sagen, Lieder und Märchen der Herzogtümer Schleswig-Holstein und Lauenburg* (Kiel, 1845). In the latter collection it is called *Das Märchen von Fru Rumpentrumpen*.
[2] Jehle's assertion, "Zu den Dichtern, denen wir nach der Romantik die schönsten Kunstmärchen verdanken, gehört Theodor Storm," has never been seriously questioned, to my knowledge, and represents a fair reflection of prevalent critical

opinion. (Mimi Ida Jehle, *Das deutsche Kunstmärchen von der Romantik zum Naturalismus*, Illinois Studies in Language and Literature, 19 (Urbana, 1935), p. 158).

[3] In a letter to Hartmuth Brinkmann, dated January 18, 1864. This and subsequent references to the Storm-Brinkmann correspondence are from Theodor Storm, *Briefe an seine Freunde Hartmuth Brinkmann und Wilhelm Petersen* (vol. 12 of Gertrud Storm's edition of the collected works), Braunschweig, 1917.

[4] The Storm-Kuh correspondence was published by Paul Kuh in *Westermanns Monatshefte*, vol. 67 (1890), pp. 99-107; 264-274; 363-378; 541-554. All references are to this edition.

[5] In the "Anmerkungen" to the *Briefe an Friedrich Eggers*, p. 85 (See note 13 below).

[6] In a letter to the Verlag Gebrüder Paetel of February 2, 1873. Cf. Albert Köster's edition of the collected works (Inselverlag, 1924), vol. 8, p. 236. Quoted also by Hertha Botzong, *Wesen und Wert von Theodor Storms Märchendichtung* (Diss. München, 1935), p. 94-95.

[7] In the preface to his *Geschichten aus der Tonne* – 1873.

[8] Jehle, *op. cit.*, p. 184.

[9] Franz Stuckert, *Theodor Storm* (Bremen, 1955), p. 251.

[10] *Ibid.*, p. 282.

[11] *Ibid.*, p. 287.

[12] *Ibid.*, p. 287.

[13] In a letter to Friedrich Eggers, dated January 16, 1856. This and subsequent references to the Storm-Eggers correspondence are from *Theodor Storms Briefe an Friedrich Eggers*, ed. Wolfgang Seidel (Berlin, 1911).

[14] Cf. Fritz Böhme, *Storms Werke* (Leipzig, 1935), vol. 9, pp. 196-97.

[15] *Ibid.*, p. 197.

[16] *Mörike-Storm Briefwechsel*, ed. J. Bächtold (Stuttgart, 1891).

[17] See note 5 above. Cf. also Botzong, p. 47.

[18] Stuckert, p. 253.

[19] J. Wedde, *Theodor Storm* (Hamburg, 1888), p. 29. Also quoted by Jehle, p. 162-63.

[20] Alfred Biese, *Theodor Storm* (3. Auflage, Leipzig, 1921), pp. 179-80; Jehle, p. 163; Botzong, p. 46.

[21] In a letter to Fr. Eggers, January 16, 1856.

[22] Stuckert, p. 252.

[23] *Ibid.*, p. 251.

[24] Botzong, p. 32-33.

[25] Jehle, p. 160-61.

[26] *Stein und Rose. (Ein Mährchen.)* [signature at end: Th. St.] in: *Biernatzki's Volksbuch auf das Jahr 1851 für die Herzogtümer Schleswig, Holstein und Lauenburg*, p. 122. Böhme (vol. 9, pp. 196-205) lists most of the significant differences between this version and the standard one. I am indebted to the Dartmouth College Library for obtaining for me a photocopy of *Stein und Rose*.

[27] *Stein und Rose*, p. 129.

[28] *Ibid.*, p. 129.
[29] Jehle, p. 162.
[30] In a letter to Heyse, August 15, 1887. Quoted by Stuckert, p. 395.
[31] Stuckert, p. 251.
[32] *Ibid.*, p. 252.
[33] *Ibid.*, p. 251.
[34] Böhme, *Storms Werke* 9, pp. 198-99.
[35] Jehle, p. 161.
[36] Todsen, *Über die Entwicklung des romantischen Kunstmärchens* (Diss. Berlin, 1906), p. 115-16.
[37] Botzong, pp. 43-44.
[38] In a letter to Kuh, Dec. 22, 1872.
[39] In a letter to Storm, June 22, 1873. Kuh, who was preparing an essay on Storm, asked his friend five "kecke Fragen," the fifth of which was "Wer waren Ihre poetischen Muster und Lieblinge?" Storm's detailed answer is contained in a letter written in two parts; the first is dated August 13, 1873, the second, from which our quote is taken, August 21, 1873.
[40] *Das Sonnenkind. Ein Mährchen von F. Röse*; in: *Der deutsche Pilger durch die Welt. Ein unterhaltender und lehrreicher Volkskalender für alle Länder deutscher Zunge auf das Jahr 1845*, 4. Jg. Stuttgart. The *Sonnenkind* is found on pp. 57-89. I am indebted to the University of Vienna Library for procuring me a photocopy of this fairy tale. The lines quoted are from page 60; subsequent page numbers are placed in parentheses after the quotation.
[41] Stuckert, p. 251.
[42] Botzong, p. 43f.
[43] *Die Schneekönigin.* In Andersen's *Gesammelte Märchen* (German version, *Goldmanns Gelbe Taschenbücher* 510-511), p. 266-67.
[44] Cf. Max Lüthi, *Es war einmal... Vom Wesen des Volksmärchens* (Göttingen, 1962), p. 37.
[45] *Kleines Literatisches Lexikon*, 3rd edition, ed. by Wolfgang Kayser (Bern, 1961). Entry *Märchen*, p. 151. For a concise summary of various *Märchen* definitions, see Max Lüthi, *Märchen* (Sammlung Metzler 16, Stuttgart, 1962), section "Name und Begriff," pp. 1-14.
[46] André Jolles, *Einfache Formen* (Tübingen, 1930), p. 241.
[47] Jolles, p. 245.
[48] *Ibid.* p. 239.
[49] *Ibid.* p. 240.
[50] *Ibid.* p. 241.
[51] *Ibid.* p. 245.

BIBLIOGRAPHY

Andersen, Hans Christian. *Gesammelte Märchen.* (German version, Goldmanns Gelbe Taschenbücher 510-11).
Arnold, P. J. "Storms Novellenbegriff." *Zeitschrift für Deutschkunde,* 37 (1923), 281-88.
Bernd, Clifford B. "Die gegenwärtige Theodor Storm Forschung. Eine Bibliographie." *Schriften der Theodor-Storm-Gesellschaft,* 3 (1954), 60-79.
Biernatzki, Johann Christoph. (ed.) *Volksbuch auf das Jahr 1850 für die Herzogthümer Schleswig, Holstein und Lauenburg.* Altona, [1849]. Also, *Volksbuch* for 1851.
Biese, Alfred. *Theodor Storm.* Leipzig, 1921 (3rd ed.).
Blankennagel, John C. "Tragic Guilt in Storm's *Schimmelreiter.*" *German Quarterly,* 29 (1952), 170-81.
Böhme, Fritz. "Vergessene Geschichten." *Westermanns Monatshefte,* 89 (1912), 116-22.
- "Ein unbekannter Novellenplan Theodor Storms." *Literarisches Echo,* 18 (1915/16), 644-47.
- *Theodor Storm, Werke.* Nach der von Th. Hertel besorgten Ausgabe, neubearbeitet und ergänzt von Fritz Böhme. Mit einer Vorrede von Hans Friedrich Blunck. Leipzig, 1935. 8 vols.
Böttger, Fritz. *Theodor Storm in seiner Zeit.* Berlin, no date [1958].
Botzong, Hertha. *Wesen und Wert von Theodor Storms Märchendichtung.* Diss. Munich, 1911.
Bracher, Hans. *Rahmenerzählung und Verwandtes bei G. Keller, C. F. Meyer und Th. Storm.* Hässel, 1909.
Brám, E. Max. *Geschichte der deutschen Literatur.* Bern, 1943. 3 vols.
Braun, Frank X. "Theodor Storm's *Doppelgänger.*" Germanic Review, 32 (1957), 267-72.
Brecht, Walter. "Storm und die Geschichte." *Deutsche Vierteljahrschrift,* 3 (1925), 444-62.
Browning, Robert M. "Association and Disassociation in Storm's Novellen." *PMLA,* 66 (1951), 381-404.

Bruch, Bernhard. "Novelle und Tragödie: Zwei Kunstformen und Weltanschauungen." *Zeitschrift für Ästhetik und allgemeine Kunstwissenschaft*, 22 (1928), 292-330.
Buck, Rudolf. "Theodor Storm: *Aquis Submersus*." *Der Deutschunterricht* (1953), Heft 1. 92-107.
Coenen, F. E. "Problems in Theodor Storm's Novellen." *Germanic Review*, 15 (1940), 32-45.
— "Death in Theodor Storm's Novellen." *PMLA*, 64 (1949), 340-49.
Eichentopf, Hans. *Theodor Storms Erzählungskunst in ihrer Entwicklung*. Diss. Marburg, 1908. (Also publ. in *Beiträge zur deutschen Literaturwissenschaft*, 11).
Engelhard, Hermann. *Theodor Storm. Werke*. Gesamtausgabe in drei Bänden, herausgegeben und eingeleitet von Hermann Engelhard. Stuttgart, 1959.
Feise, Ernst. "Theodor Storms *Aquis Submersus*." In: *Xenien: Essays in the History of German Literature*. Baltimore, 1950.
Fischer, Ottocar. "Das Problem der Erinnerung." *Literarisches Echo*, 13 (1910-11), 1717-24.
Fontane, Theodor. "Der Tunnel über der Spree. Aus dem Berliner literarischen Leben der vierziger und fünfziger Jahre." *Deutsche Rundschau*, 87 (1896), 214-49.
Fontane, Theodor. *Von Zwanzig bis Dreißig. Autobiographisches*. Berlin, 1925. (19th ed.)
Gladding, Everett B. "A Supplementary Storm-Bibliography." *Monatshefte*, 32 (1940), 381-84.
Guth, Anna. *Theodor Storms "Gartenpoesie," ihre Grundlagen und ihre Entwicklung*. Diss. Königsberg, 1928.
Heller, Erich. *The Disinherited Mind*. Cambridge, 1952.
Herrmann, Walther. "Die Entstehung von Theodor Storms Novelle *Ein stiller Musikant*." *Euphorion*, 22 (1918), 632-39.
— "Zu Theodor Storm." *Euphorion*, 23 (1922), 299-300.
Jehle, Mimi Ida. *Das deutsche Kunstmärchen von der Romantik zum Naturalismus*. (*Illinois Studies in Language and Literature*, 19). Urbana, 1935.
Jolles, André. *Einfache Formen*. Tübingen, 1930.
Kayser, Wolfgang. *Bürgerlichkeit und Stammestum in Theodor Storms Novellendichtung*. Berlin, 1938.
Kayser, Wolfgang. (ed.) *Kleines literarisches Lexikon*. Bern, 1961. (3rd ed.) Entry: *Märchen*.
Klein, Johannes. *Geschichte der deutschen Novelle*. Wiesbaden, 1954. (4th ed., 1960).
Kluckhohn, Paul. "Biedermeier als literarische Epochenbezeichnung." *Deutsche Vierteljahrschrift*, 13 (1935), 1-43.
Köster, Albert. *Theodor Storm. Sämtliche Werke*. Leipzig, 1924. 8 vols.
Krey, Enno. *Das Tragische bei Theodor Storm*. Diss. Marburg, 1914.
Kuh, Paul R. "Briefwechsel zwischen Theodor Storm und Emil Kuh." *Westermanns Monatshefte*, 67 (1889-90), 99-104, 264-74, 363-78, 541-54.
Laage, Karl Ernst. "Das Erinnerungsmotiv in Theodor Storms Novellistik." *Schriften der Theodor-Storm-Gesellschaft*, 7 (1958), 17-39.

Ladendorf, Otto. *Theodor Storm. Immensee und Ein grünes Blatt. (Deutsche Dichter des neunzehnten Jahrhunderts*, 4). Leipzig and Berlin, 1903.
Lenhartz, Rolf. *Die lyrische Einlage bei Theodor Storm. (Mnemosyne*, 14). Bonn, 1933.
Lobsien, Wilhelm. "Theodor Storms *Immensee*." *Schleswig-Holsteinsche Zeitschrift für Kunst und Literatur*, 1 (1906), 145-52.
Lockemann, Fritz. *Gestalt und Wandlungen der deutschen Novelle*. Munich, 1957.
Lüthi, Max. *Märchen. (Sammlung Metzler*, 16). Stuttgart, 1962.
- *Es war einmal... Vom Wesen des Volksmärchens*. Göttingen, 1962.
Lukacs, Georg. *Die Seele und die Formen. Essays*. Berlin, 1911.
Mann, Thomas. "Theodor Storm." In: *Leiden und Größe der Meister*. Berlin, 1935.
Martens, Alfred. "Theodor Storms *Renate*." *Zeitschrift für deutschen Unterricht*, 22 (1908), 97-106.
Martini, Wolfgang. "Theodor Storms Gedichte. Eine Untersuchung ihres seelischen Gehaltes und ihrer Ausdrucksformen." *Der Merker*, 9 (1918), 652-58.
McHaffie, M. A. and J. M. Ritchie. "Bee's Lake, Or the Curse of Silence. A Study of Theodor Storm's *Immensee*." *German Life & Letters*, New Series 16 (1962), Heft 3. 36-48.
Meyer, R. M. *Die deutsche Litteratur des neunzehnten Jahrhunderts*. Berlin, 1900.
Morgan, B. Q. "The Text of Storm's *Immensee*." *Modern Language Journal*, 7 (1923), 227-29.
Morgan, B. Q. and E. O. Wooley. *Storm. Immensee. (Heath Modern Language Series*), New York, 1927.
Mühlner, W. "Storms Märchen." *Die Grenzboten*, 70 (1911), 254-61.
Müllenhoff, Karl. *Sagen, Lieder und Märchen der Herzogthümer Schleswig-Holstein und Lauenburg*. Kiel, 1845 (4th ed.)
Müller, Thea. *Theodor Storms Erzählung "Aquis Submersus." (Beiträge zur deutschen Literaturwissenschaft*, 26) Marburg, 1925.
Pitrou, Robert. "Une interprètation nouvelle de quelques oeuvres de Theodor Storm." *Revue germanique* (1913), 588-90.
- *Le travail de "polissage" dans les nouvelles de Theodor Storm*. Diss. Caen, 1920.
- *La vie et l'oeuvre de Theodor Storm*. Paris, 1920.
- "Un livre sur Storm." *Etude Germanique*, 12 (1957), 339-42. Review of Stuckert's Storm biography (1955).
Porterfield, A. W. "*Wilhelm Meisters Lehrjahre* and *Immensee*." *Modern Language Notes*, 41 (1926), 513-16.
Procksch, August. "Der Wortschatz Theodor Storms." *Germanisch-romanische Monatsschrift*, 6 (1914), 532-62.
Reitz, Walter. *Die Landschaft in Storms Novellen*. Diss. Bern, 1913.
Rockenbach, Therese. *Theodor Storms Chroniknovellen*. Braunschweig, 1916.
Roesch, Lydia. "*Immensee* und kein Ende." *Modern Language Notes*, 49 (1934), 34-36.
Röse, Ferdinand. *Das Sonnenkind. Ein Mährchen von F. Röse*. In: *Der deutsche Pilger durch die Welt*, 4 (1845), Stuttgart. 57-89.

Rowel, Chester. "The Scene of Storm's *Immensee*." *Modern Language Notes*, 13 (1898), 194-96.
Rysan, Josef. "Theodor Storm und Psychic Phenomena." *Modern Philology*, 53 (1955/56), 39-46.
Salinger, Herman. "The 'Gartensaal' in Storm's *Immensee*: An Interpretation." *German Quarterly*, 13 (1940), 149-50.
Schmidt, Erich. *Charakteristiken*. 2nd ed., Berlin, 1902. 2 vols.
Schriften der Theodor-Storm-Gesellschaft. Heide in Holstein, 1952-62. Vols. 1-11.
Schütze, Paul. *Theodor Storm. Sein Leben und seine Dichtung*. Berlin, 1907. (2nd ed., 1911; 4th ed., 1925).
Schumann, Willy. "The Technique of Characterization in the Late Novellas of Theodor Storm." Diss. Abstracts, 20 (1959), 1029.
Silz, Walter. *Realism and Reality*. (*University of North Carolina, Studies in the Germanic Languages and Literatures*, 11), Chapel Hill, 1954. Chapter 9: Storm, *Der Schimmelreiter*, 117-36.
Storm, Gertrud. *Theodor Storm. Ein Bild seines Lebens*. Berlin, 1913.
– *Mein Vater Theodor Storm*. Berlin, 1922.
– *Wie mein Vater 'Immensee' erlebte*. Leipzig, 1924.
Storm, Theodor. *Briefe an Friedrich Eggers*, hrsg. von Wolfgang Seidel. Berlin, 1911.
– *Briefe an seine Frau*, hrsg. von Gertrud Storm. Braunschweig, 1915.
– *Briefe an seine Freunde*, hrsg. von Gertrud Storm. Braunschweig, 1917.
– *Der Briefwechsel zwischen Theodor Storm und Gottfried Keller*, hrsg. von Peter Goldammer. Berlin, 1959.
– *Briefe an seine Kinder*, hrsg. von Gertrud Storm. Braunschweig, 1916.
– *Der Mörike-Storm Briefwechsel*, hrsg. von J. Bächtold. Stuttgart, 1891.
– *Briefwechsel zwischen Theodor Storm und Eduard Mörike*, hrsg. von Hanna Wolfgang Rath, Stuttgart, 1919.
– *Heyse-Storm Briefwechsel*, hrsg. von Georg F. Plotke. Munich, 1917/18. 2 vols.
– "Briefe an Tycho Mommsen." Hrsg. von Friedrich Krüger. *Neue Rundschau*, 25 (1914), 366-81.
Stuckert, Franz. "Idyllik und Tragik in der Dichtung Theodor Storms." *Deutsche Vierteljahrschrift*, 15 (1937), 510-43.
– "Storms Menschendarstellung." *Dichtung und Volkstum*, 38 (1937), 451.
– *Theodor Storm*. Bremen, 1955.
Todsen, H. *Über die Entwicklung des romantischen Kunstmärchens*. Diss. Berlin, 1906.
Ubben, John H. *The Cultural Background of Theodor Storm's Chroniknovellen*. Diss. Chicago, 1942.
– "Theodor Storm's Debt to Gottfried von Straßburg." *German Quarterly*, 27 (1954), 245-50.
Ulshöfer, Robert. "Epische Situation und symbolisches Ereignis in der Prosadichtung. Dargestellt an Storms *Immensee*." *Der Deutschunterricht* (1956), Heft 3. 37-45.
Vlasimsky, J. "Heine-Storm." *Euphorion*, 17 (1910), 664-66.

- "Zu Theodor Storm." *Euphorion*, 17 (1910), 359-60.
- "Mimische Studien zu Theodor Storm." Euphorion, 17 (1910), 636-50. Continued in *Euphorion*, 18 (1911), 150-57 and 468-78.

Wedde, J. *Theodor Storm*. Hamburg, 1888.

Wooley, E. O. *Studies in Theodor Storm*. (*Indiana University Publications*, Humanities Series), Bloomington, 1943.
- *Theodor Storm's World in Pictures*. Bloomington, 1954.
- "*Immensee*." Schriften der Theodor-Storm-Gesellschaft, 9 (1960), 24-32.

Zieglschmid, A. J. F. "Betrachtungen zu Storms *Immensee*." *Monatshefte*, 22 (1930), 208-13.

INDEX

Andersen, Hans Christian, 131, 153, 155, 158, 159, 174, 175
Arnold, P.J., 175
Auerbach, Berthold, 79

Bächtold, J., 173, 178
Bernd, Clifford B., 175
Biernatzki, Karl Leonhard, 1, 3, 130, 166, 173, 175
Biernatzki Version (1st version of *Immensee*), 1-37
Biese, A., 135, 173, 175
Blankennagel, John C., 175
Boccaccio, 41
Böhme, Fritz, 22-37, 39, 81, 104, 151, 152, 154, 155, 166, 169, 173, 174, 175
Böttger, Fritz, 175
Botzong, Hertha, 135, 137, 138, 149, 152, 153, 155, 158, 173, 174, 175
Bracher, Hans, 170, 175
Bräm, E. Max, 167, 175
Braun, Frank X., 175
Brecht, Walter, 99, 107, 170, 175
Brinkmann, Hartmut, 1, 131, 132, 133, 134, 169, 173
Browning, Robert M., 168, 170, 175
Bruch, Bernhard, 98, 170, 176
Buck, Rudolf, 170, 172, 176

Coenen, F.E., 97, 169, 170, 176

Duncker, Alexander, 1

Eggers, Friedrich, 134, 173, 178
Eichendorff, Joseph von, 21, 152, 154
Eichentopf, Hans, 165, 166, 176
Engelhard, Hermann, 165, 166, 176

Feise, Ernst, 104, 170, 171, 176
Fischer, Ottocar, 176
Fontane, Theodor, 38, 81, 168, 176

Geibel, Emmanuel, 151, 152
Gervinus, Georg G., 1, 2
Gladding, Everett B., 176
Goethe, Johann W. von, 2, 41, 154, 170
Goldammer, Peter, 178
Grimm, Jakob & Wilhelm, 130, 131, 155
Guth, Anna, 176

Hauff, Paul, 132
Hebbel, Friedrich, 84
Heine, Heinrich, 154
Heller, Erich, 170, 176
Herrmann, Walther, 176
Heyse, Paul, vi, 150, 174, 178
Hoffmann, E.T.A., 131, 138, 151, 152, 153

James, Henry, 20
Jehle, Mimi Ida, 135, 137, 138, 139, 142, 143, 149, 151, 152, 172, 173, 174, 176
Jolles, Andrè, 160, 162, 174, 176

Kayser, Wolfgang, 174, 176
Keller, Gottfried, 170, 178
Klein, Johannes, 21, 51, 52, 55, 56, 65, 88, 90, 165, 167, 168, 169, 176
Kluckhohn, Paul, 165, 176
Köster, Albert, 169, 173, 176
Krey, Enno, 176
Krüger, Friedrich, 178
Kuh, Emil, 107, 108, 118, 130, 132, 165, 171, 173, 174, 176
Kuh, Paul R., 171, 173, 176

Laage, Karl Ernst, 176
Ladendorf, Otto, 177
Lenhartz, Rolf, 166, 177
Lobsien, Wilhelm, 177
Lockemann, Fritz, 5, 51, 52, 54, 55, 56, 78, 165, 166, 168, 169, 177
Lüthi, Max, 174, 177
Lukacs, Georg, 177

Mann, Thomas, 177
Martens, Alfred, 177
Martini, Fritz, v
Martini, Wolfgang, 177
McHaffie, M. A., 167, 177
Meyer, R. M., 169, 177
Mörike, Eduard, 131, 134, 154, 178
Mommsen, Theodor, 154
Mommsen, Tycho, 3, 166, 178
Morgan, B. Q., 166, 177
Mühlner, W., 177
Müllenhoff, Karl, 130, 172, 177
Müller, Thea, 169, 177

Novalis, 131, 138, 149, 151, 153

Petersen, Wilhelm, 173
Pietsch, Ludwig, 154
Pitrou, Robert, 177
Plotke, Georg F., 178
Porterfield, A. W., 177
Prokosch, August, 177

Rath, Hanna W., 178
Reitz, Walter, 168, 177
Ritchie, J. M., 167
Rockenbach, Theresa, 177
Roesch, Lydia, 177
Röse, Ferdinand, 151, 152, 154, 155, 156, 158, 174, 177
Rowell, Chester, 178
Rysan, Josef, 178

Salinger, Herman, 178
Schmidt, Erich, 16, 17, 81, 165, 178
Schütze, Paul, 88, 90, 138, 139, 169, 178
Schumann, Willy, 178
Seidel, Heinrich, 131, 134, 135
Seidel, Wolfgang, 173, 178
Silz, Walter, 178
Staiger, Emil, 21
Storm, Gertrud, 83, 165, 168, 169, 173, 178
Storm, Theodor, Works cited:
 Am Kamin, 38-53, 58, 133, 168
 Angelika, 134
 Aquis Submersus, 57, 69, 78, 79, 82, 83, 84, 85, 86, 87, 90, 97, 99-129, 169, 170, 171, 172, 176, 177
 Auf dem Staatshof, 38-77, 79, 80, 93, 94, 95, 97, 168
 Auf der Universität, 79, 81, 82, 85-94, 95
 Beim Vetter Christian, 78
 Bulemanns Haus, 130, 131, 132, 133, 135, 153, 161, 162
 Carsten Curator, 84

Drei Märchen, 132, 133, 161
Drauszen im Heidedorf, 78, 79
Eekenhof, 78
Ein Bekenntnis, 150
Ein Doppelgänger, 175
Ein Fest auf Haderslevhuus, 98
Ein grünes Blatt, 177
Ein stiller Musikant, 176
Eine Halligfahrt, 57, 79, 168
Geschichten aus der Tonne, 154, 173
Hans Bär, 130, 131, 161, 168
Hinzelmeier, vi, 130-164
Im Korn, 79, 80, 81, 82, 84, 85, 86, 90, 93, 94, 95, 96, 97, 169
Immensee, vi, 1-37, 41, 44, 52, 78, 79, 80, 87, 95, 96, 119, 120, 122, 131, 165, 166, 167, 168, 177, 178, 179
Im Saal, 165
In St. Jürgen, 57
(Der) kleine Häwelmann, 130, 131, 132, 133, 154
(Das) Märchen von den drei Spinnfrauen, 130, 150, 154, 161
Marthe und Ihre Uhr, 165
Posthuma, 79, 94, 95, 96, 97, 165
(Die) Regentrude, 130, 131, 132, 133, 135, 153, 161, 162
Renate, 57, 84, 177
(Der) Schimmelreiter, 78, 93, 98, 175, 178
Schneewittchen, 130
(Die) Söhne des Senators, 78
Sommergeschichten und Lieder, 1, 3, 166

(Der) Spiegel des Cyprianus, 130, 131, 132, 133, 135, 153, 161
Stein und Rose, 133, 134, 137, 139-141, 143, 145, 173
Zur Chronik von Griesbuus, 57
Storm, Theodor, Correspondence cited:
 Briefe an seine Frau, 169, 178
 Briefe an seine Freunde, 165, 169, 173, 178
 Briefe an seine Kinder, 168, 178
 Briefe an Friedrich Eggers, 173, 178
 Heyse-Storm Briefwechsel, 178
 Keller-Storm Briefwechsel, 178
 Emil Kuh-Storm Briefwechsel, 176
 Mörike-Storm Briefwechsel, 173, 178
 Briefe an Tycho Mommsen, 178
Stuckert, Franz, 2, 39, 40, 78, 80, 81, 85, 93, 94, 104, 109, 131, 132, 135, 137, 138, 141, 147, 150, 151, 152, 157, 165, 167, 168, 169, 171, 172, 173, 174, 178

Todsen, H., 138, 151, 152, 174, 178
Tolstoy, Leo, 149

Ubben, John H., 178
Ulshöfer, Robert, 167, 178

Vlasimsky, J., 178
Voltaire, 157

Wedde, J., 135, 138, 139, 173, 179
Wooley, E.O., 166, 179

Zieglschmid, A.J.F., 179

www.ingramcontent.com/pod-product-compliance
Lightning Source LLC
Chambersburg PA
CBHW031313150426
43191CB00005B/213